Introduction to Information Literacy for Students

Introduction to Information Literacy for Students

By

Michael C. Alewine and Mark Canada

WILEY Blackwell

Registered Office
John Wiley & Sons, Ltd, The Atrium, Southern Gate, Chichester, West Sussex, PO19 8SQ, UK

Editorial Offices
350 Main Street, Malden, MA 02148-5020, USA
9600 Garsington Road, Oxford, OX4 2DQ, UK
The Atrium, Southern Gate, Chichester, West Sussex, PO19 8SQ, UK

For details of our global editorial offices, for customer services, and for information about how to apply for permission to reuse the copyright material in this book please see our website at www.wiley.com/wiley-blackwell.

Library of Congress Cataloging-in-Publication Data applied for.

Hardback ISBN: 9781119054696
Paperback ISBN: 9781119054757

A catalogue record for this book is available from the British Library.

Cover Photo: monkeybusinessimages/Gettyimages

Set in 10.5/13pt MinionPro by Aptara Inc., New Delhi, India

1   2017

For Aedan and Andrew, who are growing up in this
information-driven world
Michael

For my parents, Alan and Mary Canada, who taught me early
the value of knowledge
Mark

Contents

List of Figures

Preface

Today, more than ever, progress—even survival—in science, business, criminal justice, and every other field depends on information literacy. People who can find, evaluate, and use this information will make the difference between success and failure, victory and defeat, life and death.

Introduction to Information Literacy for Students will help you transform your students into those successful movers, shakers, designers, explorers, educators, and leaders. A guide to doing every kind of academic research—from research papers to dissertations to multimedia TED talks—it presents a stable, practical, accessible method that students at any level working with any kind of source in any form of assignment can use.

Research: A Way to Understand

This book discusses research in terms familiar to every human being—that is, as a means of understanding. You don't have to be a historian or a chemist to be curious. Indeed, we spend much of our lives, even much of our time on any given day, trying to understand the people, things, and situations around us. In our daily lives, understanding is often slow and haphazard. The individual pixels come to light one at a time until, if we're lucky, a pattern emerges.

Academic research, on the other hand, is—or should be—more methodical. Although they may not realize it because they have internalized the process through their long experience and follow it unconsciously, scholars of all stripes follow a series of steps when they conduct research. For most students, who must face the library stacks or the vast, invisible "Web" without the benefit of this experience, research is often mystifying, chaotic, frustrating, and, in the end, unsuccessful. If only there were a clear, explicit method for finding, evaluating, and using information, students could start to become expert researchers in their own right.

There is, and they can.

The Method

Drawing on our own experiences as researchers and teachers, we have articulated a straightforward, effective method for navigating the information universe, one that any student can use to move successfully, expeditiously, and relatively painlessly through the research process. The method consists of seven discrete steps, from adopting a research mindset to mining sources. Individual chapters in the first half of the book walk students through each of these steps, providing practical strategies for completing each step. The second half of the book features chapters on various types of sources, organized in the order that students may wish to consult them to develop a well-rounded understanding of their topics. The final chapter helps students see how they can apply what they have learned to future research challenges in other courses, graduate school, careers, and personal and civic lives.

1: *Think Like a Detective* helps students develop a research mindset. It discusses various literacies, including information literacy, and, through an analogy with detective work, describes both the purpose of research and the central role it plays in the academic world.

2: *Ask a Compelling Question* helps students generate research questions that can drive productive research.

3: *Search for Answers* covers foundational research strategies, such as crafting keyword searches and setting up a research log.

4: *Explore Possible Sources* surveys numerous kinds of primary, secondary, and tertiary sources.

5: *Evaluate Sources* prepares students to evaluate sources based on timeliness, relevance, and credibility.

6: *Create a Paper Trail* covers ethical uses of information and appropriate forms of attribution and documentation, equipping students to record and cite relevant source material as they encounter it (instead of trying to add documentation later and risking plagiarism, misrepresentation, or simply errors in documentation).

7: *Mine Your Sources* introduces students to the crucial skill of mining sources for the right kinds of information.

Types of Sources

8: *Reference* covers encyclopedias, subject encyclopedias, dictionaries, and other foundational sources, which students can use to get a bird's-eye view of their topics, along with relevant definitions, common themes and issues, bibliographies, and more.

9: *Books* covers both printed and electronic books, as well as call numbers and catalogs.

10: Periodicals covers databases and various kinds of periodicals, general and discipline-specific scholarly journals, as well as popular magazines, newspapers, and more.

11: Statistics helps students navigate statistical sources, not only those available online, but also a few hidden gems available in print format.

12: Government Sources provides an overview of various sources maintained by local, state, and federal agencies, as well as international organizations.

13: Webpages covers various kinds of Internet sources, as well as search engines and ways to set limits for results and otherwise narrow searches.

14: Other Sources points to many kinds of new media, such as podcasts and social media sites, as valuable sources of information.

15: Now What? helps students apply what they have learned to future classes, their careers, and their personal and civic lives.

Like you, we want to help enable students to become people who make a difference. As an English professor who has taught many composition classes (as well as literature, linguistics, and freshman seminar classes), Mark has worked with thousands of students since the 1990s. He also regularly locates and uses information in his own research on American literature, pedagogy, and student success. As an academic librarian, Michael has worked with thousands of students since the 1990s and taught library research, composition, and freshman seminars. We know what works, and we know the obstacles that students often encounter when they are seek information for course assignments. To help students face these challenges, now and later, we have interspersed among these chapters a number of tips, shortcuts, and strategies for using search limits strategically, setting up an interview, taking notes on sources, and more.

By the way, although students will see some screenshots of various item records and search boxes, this book does not take the "Click here" approach to research instruction. (After all, every database is a little bit different from another, and every one seems to change at least a little every month.) Instead, the book teaches students basic principles, common tools, and, most important, ways to *think* about information and research. What they learn here will help them navigate any database, evaluate any source, integrate any fact or statistic.

The method described here is probably new to most students, but don't worry. We won't let anyone get lost in the stacks (or the cyberstacks). The first page of each chapter features a flowchart showing the entire process with the current step highlighted. While some steps, such as evaluating sources, are essential for any project, other steps may not apply to certain projects. You should feel free to assign or use the steps you feel that your students need.

The Approach

Our goal in this book is the same goal we pursue in our classrooms: to teach in a way that both engages students and equips them to succeed in the world of research.

That means including real-life examples, connections to careers and the larger world, "Think Fast" review questions, "Quicktivities," "Steps to Success," and conversational language (as well as a few attempts at humor along the way). The chapters cover all the basics—keywords, Boolean operators, periodicals, paraphrasing, and scores of other terms and concepts—but they also teach students how to use hypernyms to broaden a search, how to take notes on sources (and what to include in them), how to use indexes and bibliographies strategically, how to capture online sources before they disappear, and more. We also have included, in boxed "Insider's Tip" features, suggestions from a variety of professionals, including a detective, a professional basketball coach, a university career specialist, and more. By the time they are done, your students just might feel like concertgoers with back-stage passes, enjoying access to all the tricks "behind the scenes" of information literacy. It's a shade less sordid than what they might see with those back-stage concert passes, but it's every bit as interesting—and incalculably valuable.

What This Book Can Do for Students (and You)

You and your students can use this book in one of two ways. If you are teaching a course in information literacy or a course that requires students to conduct a lot of research and share the results in a project, you probably will want to move through the chapters in order. Each chapter gives students exactly what they need when they need it. On the other hand, if you are teaching a content course that includes a research component, you might assign chapters or parts of chapters as appropriate. In either case, you and your students can count on this book for clear, practical strategies, complete with examples, instructions, activities, and more.

Information literacy, as the first chapter explains, is a crucial skill in this Information Age. This book can help you empower your students to become masters of information: the kinds of people who can use facts and interpretations, both the types they find in others' research and the information they turn up in their own work, to improve the world.

Acknowledgments

The authors would like to thank the following for all of their crucial assistance, encouragement, and support.

First, we would like to thank our very patient and supportive family members. Michael thanks Aedan, Andrew, Brian, Cynthia, and Stacey. Mark thanks Lisa, Essie, Will, Alan, and Mary.

A special thanks goes out to Robert J. Arndt, Reference/Instructional Services Librarian at the University of North Carolina at Pembroke, for providing technical advice, test-driving our chapters with his students, and providing us with their crucial feedback.

We also wish to thank Christopher Bowyer, University Library Technician for Government Documents/Development & Primary Web Information Coordinator at the University of North Carolina at Pembroke, for being our photographer.

Thanks also go to Leighana Campbell for being our student model and to Rob Wolf, Electronic Resources Librarian at Farleigh Dickinson University Libraries, for his valuable technical assistance and for his help with creating a companion site and materials for the text.

Thanks to all of our colleagues and friends at the Mary Livermore Library and the University of North Carolina at Pembroke.

Thanks to our editorial and production team, Graeme Leonard and Manish Luthra.

Thanks to Steve O'Dell and Jodi Ezell at EBSCO.

Thanks to Carol Schlatter at OCLC.

Thanks to Corye L. Bradbury at ProQuest.

Thanks to Carolyn Shomaker, Federal Documents Coordinator; Gwendolyn Hope Smith, United Nations and International & State Documents Coordinator; Jacqueline Solis, Director of Research and Instructional Services; and Kimberly N. Vassiliadis, Instructional Design and Technology Librarian, at the University of North Carolina at Chapel Hill Libraries.

Thanks to Karen Vaughn, Digital Services Coordinator, Perry Library, Old Dominion University.

Flowchart

Research is not always a totally linear process, but it helps to try to conduct steps in the order listed below. For example, it makes sense to settle on some keyword combinations before you start searching for sources. Also, because reference sources will expose you to basic terms and background, it's a good idea to consult them before moving on to other sources.

The flowchart below shows the various steps of the research process in an order that should prove helpful to you. You will see this same flowchart at the beginning of each chapter, where the current chapter will be highlighted. You may need to return to an earlier step from time to time. That's OK. For example, as you look through sources, you may come up with some new keyword combinations or even a new research question. When you do, use the flowchart to get back in the flow.

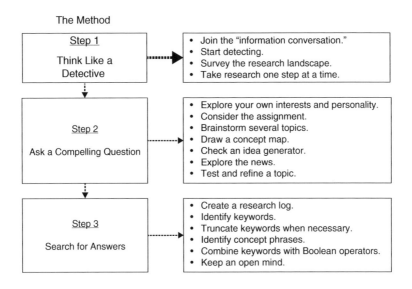

The Method

Step 1
Think Like a Detective
- Join the "information conversation."
- Start detecting.
- Survey the research landscape.
- Take research one step at a time.

Step 2
Ask a Compelling Question
- Explore your own interests and personality.
- Consider the assignment.
- Brainstorm several topics.
- Draw a concept map.
- Check an idea generator.
- Explore the news.
- Test and refine a topic.

Step 3
Search for Answers
- Create a research log.
- Identify keywords.
- Truncate keywords when necessary.
- Identify concept phrases.
- Combine keywords with Boolean operators.
- Keep an open mind.

Flowchart

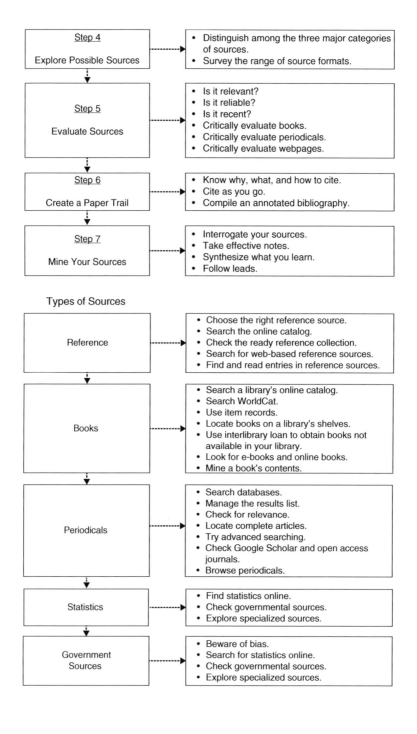

Step 4

Explore Possible Sources

- Distinguish among the three major categories of sources.
- Survey the range of source formats.

Step 5

Evaluate Sources

- Is it relevant?
- Is it reliable?
- Is it recent?
- Critically evaluate books.
- Critically evaluate periodicals.
- Critically evaluate webpages.

Step 6

Create a Paper Trail

- Know why, what, and how to cite.
- Cite as you go.
- Compile an annotated bibliography.

Step 7

Mine Your Sources

- Interrogate your sources.
- Take effective notes.
- Synthesize what you learn.
- Follow leads.

Types of Sources

Reference

- Choose the right reference source.
- Search the online catalog.
- Check the ready reference collection.
- Search for web-based reference sources.
- Find and read entries in reference sources.

Books

- Search a library's online catalog.
- Search WorldCat.
- Use item records.
- Locate books on a library's shelves.
- Use interlibrary loan to obtain books not available in your library.
- Look for e-books and online books.
- Mine a book's contents.

Periodicals

- Search databases.
- Manage the results list.
- Check for relevance.
- Locate complete articles.
- Try advanced searching.
- Check Google Scholar and open access journals.
- Browse periodicals.

Statistics

- Find statistics online.
- Check governmental sources.
- Explore specialized sources.

Government Sources

- Beware of bias.
- Search for statistics online.
- Check governmental sources.
- Explore specialized sources.

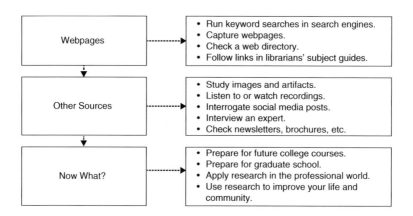

| Webpages | • Run keyword searches in search engines.
• Capture webpages.
• Check a web directory.
• Follow links in librarians' subject guides. |

| Other Sources | • Study images and artifacts.
• Listen to or watch recordings.
• Interrogate social media posts.
• Interview an expert.
• Check newsletters, brochures, etc. |

| Now What? | • Prepare for future college courses.
• Prepare for graduate school.
• Apply research in the professional world.
• Use research to improve your life and community. |

Part I
The Method

1

Think Like a Detective

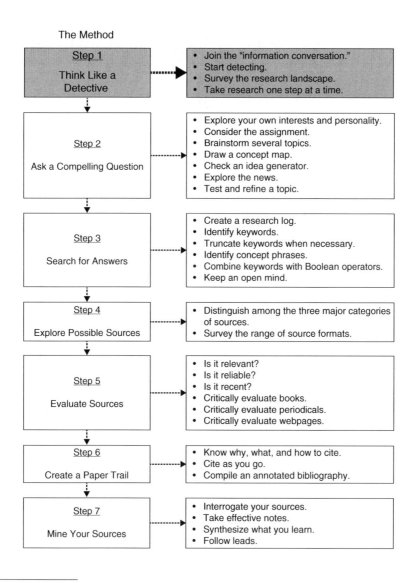

The Method

| Step 1
Think Like a Detective | • Join the "information conversation."
• Start detecting.
• Survey the research landscape.
• Take research one step at a time. |

| Step 2
Ask a Compelling Question | • Explore your own interests and personality.
• Consider the assignment.
• Brainstorm several topics.
• Draw a concept map.
• Check an idea generator.
• Explore the news.
• Test and refine a topic. |

| Step 3
Search for Answers | • Create a research log.
• Identify keywords.
• Truncate keywords when necessary.
• Identify concept phrases.
• Combine keywords with Boolean operators.
• Keep an open mind. |

| Step 4
Explore Possible Sources | • Distinguish among the three major categories of sources.
• Survey the range of source formats. |

| Step 5
Evaluate Sources | • Is it relevant?
• Is it reliable?
• Is it recent?
• Critically evaluate books.
• Critically evaluate periodicals.
• Critically evaluate webpages. |

| Step 6
Create a Paper Trail | • Know why, what, and how to cite.
• Cite as you go.
• Compile an annotated bibliography. |

| Step 7
Mine Your Sources | • Interrogate your sources.
• Take effective notes.
• Synthesize what you learn.
• Follow leads. |

Introduction to Information Literacy for Students, First Edition. Michael C. Alewine and Mark Canada.
© 2017 John Wiley & Sons, Ltd. Published 2017 by John Wiley & Sons, Ltd.

Chapter Summary

Prepare to become a master of information, the most powerful tool on earth. In this chapter, we welcome you to the two sides of the "information conversation": hearing and making yourself heard. We will make the case for both information literacy—the ability to find, evaluate, and use information—and research, a kind of detective work that can be every bit as fascinating and exciting as the investigations we love to watch on television and in movie theaters.

Key Terms: research, information literacy, text, visual literacy, media literacy, academic libraries, librarian

Chapter Objectives

- Describe the role of information and research in the "Information Age."
- Identify the various components of information literacy and their connection to academic research.
- Describe other literacies that are important for carrying out academic research.
- Explain the connection between academic research and libraries.

Information: The Key to Just about Everything

When you hear the word *information*, what comes to mind? Thrills and chills? Success and failure? Life and death? Consider the following:

- The FBI, CIA, and other law-enforcement agencies employ thousands of experts who put their information skills to work to track down missing persons, abducted children, and criminal suspects.
- Coaches of college and professional teams depend on information—about their own players' strengths and weaknesses, as well as the assets and liabilities of their opponents—to win games.
- Before a film's release, researchers behind the scenes deploy their information skills to discover details—of explosives, fashion, language, and more—that will make the movie pop on the silver screen.

Every field—including the one you will choose if you pursue a career—thrives on information, and the people who can find, evaluate, and use it are the ones who will make the difference between success and failure, victory and defeat, even life and death.

This book can help you make a difference. By giving you the knowledge, strategies, and tools you need to master information, it will empower you to solve crimes, win games, make movies, whatever you want to do. You will learn the valuable skill (and fascinating endeavor) of **research**, a process that all of the occupations mentioned above—and hundreds of others—use to find answers to questions. Along the way, you will learn how to mine sources for clues, follow leads, conduct interviews, collect and manage various kinds of intelligence, and turn it into the kind of knowledge that can move people, organizations, and whole nations. In short, you will learn to deploy information, the most powerful tool in the world, to do great things.

In this chapter, we will help you master the first step, which is to adopt a research mindset:

1   Join the "information conversation."
2   Start detecting.
3   Survey the research landscape, particularly libraries and the online world.
4   Take research one step at a time.

Now let's begin by bringing you into the information conversation.

Insider's Tip: Winners Use Research

Research is vitally important for any professional coach. I have spent many hours researching opponents' tendencies so I can give my players the best chance to compete. I study the kind of defenses these opponents play through-out the game or what offensive sets they are going to run, and I use statistics to establish which opposing players are very good shooters and which ones aren't. This kind of research is invaluable for my players. For example, it can assist them during the game if they know the player they are guarding is an effective outside shooter or not. We also watch film of opponents to get a sense of their strengths, weaknesses, and tendencies. Research also helps me set my lineups. For example, if I learn that an opponent tends to use a zone defense, I might favor players who are strong outside shooters.

Research helps me to understand my own players, too. I use statistics to gauge their success in various areas. This research starts at the beginning of the season and continues all the way until the end. By tracking the ebbs and flows of shooting percentage, free throw percentage, rebounds per game, deflections, and more throughout a season, I get a sense of where players need to improve and can, in turn, develop appropriate training regimens. For example, if statistics show that players are shooting poorly at the ends of games, I might incorporate certain kinds of conditioning and shooting drills into practice.

> Finally, research is a tool for skill improvement in general. When I coach youth players, I look for challenging, enjoyable drills that develop fundamentals. I often develop my own drills, but I also spend a lot of time researching drills that other coaches have used and found effective.
>
> –Mike Oppland, professional basketball player (Black Star Mersch, Luxembourg) and youth basketball coach

Join the Information Conversation

You probably have heard the expression "There's no sense in reinventing the wheel." Over the thousands of years humans have been on earth, they have figured out a few things, from how to build a fire to how to put satellites into space and use them to track people on the ground. Thanks to the ancient Greek philosopher and mathematician Pythagoras, we can calculate the length of the hypotenuse of a right triangle if we know the lengths of the other two sides. Biologist James Watson and physicist Francis Crick discovered the structure of DNA. Others, through their own research, have revolutionized the way we think about economics, education, psychology, and other fields.

Imagine what life would be like if we lost all of this information. We would have to, well, reinvent the wheel—as well as the telephone, the airplane, the computer, and millions of other devices. We also would have to recount, recalculate, reimagine everything humans have ever known. All this re-ing would take a lot of time and energy, and we might not get everything right this time. When people begin to plan a job or design a product or complete any other complex task without first determining what already is known about it, they are putting themselves in a similar position, setting themselves up to waste time and energy and possibly fail because they don't have the information that others already have discovered or developed. They are, essentially, working in an empty room instead of one filled with knowledgeable experts.

Successful people know better. Rather than going it alone, they get in on the exchange of information that goes on every hour of every day. Some people call it the "information conversation." Imagine a gigantic room filled with people—professors, lab researchers, doctors, engineers, athletes and coaches, journalists, politicians, police officers, parents, people with every kind of degree and job and personal experience—all talking, sharing what they know about history, science, medicine, technology, sports, news, politics, crime, children, and hundreds of other subjects. You could learn a lot in this room, couldn't you? Gatherings like this one—but on a smaller scale and on a narrower group of subjects—actually occur frequently and go by the name of **conferences**. Thanks to all the forms of communication we have, though, we don't need to be in the same room to exchange facts and ideas. The information conversation can take place around the clock in the form of email, social media posts, Tweets, blogs and vlogs, YouTube videos, podcasts, newspaper and magazine articles, books, radio talk shows, television documentaries, and dozens of other forms of communication.

Science, politics, sports, and all those other subjects are complex. Sometimes the experts in the room can provide clear answers, but sometimes they don't know the answers, and sometimes they don't agree about the answers. Let's face it: information, though crucial, is not always a definite quantity. Ever since Sigmund Freud invented modern psychology, various scientists have offered different theories for human thought and behavior. Interpreters of art, music, sculpture, and literature regularly offer different ways of understanding these forms of expression. Even science and mathematics, sometimes thought of as disciplines where there are "right" and "wrong" answers and less room for interpretation, have any number of ways of approaching or explaining the same phenomena. In all of these fields and others, theories and interpretations abound, sometimes merely existing side by side and other times contradicting one another.

Because the voices in this room are so many and so varied, it often can be difficult to make sense of all the conversation, but the important thing is to be in the room. "The man who does not read good books," Mark Twain said, "has no advantage over the man who can't read them." The same is true of all information. When you can *and do* use information, you have power. It's easy to join the conversation. Anyone with Internet access and a computer can create a blog or a vlog, comment on YouTube videos and news articles, contribute to Wikipedia articles, and create and manage their own websites. You don't have to be a professor or a lab scientist to attend a conference or publish your work: many college students, in fact, present information in conferences and publications designed for undergraduates. In this large and open conversation, you don't have to convince a magazine editor or an acquisitions editor at a publishing company that you have something worthwhile to say (and the ability to say it in a clear, engaging way) to have a voice in the room. You can just start talking!

Of course, having the opportunity to talk does not guarantee that anyone will be listening, especially since some people in the room—because of money, access, or status—always seem to be carrying microphones and amplifiers. For example, a billionaire can buy television or Internet ads that would not be affordable for most of us. Owners of radio stations and other media outlets, people who work in the media, and people who have friends in the media business are likely to have an easier time expressing their views in commentaries or shaping the news and other information going out to the public. Finally, politicians, celebrities, and even less well-known leaders in noteworthy positions, because of their status, have a kind of "bully pulpit" they can use to command attention. (President Theodore Roosevelt famously used this term to express a president's influence in the public sphere: when a president talks, people listen.)

This information conversation has both pros and cons. Access means that everyone, including you, can have a say, but it also means that you have to be careful, since some of the speakers may not be reliable. The system does privilege "insiders," providing a degree of quality control, but this same feature can be a disadvantage if you are not one of those insiders. In this book, you will learn to make the most of the system. For example, you will learn ways to evaluate the information you encounter so that you will not be easily taken in by unreliable voices. You also will find here dozens of tools and strategies that will help you to think, work, and communicate like an insider. When you're done, you will be able to enter the room, join the information conversation, and feel right at home.

Quicktivity: The Information Conversation Online

Use the metaphor of the information conversation to explain the kind of information exchange that takes place online—via Twitter or Tumblr, for example. Who gets to talk? What kinds of factors shape the conversation?

You can't help but notice this conversation. It's everywhere, from conferences to libraries to little screens on pumps at the gas station. (They don't call it the "Information Age" for nothing.) All of us encounter information on a daily, even an hourly basis, whether we are checking out classes and professors, shopping for a cell phone or a car, considering political candidates, or making any number of other decisions. Even if we are not consciously setting out to make a specific decision, we are using information to broaden and deepen our understanding of current events, as well as timeless questions about free will, our place in the world, and more. If air, food, and water are the keys to basic survival, information is the key to just about everything else: safety, enrichment, entertainment, comfort, progress. Consider war, poverty, hunger, oppression, intolerance, and disease. How many of these problems could be alleviated through better understanding?

Information, though, is only as good as our ability to make sense of it and deploy it to make progress—thus the case for **information literacy**, which the Association of College and Research Libraries (ACRL) defines as "the set of skills needed to find, retrieve, analyze, and use information." Information comes in a variety of forms, especially in the digital age. Because language is so important to humans, **text**—that is, the words and sentences found in books and other documents—has long been the dominant means for storing and conveying information; however, thanks in part to the rise of the Internet since the 1990s, images and sounds now form important parts of the world of stored information. For this reason, information literacy involves the ability to find, evaluate, and use not only books and articles, but also YouTube videos, podcasts, images posted on social media sites, and more. Some people and organizations use different terms, such as **visual literacy** or **media literacy**, for the skills involved in working with these various kinds of sources. For example, the ACRL uses the term *visual literacy* for skills involving working with images, and the National Association for Media Literacy Education explains that *media literacy* involves the skills of retrieving, analyzing, evaluating, and conveying both printed and digital information. In this book, *information literacy* is a general term for finding, evaluating, and using all kinds of information, including textual, visual, and audio material, as well as information stored in printed or digital formats.

In any conversation, information flows in two directions. Information-literate people know how to make sense of all the talk around them, but they also can make worthwhile contributions to the conversation. They can use the information they hear, find additional information, and put it all together to say things that will help other people to understand technology, art, politics, education, or another subject. In other words, they know how to do research—which, as you will see, is really a kind of detective work.

Think Fast: Information Literacy

Define *information literacy* in your own words.

Start Detecting

For many people, *research* is an ugly word, something that conjures up images of confusing articles and desks littered with paper, as well as feelings of boredom, anger, and frustration. Mention the word *investigate* or *detective*, on the other hand, and you often will get a much more enthusiastic response. Millions of people have spent millions of hours watching detective shows such as *NCIS*, *CSI*, *CSI-Miami*, *CSI-New York*, *CSI-Cyber*, *Forensic Files*, *The X-Files*, *The Dresden Files*, *The Rockford Files*, and a few hundred other shows, even some that don't have *C*, *S*, *I*, or *Files* in their titles. In fact, many college chemistry and criminal justice professors will tell you that the *CSI* shows alone have inspired many students to study their subjects. Countless people will rush to watch a detective show or movie, play an investigative videogame, read a murder mystery, or earn a degree with the hope of becoming detectives themselves, but many of these same people will move even faster to dodge anything clearly labeled "research." Investigation is often seen as a form of recreation, one for which people will pay good money, while research is viewed as drudgery, something many would—if they could—pay to avoid.

What's the difference?

In terms of purpose and process, there is no difference. Both detectives (FBI agents, police investigators, forensic scientists) and other kinds of researchers (geologists, historians, psychologists) seek answers to questions, and they study evidence to find those answers. For detectives, the evidence consists of physical objects (traces of DNA, fingerprints, murder weapons), testimony (from eyewitnesses and experts), and paper and electronic documents (financial records, email correspondence, handwritten notes). For other kinds of researchers, the evidence includes— you guessed it—physical objects (artifacts such as paintings and buildings), testimony (from scholars), and documents (books, articles, letters, webpages). In fact, many detectives and other researchers use exactly the same kinds of evidence, particularly manuscripts, government statistics, and scientific reports.

As you can see, investigation and research are the same things. Both involve finding answers, something that appeals to a natural curiosity that all humans have. In fact, every person who has ever lived has been curious about something. The proof is right there in their behavior as children, who are constantly reaching out to touch things and repeatedly asking their parents "Why?" So how did research get such a bad rap? We have a few ideas:

1   Many people don't see research as investigation and thus don't engage their curiosities.
2   In school, students often feel forced to explore topics that don't interest them.
3   Most students don't have a straightforward, logical method for conducting research, so they wind up spending too much time finding too little good information to earn too-low grades, ultimately feeling angry, frustrated, and disappointed.

Are you ready for some good news? Here goes:

1   This book approaches research as a form of investigation (sometimes using detectives and forensic scientists as examples), often describing it in a way that captures the elements that make detective work so interesting: the captivating questions, the clever strategies, the thrilling car chases—no, scratch the car chases; they were going to take us over budget!
2   Research is most engaging—and most successful—when people try to answer questions about the things that interest them. The next chapter, in fact, offers several tips for exploring your own interests and either turning them into research questions or finding just the right angles on course assignments so that you can tailor them around your interests or your personality.
3   This book presents a step-by-step method that makes the research process both manageable and effective.

The goal is to help you become not only an effective researcher, but also an enthusiastic one, someone who sees bits of information as interesting, valuable clues that can help us satisfy our own natural curiosities.

Quicktivity: Compare Research and Investigation

Find the definitions of *research* and *investigate* and compare them. What do you notice? Now, reflect on how you found the definition of each word. Does what you did count as research? Explain.

While detectives and other researchers have a lot in common, detectives' goals tend to be narrow and immediate: the identity of a thief, the location of an abducted child, the time of a criminal plot. Detectives usually are trying to answer the questions that begin with *Who, Where,* or *When.* On the other hand, biologists, political scientists, linguists, and other scholars engaged in what we call academic research ask broad questions that don't require an immediate answer. Often their questions begin with *Why* or *How* (although some do begin with *Who, Where,* and *When,* as well as *What* and *How many*). These researchers, you might say, are often concerned with the "big" or "deep" questions, and their answers help to create the information we use to understand our world, from its nature to its politics to its languages and beyond. In doing so, they often pursue answers just because they want to *know.* They're curious—like you. You wonder about things, don't you? How do people fall in love (and how can I get this incredible person I just met to fall in love with me)? Can we adequately feed everyone in the world? Are we alone in the universe? Why do so many analog watches in advertisements read 10:10? (They really do. See for yourself.)

Academic research is just another way to understand—that is, to use information to get a better grasp on some aspect of our world or our experience. Researchers, whether they are professionals or students, start with an idea, search for information about that idea, and use information they find to expand our understanding of some aspect of the world. Your immediate motivation in college may be to earn a stellar grade on an assignment or to earn a degree, but research also will help you do much more. You will develop skills that will enable you to make meaningful, useful contributions in the information conversation and ultimately to help us all understand the world and ourselves better.

Think Fast: The Purpose of Research

Why do people conduct research?

Now, if you reflect on your own attempts to make sense of things, you probably will agree that understanding can be a messy, chaotic process. When you went on that first date, you probably didn't bring a list of interview questions (and, if you did, you probably didn't have to worry about scheduling a second date). Still, you also may have noticed that *some* order does help when you are seeking to understand. When you want to make Swedish crepes, you don't start by researching the geography of Sweden or the history of crepes. You start with the basics. You also go to the people who know about cooking, not just the first person you bump into on the street. You buy the ingredients. You try to be careful when you mix them. If you are serious about getting those crepes right, you try again and refine your steps. Maybe you seek out someone else who knows about cooking, or you try some different ingredients. In other words, you follow a rough *method* for understanding.

Research works the same way—or, at least, it should. In this book, we outline, step by step, a very effective method for understanding things through research. It still will be messy at times, as detective work often is, but following this process will make the entire experience easier, less frustrating, more satisfying, and more productive. In fact, if you have ever tried to conduct research the way a lot of people do—haphazardly and superficially, that is—you may be amazed how manageable research is when you follow this method.

As a student, you often will have the opportunity not only to think like a researcher, but also to work like one. In many of your courses, your instructors will expect you to investigate the same kinds of questions that they themselves—as scientists, historians, management experts, and scholars of everything from art to zoology—do in their work outside the classroom. Sometimes, you may do your research in a laboratory. Other times, you will work in a library environment—either a physical library (with shelves and books) or a virtual library (with digital information you can access from home with your laptop or mobile device). In college, you probably will work in or with **academic libraries**, the kind of well-stocked libraries found on campuses and used by serious researchers. In still other cases, you may collect information from the world around you through observations and interviews, as well as close studies of social media, images, and other kinds of sources. After finding, interpreting, and assembling your information, you will share your findings with your instructor or classmates in a research paper, presentation, blog, vlog, podcast, or some other form. In short, your success in college depends largely on your ability to find, evaluate, and use information, including the kind found in physical and virtual libraries, as well as the kind that exist all around you—on Twitter and Tumblr, in images and recordings made by both amateurs and professionals, even in objects you can observe and people you can interview.

Sound overwhelming? Relax. Research is challenging, but the process is certainly manageable (as this book will show you), and often it's exhilarating. It's a way to satisfy your curiosity—and help your fellow human beings make a better world. After all, information makes progress possible, and who doesn't want progress?

Insider's Tip: Become an Expert

In colleges and universities across the country, students are exploring topics that interest them, developing expertise, and even presenting and publishing their work. Student research, in fact, is a point of focus for many institutions, including both of the ones where I have worked in recent years. As an English professor who has worked with thousands of students, I have seen some of them become experts in specific areas, such as Thomas Wolfe's drama or Truman Capote's nonfiction novel, and I have sometimes asked them to talk to one of my classes or even just asked them for some information—just as I would ask a professional colleague. Why wouldn't I? In the course of their research, these students have developed their own expertise. In their niche areas, they sometimes know more than I do.

You can be this kind of student, too. After all, there's a lot of ground to cover out there, not only in the study of Wolfe and Capote, but also in countless niches in art history, astronomy, finance, psychology, criminal justice, and other disciplines. There's room enough for every one of us to become an expert in something.

–Mark

Survey the Research Landscape

The Internet has made research much easier than it once was, even to the point where some people may think that finding information is as easy as googling it and reading the first page that comes up on the results page. Want to know the percentage of nitrogen in the earth's atmosphere? Google it. Need some tips on fielding a ground ball? Watch a video on YouTube. Interested in some expert commentary on the effects that the Panic of 1837 had on the book-publishing industry? Hmmm. Try googling that information, and you might not be so lucky. Until now, you may not have worried too much about understanding this kind of thing, but the kinds of information challenges you will face in college, in your job, and in other aspects of your life (as a citizen, as a parent, as a coach) often involve questions not easily answered with a Google search.

Part of the problem is that vast amounts of information are simply not available on the public form of the Internet and thus not accessible through Google or any other public search engine. (Google, through projects such as Google Scholar, is trying to expand the amount of information publicly available on the Internet, but this work may take a while, particularly because of limits imposed by copyright law.) Furthermore, because anyone with Internet access can post information there without submitting it to be checked or edited, much of this information is subject to error or is just plain confusing.

The Internet—along with Google and the many other companies involved with shaping the way we use it—is evolving, and we eventually will be able to find most or even all of the information we need there. Until that time, which may be many years away, true information literacy—the kind that you will need to succeed during and after college—requires that you be able to find, evaluate, and use not only information available on the Internet, but also information stored in and by libraries in the form of books, periodicals, government documents, and other kinds of printed and digital media. Fortunately for you and the rest of the world's researchers, these libraries employ information specialists—called, of course, **librarians**—who understand the common systems for organizing information and can help you find what you need. In fact, many large academic libraries have librarians who specialize in particular subject areas, or disciplines. Both general and specialist librarians keep on top of new sources of information, changes to databases, and specific Web-based resources. They can suggest useful research strategies such as using descriptors, keywords, and subject headings—although you may need little or no help with such tools after you finish reading this book! In short, librarians can help you with all aspects of the academic research process. Help them help you by setting up appointments for research consultations well in advance of due dates. Bring your syllabus, descriptions of assignments, and notes from meetings with your instructors.

Take Research One Step at a Time

"Where do I start?" Librarians hear this question all the time—not just from anxious first-year college students, but from experienced seniors, graduate students, even professors. Research starts with an idea, ideally one that interests you, and then becomes a process of discovery. Remember, research is a way of understanding. Starting with a topic you want to explore or a question you want to answer, you will gather information from a variety of sources—from webpages to books to interviews with experts—to deepen your understanding. Along the way, as you study the information you find, you will think about how that information relates to your initial thought or start moving in a different direction. In the end, if you are successful, you will have expanded your understanding of your topic *and* produced something, such as a paper or presentation, that will expand others' understanding, as well; thus, your product will become a new source of information for others to use.

That's the general direction that research takes. It sounds pretty murky, doesn't it? How exactly are you supposed to come up with that first idea? Where can you find the best information? How do you study the information, draw out the relevant parts, and use them in your own project? Let's face it: if you don't know what you're doing, information can be intimidating, research can be frustrating, and the entire experience of trying to find and use information can be confusing, even maddening.

It doesn't have to be that way. This book describes a step-by-step method for working with information, one that makes the research process manageable, effective, and satisfying. This book will take you through this method one step at a time. By the time you finish this chapter, you will have completed the first step, which is to think like a detective. The next six chapters describe the rest of the seven steps in the method:

2: Ask a Compelling Question
3: Search for Answers
4: Explore Possible Sources
5: Evaluate Sources
6: Create a Paper Trail
7: Mine Your Sources

Each of these chapters describes specific strategies you can use as you work through each step in the method. In the chapter on asking a compelling question, for example, you will learn how to explore your own interests, consider the assignment, brainstorm ideas, draw a concept map, check an idea generator, explore the news, and test and refine a topic.

The chapters in the second half of the book provide you with everything you need to know to find and use specific kinds of sources:

8: Reference
9: Books
10: Periodicals
11: Statistics
12: Government Sources
13: Webpages
14: Other Sources

The order of these chapters aligns with the order you will want to explore each kind of source, at least while you are learning the ropes of research. For example, reference sources come first because the overviews, definitions, and bibliographies they contain make them the ideal places to start doing research on a topic. As you become a more experienced researcher, you may wind up exploring sources in a different order—checking out government sources before books, for example—but this order serves as a basic way to approach the wide variety of sources available to you.

The final chapter offers several ideas of how you can use what you have learned in the book to conduct research in other courses, on the job, and in your personal and civic lives.

Each chapter begins with an overview (featuring a chapter summary, terms, and objectives) and then walks you through specific strategies for completing a step in the research process or exploring a specific kind of source. Other features—including Think Fast questions, Quicktivities, tips from insiders such as a detective and a basketball coach, examples from various disciplines, images of online resources, and Steps to Success—provide opportunities to review what you have learned, witness strategies and tools at work, and apply the strategies you are learning to a particular research project.

You already have seen one of our Quicktivities. Below is another. Use these exercises, along with the "Think Fast" questions and "Steps to Success" at the end of this chapter, to review and apply what you already have learned about information literacy and research.

Quicktivity: Compare the Internet and Libraries

In "Information Literacy Makes All the Wrong Assumptions," librarian Stanley Wilder argues that the typical first-year college student accustomed to the Internet might rightly fault libraries for their numerous interfaces and search systems. If you have tried to find information on the Internet and through a library, compare your experiences. (If you have not, take a few minutes and try to find the same piece of information in both places.) Which resource, the Internet or the library, did you find easier to use? What would make either one easier to use?

Conclusion

As you know from reading this chapter, information literacy involves both taking in information (discovering and thinking) and producing it (doing) through research. Knowing how to understand and use information can improve every part of your life—from buying a car to parenting children to improving your community and the world. Perhaps this introduction has given you a new appreciation for the value of information and the various forms it takes, as well as an understanding of the concepts of information, visual, and media literacy. Maybe you are feeling a little more confident and comfortable with the research process, now that you know that it can be managed as a series of steps. The next chapter will walk you through the next step: asking a compelling question.

Steps to Success

1   Think of a specific time you needed information—when you were considering various colleges or shopping for a phone. Where did you get your information? What obstacles did you encounter, and how did you overcome them? Now that you have read this chapter, can you think of any things you would do differently? How so?

2   Look over the syllabi for your various courses and identify the research projects on the horizon in the coming weeks. Develop a plan for completing these projects, noting deadlines along the way. Include at least one meeting with each instructor and one meeting with a librarian.

3   Focus on one of your research projects and consider the various forms of information—webpages, books, articles, social media, podcasts, and more—mentioned in this introduction. How might you tap a wide variety of sources for a single project? For example, if you were researching the effects of texting on teenagers' driving, you might check out government statistics on traffic accidents linked to texting, listen to some online news reports, interview or survey several teen drivers, and perhaps even observe some of these drivers.

Works Cited

Association of College & Research Libraries (ACRL). (2000). ACRL Information Literacy Competency Standards for Higher Education, Retrieved from http://www.ala.org/acrl/standards/informationliteracycompetency#ildef, accessed August 1, 2016.

Association of College & Research Libraries (ACRL). (2011). ACRL Visual Literacy Competency Standards for Higher Education, Retrieved from http://www.ala.org/acrl/standards/visualliteracy, accessed August 1, 2016.

National Association for Media Literacy Education (NAMLE). (2015). "Media Literacy Defined." Retrieved from https://namle.net/publications/media-literacy-definitions/, accessed August 1, 2016.

Wilder, Stanley. 2005. "Information Literacy Makes All the Wrong Assumptions." *The Chronicle of Higher Education*, January 7, 2005: 13. Retrieved from http://chronicle.com/article/Information-Literacy-Makes-/21377/, accessed August 1, 2016.

2

Ask a Compelling Question

The Method

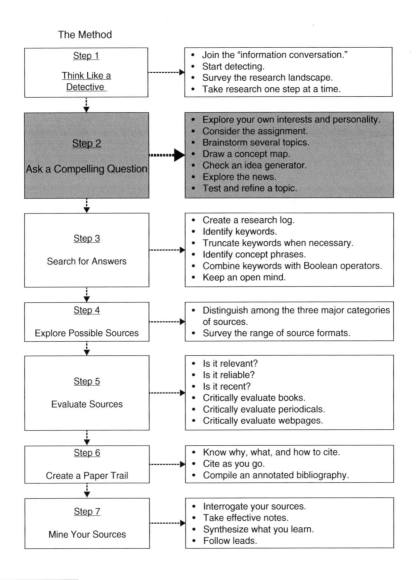

Step 1		
Think Like a Detective	- Join the "information conversation." - Start detecting. - Survey the research landscape. - Take research one step at a time.	

Step 2		
Ask a Compelling Question	- Explore your own interests and personality. - Consider the assignment. - Brainstorm several topics. - Draw a concept map. - Check an idea generator. - Explore the news. - Test and refine a topic.	

Step 3		
Search for Answers	- Create a research log. - Identify keywords. - Truncate keywords when necessary. - Identify concept phrases. - Combine keywords with Boolean operators. - Keep an open mind.	

Step 4		
Explore Possible Sources	- Distinguish among the three major categories of sources. - Survey the range of source formats.	

Step 5		
Evaluate Sources	- Is it relevant? - Is it reliable? - Is it recent? - Critically evaluate books. - Critically evaluate periodicals. - Critically evaluate webpages.	

Step 6		
Create a Paper Trail	- Know why, what, and how to cite. - Cite as you go. - Compile an annotated bibliography.	

Step 7		
Mine Your Sources	- Interrogate your sources. - Take effective notes. - Synthesize what you learn. - Follow leads.	

Introduction to Information Literacy for Students, First Edition. Michael C. Alewine and Mark Canada.
© 2017 John Wiley & Sons, Ltd. Published 2017 by John Wiley & Sons, Ltd.

Chapter Summary

Chart a course for success by choosing a topic that compels attention—first from you and then from your audience. In this chapter, you will learn how to immerse yourself in a subject, ask provocative research questions, and refine your topic to something manageable and appropriate for your task. You will find examples from a wide variety of subjects—including some that you may have never thought were appropriate for academic research or that you never even knew existed—as well as tips for turning these subjects into compelling papers, presentations, and more.

Key Terms: topic, research question, brainstorming, concept mapping, idea generator

Chapter Objectives

*   Explore your interests to identify possible areas for research.
*   Use various strategies to identify and narrow research topics.
*   Test a topic to determine whether it is too broad or too narrow.

It All Begins with a Research Question

As you learned in the previous chapter, research is simply a way of understanding something. The word for that something is **topic**—that is, the specific idea that a researcher is trying to understand. Often researchers frame their topics in the forms of something they call **research questions**—that is, questions they pose about specific people, things, or phenomena and then try to answer through their research.

In many cases, researchers generate their own topics and questions. Professors of communication, chemistry, psychology, and other fields, for instance, regularly plunge into their subjects to try to shed light on phenomena that are not yet fully understood. In other cases, researchers are working with a topic that someone—probably an instructor or a boss—has assigned to them. For example, a company executive may have a public relations officer research publicity campaigns conducted by other companies and produce a report.

When you can write on just about anything, as is often the case in first-year composition classes, you have a lot of control over the success of your project because you can choose something that interests you. Your interest in the topic probably will translate into a provocative research question, as well as a lot of time spent trying to answer this question. Even when an instructor or boss gives you a research assignment, you often still have a lot of freedom to "craft" your topic—that is, to narrow it to a specific thread or put your own spin on it. If, for example, your political science professor asks you to explore presidential power, you could choose to focus on formal or informal power, power with the public or power with Congress, power in a first term or power in a second term, power in a time of war or power in a time of peace, and so on.

This chapter will provide you with guidance you can use in either situation, taking you through a series of strategies you can use to craft the perfect research question about a topic you can investigate:

1 Explore your own interests and personality.
2 Consider the assignment.
3 Brainstorm topics.
4 Draw a concept map.
5 Check an idea generator.
6 Explore the news.
7 Test and refine a topic.

Whether you come to it or it comes to you, the topic matters a great deal to the success of your project. It can make the difference between exhilaration and despair, satisfaction and disappointment, success and failure. It may well be the difference between feeling like an explorer expanding the world's knowledge and an exhausted gerbil trapped on a spinning wheel to nowhere. Which one do you want to be?

Think Fast: Research Question

What is a research question, and how does it drive your research process?

Explore Your Own Interests and Personality

Already you can tell that crafting the right topic is crucial to both your success and your sanity, but how can you tell if a topic is "right"? That depends a lot on you—specifically what matters to you. You probably have something that makes you tick, something that fascinates you, something you do for nothing, except the satisfaction it brings you (or would do if you had the time). You can't help it. You're just wired that way. You may not even know what it is yet, but there is at least that one thing, maybe several things. When you think about this thing or do it, you get excited, you ask questions, you want to find answers, you want to think more about it or do more of it. You want to *understand* it. Like the detective driven to solve a crime, you are driven to find answers to your questions. When you have this kind of natural interest in something, a research project is more than a chore; it's an opportunity to satisfy your own curiosity while also advancing other people's understanding of it. That's what research is all about, and it's why so many people thoroughly enjoy doing research—and why you're likely to find that you enjoy it, too.

The first part of the step of crafting a topic, then, is to do some soul-searching and try to determine the kinds of things that naturally engage you. Consider your hobbies, your major, your intended profession, something that you or a loved one is experiencing. Are you on a team? Do you have a volunteer job? Are you into a certain kind of music or game? Any of these experiences or interests can be the sources of research questions. Think, too, about your own personality. Are you a "people person," or do you gravitate toward things—plants, animals, rocks, machines, numbers, policies? Do you prefer the concrete or the abstract? Do you often catch yourself asking "Why?" or are you more of a "How?" person?

Another way to tap the personal sides of topics is to reflect on your own experiences, as well as those of your friends and family. For example, your father may have diabetes. You could write about this topic from two angles. First, you could explore the ways the disease has affected his diet, activity, or emotions. Maybe you could seek to learn something new about ways to make diabetes more manageable or less stressful, something that will have a direct effect on your father's life. Another angle is to examine the impact of diabetes on you. After all, you can talk knowledgeably about what it is like living with diabetes in the home: the day-to-day issues, for example, or the financial and other pressures that the disease puts on families. Your own observations and experiences not only can spark ideas to explore, but also serve as supporting evidence. (You will hear more about evidence in a future chapter.)

Diabetes in the home is just one example. Maybe you have a little brother with dyslexia, a roommate with a shopping addiction, or an uncle who lost his job when a corporation moved a factory overseas. Then there's your own experience. Are you a veteran, a volunteer, an immigrant, a photographer, a martial artist, a skateboarder, a computer geek, a foodie, a fashionista, or a good ol' boy? Any of your identities or hobbies are sources of potential topics.

Professionals do research because it has meaning and value for themselves and others. When you draw on the experiences that you, your family, and your friends have had, you will see meaning and value in topics, and these things will help engage you in your work. Not only will the topic matter; it will matter to *you*.

Quicktivity: Know Thyself

Use the prompts below to explore your own interests and personality.

1 What do you like to read or watch?
2 What kinds of games or sports do you play?
3 If you had a month (and enough money) to do anything, what would you do?
4 If you could design a class on any subject and take it for college credit, what would you choose?

Circle all of the following words and phrases that interest you:

People (relationships, celebrities, families, children)
Other living things (plants, animals)
How things (natural and manmade) work
Why events (wars, demonstrations, social change) happen
"Deep questions" (Why are we here? Is there life outside Earth? What's right?
    What matters?)
Expression (art, literature, music)
Experience (travel, food, entertainment)

Consider the Assignment

Following your own interests sounds great, but let's face it: your classes (and eventually your jobs) are not entirely about *you*. Much of the time, especially in school and on the job, we all have to consider others' needs, goals, and preferences. In the case of research assignments, your topics will generally have to fit within limits set by your instructors. Some will provide only minimal guidelines. ("Complete a 10-page argumentative paper on a topic of your choice.") Others make very specific assignments. ("Argue for or against the use of drones to catch students cheating.") Still others will fall at various points between these extremes, as in a themed course.

It's a balancing act. Working with a topic that interests you is a great idea, but you still need to stay inside the boundaries of the instructor's assignment. If the boundaries are large or flexible, aligning the topic with your own interests is fairly easy: you can explore the impact of diabetes on a family's home life, the reasons behind the rise of tattoos, the case for or against restrictions on gaming, or whatever intrigues you and makes you want to know more.

If the subject matter is not up for grabs, you probably still have some freedom to choose something that interests you. Try to identify with some aspect of the subject. Maybe you don't gravitate toward history, but remember that people in the past had sports, fashion, love, pain, intrigue, even technology. (Eli Whitney's cotton gin and Benjamin Franklin's lightning rod didn't come with apps, but both were at least as revolutionary as the iPhone.) Ancient history had Hammurabi's Code, which called for chopping off thieves' hands, and ancient Rome had Julius Caesar, who was killed by a pack of angry senators. Science may not be your thing, but there's probably a scientific side to some things that interest you. For example, physics, biology, chemistry, psychology, and sociology all help to explain much of what happens in sports, as well as many of the phenomena and events covered in the daily news. Airline travel helps to spread contagion throughout the world—are we on the brink of destruction? Many of us eat genetically modified food—what, if anything, is this food doing to us? Put your instructors to work for you by asking them what questions they or their colleagues are still trying to answer. After all, these instructors are the subject matter experts—they know their fields. In many cases, they are reading articles and studies that try to answer these questions, or they are doing their own research to try to answer them.

Finally, even if your instructor chooses the topic, try to turn on your own natural curiosity. Think of this topic as a mystery to be solved and of yourself as the investigator. Look for a way to draw on your own personal likes and concerns to craft a compelling angle on this topic. Knowing something about your personality is especially useful in these situations when you have to craft an angle on a particular topic. To take the example we mentioned above, someone who is attracted to policies and rules might want to look at a president's formal powers, as granted in the Constitution or established by legal precedent, whereas a person who thinks a lot about relationships might prefer studying informal powers, as exercised in a president's interactions with lawmakers, the media, and the public.

As you can see, you almost always have some control over your topic or at least your angle on that topic. Exercise this control. Putting your own curiosities to work for you is the first step toward a strong research project, one that earns a good grade and, more important, results in discovery and satisfaction for both you and your audience.

Sometimes, exploring your own interests and aligning them with your assignments is enough to generate topics, but at other times you may need some help. Let's take a look at several tools you can use to come up with ideas for research projects. We will begin with one that probably is already familiar to you, although you may not have used it to generate research topics.

Insider's Tip: Embrace Your Obsessions

I'll never forget what Keith Richards, the legendary guitarist for the Rolling Stones, said about making music. He said he loved it so much he didn't want to stop to take a pee.

Now, I'm crazy about the Rolling Stones, but I think the reason that line stuck with me has less to do with Richards's riffs and more to do with the drive he was describing. I know that drive. I don't play the guitar, but I have loved a few things as much as Richards loves making music. One of them is writing. Give me the opportunity to write without interruption for hours, and I will. I lose myself in the work, and hours fall away. It's a Zen-like experience for me. The other is baseball. As a teenager, I spent countless hours playing it, reading about it, studying statistics. (True confession: I am an English professor, and I have read hundreds or thousands of novels, stories, poems, and plays, but I can't say I have relished reading anything more than the *Baseball*

Abstracts that master sabermetrician Bill James published in the early 1980s.) The point is I have been fortunate enough to find a few things that fascinate and motivate me.

What are yours?

–Mark

Brainstorm Ideas

So where do ideas come from anyway? Why not start with your brain? All day long and even when you are asleep, it's collecting ideas and impressions, and you probably don't do much with many of them. You need something to help you rediscover this useful material in your own brain.

Enter **brainstorming**, a popular strategy for getting ideas out of people's heads and onto paper (or a computer screen). Start with a subject, such as social networking, and keep following your thoughts, writing down more and more things that come to mind. Try to combine some of the things that occur to you and write some research questions about them.

If one brain contains a lot of ideas, how many do two or three or ten contain? Find out by brainstorming with some other people. Each student in your group will bring different experiences and different types of awareness that may in turn lead you to a topic that you find interesting. For example, maybe Joe's little brother was caught illegally downloading music and their parents received a court summons. Jamal regularly purchases his music off iTunes, but finds the rising costs too much. Tonya's best friend has a band, which shares its music on YouTube, but the members also want to make money from their music someday. Michael … well, Michael just wants to get lunch right now and wonders if we can talk about this stuff later.

Not so fast, Michael. We have a research question here: how does illegal downloading music affect different groups of people—bands, music listeners, music companies, parents? Group brainstorming has the potential to expose the more personal sides of a topic—and may help you generate a research question.

Example: Brainstorming in Media Studies

Brainstorming begins with a broad subject. In a course on Mass Communication, you might begin with the subject of social networking. What kinds of things come to mind when you think of social networking? Make a list:

- Facebook
- Tumblr
- Twitter

- Vine
- Pinterest
- file sharing
- Instagram
- teens
- privacy
- friends
- videos
- blogs
- photos
- stalking
- advertising
- money
- image

The next step is to choose one of these words and do the same thing for it:

File sharing

- Dropbox
- Google Docs
- HotFile
- music downloads
- P2P
- viruses

You can repeat this process any number of times:

Music downloads

- communities
- copyright
- ethics
- law
- LimeWire
- Pirate Bay
- indies
- record labels

Before long, you probably will start to see possible topics. Try combining items from the same list or different lists:

- Facebook and stalking
- teens and music downloads and indies and record companies
- social networking and privacy and image

Finally, ask yourself some questions that come to mind when you think of these words or combinations:

- Can stalkers use Facebook to identify targets or to gather details about people they already know? Should parents monitor their children's Facebook pages to protect them from stalkers?
- Do sites that offer music downloads help indie bands get off the ground? Should the government restrict music downloads to protect the profits of record companies?
- How do social networking sites shape the users' images in the eyes of prospective employers? Should companies monitor these sites to evaluate potential employees?

These research questions can guide your research.

Quicktivity: Brainstorm Possible Topics

Following the process illustrated in "Example: Brainstorming in Media Studies," brainstorm some possible topics for your research project. You may work on your own or with a group—or, even better, brainstorm both ways. Identify a general subject that interests you (martial arts, fashion, travel, etc.) What are some things that come to mind when you think about this subject?

Look at the list you just made and identify one thing that seems especially interesting. Now make a list of things that come to mind when you think of this thing.

Combine at least three of these items.

Now work these combinations into some research questions. Try beginning a question with each of the following:

Why _____?
How _____?
What are the causes of _____?
What are the effects of _____?
What should we do to change _____?

Draw a Concept Map

Concept mapping is similar to brainstorming with an extra visual component. Start with a concept and write a cluster of words or phrases around that concept. Then take one of the concepts and repeat the process. Take another and put more

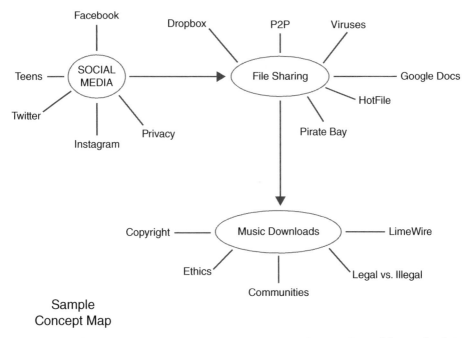

Sample
Concept Map

Figure 2.1 Concept mapping in mass communication. Source: Created by Michael C. Alewine.

concepts around that. (See Figure 2.1.) As in brainstorming, you can start to draw some possible connections between the groups of concepts (e.g., teens and P2P and copyright).

Quicktivity: Use Concept Mapping to Generate Possible Topics

Following the example in Figure 2.1, use concept mapping to generate some possible topics.

Check an Idea Generator

If you're like many other people, you spend a lot of time online. In fact, you've probably already been online at least once today via your laptop, desktop, smartphone, or tablet. Could there be some topics there? Of course there are, but how do you find one that interests you? Try running a search for a word or phrase that appears in one of your reflections on personal experiences, brainstorming lists, or concept maps, followed by words such as *links, topics, hot topics,* or *idea generator*. For example, you might search for "file sharing hot topics" or "diabetes links." When you run this kind

Health Sciences

abuse in nursing homes	fluoride treatments	plastic surgery dangers
acne	Foley catheter	politics of health care funding
acupuncture	food additives	postnatal (postpartum) depression
ADD/ADHD controversial	foodborne illnesses	post-traumatic stress disorder
treatments	food contamination	(PTSD)
addictions in health professionals	gastric bypass	prayer & healing
AIDS testing	gene therapy	prison health care
alcohol abuse	gingivitis	pulmonary embolism
allergies	ginseng	radiation
alternative medicine	Gulf War illness	radiation exposure
Alzheimer's disease	health care for non-English	regional anesthesia
anesthesia, awareness during	speaking patients	rehabilitation engineering
anosmia (absence of the sense of	health food products	remote sensing and disease vectors
smell)	health hazards of radon	role of calcium (or other element)
anthrax	herbal medicine	in the body
antibiotics, hoarding	HMOs	SAD (seasonal affective disorder)
antibiotics, overprescription	holistic medicine	sand tumors: psammoma bodies
Asperger's Syndrome	home diagnostic kits	SARS (severe acute respiratory
asthma: on the rise	hormone therapies	syndrome)
autism	human gene map implications	scaling
avian flu	humor	school-based health clinics/centers
back pain	hypervitaminosis	sexually-transmitted diseases
"bedside manner"	imaging techniques	(STDs)
bereavement assistance	immunizations	"sick" buildings
biological/chemical warfare--effects	infant motality	SIDS (sudden infant death
bird flu pandemic	infection controll	syndrome)
bone marrow transplantation	influenza	skin cancer: on the rise
breast implants	inhalation therapy	sleeping disorders
breastfeeding	iodine	smoking cessation
caffeine effects on health	lactose intolerance	sports injuries
carpal tunnel syndrome	latex allergy risks	"staph" infections

Figure 2.2   Idea generator (Old Dominion University Libraries). Source: Patricia W. and J. Douglas Perry Library, Old Dominion University. Reproduced with permission of Old Dominion University.

of search, you often can find lists of topics, sometimes known as **idea generators**, that can draw your attention to topics that may not have occurred to you. Some of these lists, often compiled by librarians or teachers, are just lists of words, but others are interactive. One we highly recommend, located on Old Dominion University's website, features columns of specific words under broad headings. (See Figure 2.2.) Just pick a heading that looks interesting and skim the columns. Try combining words or phrases, such as "avian flu" and "food contamination," to generate even more topics.

Running this kind of search sometimes will turn up lists prepared by relevant organizations. A search for "political science topics," for example, leads to several useful sites, including one hosted by Western Michigan University. A search for "environmental science topics" turns up a topic site, hosted by the United States Geological Survey, with a list of various science-related topics, including contamination and pollution, health and disease, human impacts, land use, mine drainage, oil spills, recreation, water quality, and more.

If you know the name of a professional organization in a field, try adding its name to your search. For example, you might try searching "American Psychological Association" and "psychology topics." (See Figure 2.3.)

One of the first results in the list is the American Psychological Association's site for psychology-related topics. Just a quick glance at this site shows that it contains

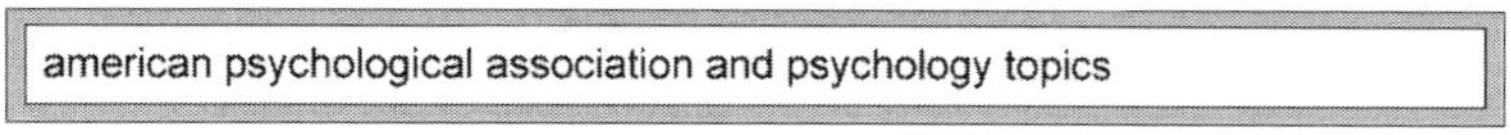

american psychological association and psychology topics

Figure 2.3 Internet search for psychology-related research topics. Source: Created by Michael C. Alewine.

numerous topic words. Each linked term takes you to more information about that particular topic in articles, books, and videos. More popular topics appear larger than less popular topics.

Quicktivity: Google for Topics

Using what you have learned in this section, run some Internet searches to find topic lists. Include the name of a professional organization in at least one of your searches. Try using both general terms ("sociology topics") and specific phrases ("drug testing topics"). Record several topics in the lists you find.

Explore the News

Journalists produce countless ideas for research just by disseminating the news every day. Just glancing at a newspaper, news magazine, or online news source can give you dozens of ideas for research projects. For example, a search of the CNN website on June 10, 2015, turned up news stories discussing ISIS, troops in Iraq, violence in Egypt, sanctions on Russia, terrorism, MERS (Middle East Respiratory Syndrome), preserved dinosaur cells, human rights, Uber cars, and drones.

Here are a few other news sources where you can find ideas for topics:

News magazines

- *Newsweek*
- *Time*
- *U.S. News & World Report*

Newspapers and wire services

- *Associated Press*
- *Los Angeles Times*
- *New York Times*
- *Wall Street Journal*
- *Washington Post*

Other news sources

- *The Daily Show*
- *Huffington Post*
- *The Raw Story*
- *ScienceDaily*

Television news sites

- ABC News
- BBC
- CBS News
- CNN
- HLN
- NBC News

When you come across stories that interest you in these sources, jot down keywords or questions. Since these sources cover a mixture of general and specific topics, from the positive effects of exercise to a specific crime that a celebrity committed yesterday, you may need to narrow or broaden the focus. You can do additional searches to find more general or more specific information. For example, a story about violence in the Middle East might lead you to explore fundamental differences between Sunni and Shiite Muslims. News stories may also refer to specific scientific studies that you can find and read for more information. As in the case of brainstorming and other techniques, you eventually can turn topics into research questions. For example, a story about the positive effects of exercise may lead to these questions:

1 Should public high schools require four years of physical education?
2 How might schools improve physical education, perhaps by emphasizing sustainable fitness routines?
3 Could businesses improve employees' performance by building fitness hours into their workdays?

A story about a celebrity's crime might fit within another framework, raising questions such as these:

1 What effect does criminal behavior by celebrities have on young people?
2 Should judges sentence celebrity criminals to community service or jail time?
3 What relationship, if any, is there between fame and crime?

As you can see, a simple news story can lead you off in unexpected—and promising—directions.

Quicktivity: Mine the News for Topics

Visit a news site or flip through a magazine. Write down three topics that interest you. Look for some more general information and some more specific information about one of these topics.

Test and Refine a Topic

If you have reflected on your interests and experience, brainstormed alone and with a group, drawn some concept maps, checked out some news stories, and played around with some idea generators, you should have some promising topics. Now it's time to test one or more of these topics. After all, they might not be appropriate for your instructor's assignment, or maybe they're too broad or too narrow. (Usually, they're too broad for what you can do in a course project.) To see if a topic is appropriate for the assignment, of course, you can run it by your instructor, but how can you tell if a topic is too broad or too narrow?

One easy way is to try searching for information on it. If you run a search on the Web and find entire books or documentaries on your topic, it might seem just right, but you aren't writing a whole book. Instead, you probably have to cover this topic thoroughly in just a relatively short paper or presentation, a poster, a blog, or another short form. If you try to cover a really broad topic in a short amount of space, you won't be able to get very far beyond stating some general points with perhaps a small number of examples or just a bit of elaboration. In short, you need to narrow your topic. Try limiting your research to a particular time period, region, or aspect. For example, if you run a search for "physical education" on the Internet, you will find many thousands of sites. You can't cover all this information in a short paper or presentation, even if you look at only university PE classes. Perhaps you could look at the PE requirements at your university and propose some specific changes to improve students' experiences. Another approach is to note some of the specific questions that others are raising about PE in their blogs, tweets, and posts. Perhaps you can focus on one of these questions.

Sometimes you may encounter an opposite problem. Perhaps you conducted some test searches and found very few sites that address your topic. For example, the "prevention of child abuse in Smith County" may produce few specific results, but a more general approach probably would turn up more information. For example, you might try "child abuse prevention in rural areas." If you continue to struggle, talk to your instructor, who might have other ideas for narrowing or broadening your topic.

There's one more thing to keep in mind: a topic or research question is only a starting point. Even after you have narrowed or broadened it, it may change as you research it. After all, you don't know what you are going to learn about it until you plunge into all the articles, books, blogs, podcasts, posts, documentaries, and other sources you will encounter in your research. In Chapter 4, we will take you on a tour of several kinds of sources where you can explore your topic, but for now we just want you to remain flexible. As you can see in "Insider's Tip: Let Your Research Be Your Guide," research is not a flight to a predetermined destination, but a road trip of discovery. See where your trip takes you.

Insider's Tip: Let Your Research Be Your Guide

Research has a way of guiding you and leading you to new ideas. When I was in graduate school, I often found that my research introduced me to new ideas and forced me to reexamine my thoughts on a topic.

For one of my graduate classes, African American Literature and Ecocriticism, I was interested in the use of dialect and the role of "conjure"—another term for folk beliefs and magic—in Charles W. Chesnutt's *The Conjure Woman*. I eventually found myself reading dozens of articles and books on the origins of conjure. As my research unfolded, it shaped my interests. In the end, my project had nothing to do with *The Conjure Woman*, but instead examined three different regions and the respective folk beliefs of those regions. Thankfully, my professor was excited about what I was learning and supported the new direction I was taking. During my research, I learned a lot of surprising things about earth-centered religions. I hadn't realized the degree of overlap between these older spiritual practices and modern religious and secular practices. Although my class has long ended, my fascination with folk tales, mythology, earth-centered religions, and the history of religions has continued, all thanks to one paper assignment.

In your own research, you will start with one idea, but your sources may lead you in another direction. Let it be and go with the flow. Following your research to where it's leading is one of the joys of research and writing. Enjoy the surprises and discoveries along the way. In school we sometimes become fixated on finished products—essays, presentations, grades—but let yourself enjoy the journey. Following and accepting new ideas makes education—and indeed life—a lot more interesting.

–Nami L. Montgomery, ESL Specialist, co-editor of *Thomas Wolfe Remembered*

Conclusion

By now, we hope, you have one or more possible topics that are just right for starting your project. You also have a set of strategies and resources—personal reflection, brainstorming, concept mapping, idea generators, and news sources—you can use to generate topics for future projects. Finally, you know how to narrow or broaden a topic, and you realize that you need to remain flexible over the course of your research journey. The next step is to run some searches to find information on your topic.

Steps to Success

1 Review the various topics you generated through brainstorming, concept mapping, and other strategies you used to complete the Quicktivities in this chapter. Choose the three that seem the most interesting to you. Write two research questions for each topic.

2 Use a notepad or a mobile device to track your thoughts for a day. What kinds of things did you wonder about as you encountered the people, places, and situations that filled your day? What do your thoughts reveal about your interests and personality? Drawing on what you learned from this exercise, test each of your research questions. Do they align with your interests, personality, or experience? If not, look back over the thoughts you recorded today and revise your questions so that they better match the kinds of things that matter to you.

3 Once you have a research question that matters to you, use what you learned in this chapter to test it for sufficient focus and, if necessary, narrow or broaden it. Record your research question in a prominent place—on a mobile device or sheet of paper you can carry around with you. Review it from time to time. Think about what you want to learn and where you might find information. You're ready to take the next step on your research journey of understanding.

3

Search for Answers

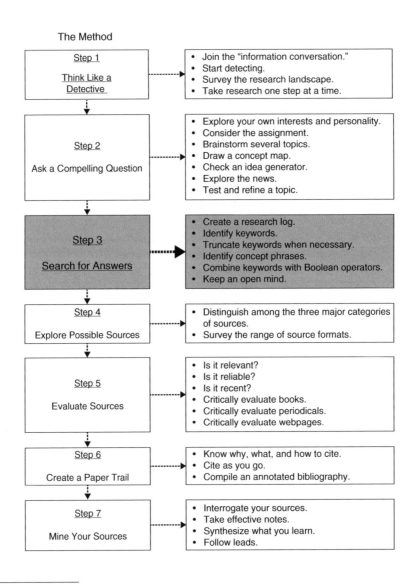

The Method

Step 1 — Think Like a Detective	• Join the "information conversation." • Start detecting. • Survey the research landscape. • Take research one step at a time.
Step 2 — Ask a Compelling Question	• Explore your own interests and personality. • Consider the assignment. • Brainstorm several topics. • Draw a concept map. • Check an idea generator. • Explore the news. • Test and refine a topic.
Step 3 — Search for Answers	• Create a research log. • Identify keywords. • Truncate keywords when necessary. • Identify concept phrases. • Combine keywords with Boolean operators. • Keep an open mind.
Step 4 — Explore Possible Sources	• Distinguish among the three major categories of sources. • Survey the range of source formats.
Step 5 — Evaluate Sources	• Is it relevant? • Is it reliable? • Is it recent? • Critically evaluate books. • Critically evaluate periodicals. • Critically evaluate webpages.
Step 6 — Create a Paper Trail	• Know why, what, and how to cite. • Cite as you go. • Compile an annotated bibliography.
Step 7 — Mine Your Sources	• Interrogate your sources. • Take effective notes. • Synthesize what you learn. • Follow leads.

Introduction to Information Literacy for Students, First Edition. Michael C. Alewine and Mark Canada.
© 2017 John Wiley & Sons, Ltd. Published 2017 by John Wiley & Sons, Ltd.

Chapter Summary

Devise search strategies that will guide you through the vast amount of information available online, in libraries, and in the larger world. In this chapter, you will learn some crucial concepts and strategies that can turn long, tedious, wild goose chases that leave you tired and frustrated into efficient searches that turn up detailed, credible information on exactly the topic you want to research.

Key Terms: research log, keyword, synonym, jargon, hypernym, hyponym, truncation, false hit, concept phrase, Boolean operators

Chapter Objectives

- Create a research log to record searches.
- Use your own knowledge, as well as a variety of sources, to identify keywords that accurately capture the subtleties of your topic.
- Refine searches by using synonyms, hypernyms, hyponyms, truncation, and Boolean operators.

Good News and Bad News

A detective investigating a case has learned that a suspect may have bought an item used in the crime at an Army surplus store, so she heads over to the store to try to get her hands on a receipt. The shop owner is there, and he recognizes the face in the mugshot the detective has brought with her. "I'd like to see the receipt for the purchase," the detective tells him. The owner replies, "Follow me." Before he opens the door to the backroom, he says, "The good news is that I have it." He then opens the door to a dark room where little slips of paper are piled high on a desk, pinned on bulletin boards, taped on the wall, and scattered around the floor. "The bad news," the shop owner says, turning around, "is that it's in here—somewhere."

As a researcher, you have a similar problem. Consider these facts: the United States has more than 85,400 business professors, 24,800 chemistry professors, 70,200 education professors, 74,800 English professors, and 20,300 sociology professors (BLS, 2015). Then there are all those thousands of professors of accounting, art history, biology, engineering, finance, forestry, geography, music, nursing, pharmacology, and many other fields. In addition to teaching courses such as the ones you are taking this semester, many of these professors also conduct research in their fields and publish their findings in books and articles. Of course, they cannot merely report the same things that others have published; they have to conduct new research and report new knowledge.

It doesn't take a mathematician (yet another kind of researcher, by the way) to see that hundreds of thousands of professors continually publishing their findings year after year, decade after decade, generate a lot—millions, in fact—of books and articles. No matter what your interest—the American Revolution, lasers, fungi, diabetes, game theory, computer signal processing, the dash in Emily Dickinson's poetry—there almost certainly is a book or an article on it. In fact, there are probably a hundred or a thousand. Like the detective standing in that shop owner's backroom, you face good news and bad news. The good news is that you almost never need to worry that there isn't any information on a topic that interests you. The bad news is that it's out there—somewhere.

There's more good news, though. You don't have to wander through a dark room at a surplus store—or through the stacks at a library or all over the Internet. You almost always can find the information you need if you know how to run an effective search. This chapter will take you through the search process, showing you exactly the strategies you need to find information on your topic:

1   Create a research log.
2   Identify keywords.
3   Truncate keywords when necessary.
4   Identify concept phrases.
5   Combine keywords with Boolean operators.
6   Keep an open mind.

You will begin by creating a research log where you can keep track of your keywords, actual searches, and more.

Create a Research Log

Are you a planner? If you aren't a planner, you may know one. This is the kind of person who makes lists, keeps calendars, and checks things off. Planners drive non-planners crazy—they're just so ... *organized*. The non-planner takes one look at the planner's phone or tablet or notebook, where everything is alphabetized and color-coded, and says, "Relax, dude."

Whether you are the type to go to the grocery with your shopping items meticulously organized in a fancy mobile app, scrawled on the palm of your hand, or vaguely conceived in some dark corner of your brain, you will want to be a planner when it comes to research. A grocery can be mildly disconcerting—jelly or jam? waffle or shoestring? rigatoni or tortellini?—but it's nothing—*nothing*—compared to a large research project, which may involve a variety of databases, dozens or even hundreds of sources, and—the topic of this chapter—many variations of keyword searches.

Relax, dude. That's what a research log allows you to do. A **research log** is simply a record of the *process* of your research. (The actual notes you take on your sources are a different matter—and a subject in Chapter 7.) By helping you to keep track of what you need to do and what you already have done, a research log makes the research process manageable and efficient. At first, it seems like an unnecessary step, like extra work. After using it for just an hour or less, though, you may begin to realize how much time and stress it can save you, especially if you have tried doing research the haphazard way: with a Google here and a YouTube there and—wait, have I already seen this site? Where did I read that fact about … ?

One reason that a research log is so important is that you cannot complete all of your research at once. Instead, you may spend a half-hour during workshop time in class, another half-hour the next day, two more hours over the weekend, and three hours—spread out over 30- and 45-minute increments—over the next week. You need some way to remind yourself of your many tasks so that you won't forget to explore a particular database or waste time exploring it twice.

You can keep a physical research log (in a spiral notebook, for example) or a digital one (on a laptop or a tablet, for example). We recommend a digital research log, which can be easily searched and copied. If you keep it on certain apps, such as Evernote, you can even have access to it on multiple devices: not only your own laptop or phone, but also any computer with Internet access. This access is very handy when you are running searches in different places.

Insider's Tip: Plan Your Investigation

When I joined my agency's Evidence Response Team – ERT (the federal version of CSI), I assumed I would be working in a world like the one seen in television shows, where specialists with a divining sense effortlessly locate crucial evidence, identify suspects, and ultimately obtain a confession—all in the span of an hour. As I learned on the job, real cases can take years to develop, and our crime scenes are more likely to resemble an episode of *Hoarders* than *CSI*. If I had to choose one word for the type of work investigators do on a real-world crime scene, that word would be *methodical*. A crime scene is a large data set where only some of the available information is relevant to our investigation. Our job is to cull through the set to find what is relevant to solving the crime. It can be complex, especially when you enter a location with an overwhelming amount of "stuff." What is important? What is secondary? And what is just trash?

To sort things out, we approach the scene with a plan that helps us to identify *what* we hope to find, *where* we might find it, and *how* we will collect it. Randomly wandering around hoping to uncover a hair or fiber or fingerprint is not realistic. We have to be strategic. Where might the suspect hide a weapon? Where did they sit? What did they touch? Did they try to clean the scene? Can we use a technique to uncover this attempt? What do we expect to find (or not find)? Researchers of all types—including you—can benefit from a similar approach; that is, start with a plan that helps you separate the important from the not-so-important. In academic research, the core of that plan will be your research question.

   Whether you are a federal investigator or an academic researcher, technical skill combined with curiosity and diligence can help you tame even the most complex of questions. With practice and dedication, you can develop an expertise that may not be suspenseful or glamorous, but is certainly stimulating and rewarding.

–Kerrie Harney, federal investigator

"Example: A Research Log in Sociology" shows several kinds of information you can track in a research log. As you can see, you can use this log to record not only keywords and the like, but also databases where you have run searches, contact information for people who can help you, questions to answer, and more. For now, you can use it to record keywords, truncation strategies, and actual searches you have conducted. Make sure to revisit it as you work through the research steps covered in the remaining chapters. As you complete these steps, you often will use your research log to keep track of other things, such as specific sources you have explored.

Example: A Research Log in Sociology

Research question: why do many teenagers drink excessively?

Keywords (truncations)	Synonyms	Hypernyms	Hyponyms
teenager (teen*)	adolescent (adolescen*)	youth	16-year-old
alcohol	liquor	substance	beer
	booze		wine cooler

Concept phrases

binge drinking
peer pressure

Keyword combinations

(teen* or adolescen*) and binge drinking
(teen* or adolescen*) and alcohol
(teen* or adolescen*) and beer
youth and alcohol

Search engines	Databases	Libraries	Other
Google	Sociological Abstracts	UPenn library	Public archives
Bing	ProQuest Sociology	Temple library	

Resources

Professor Zhang (expert on binge drinking; Professor Amos introduced me to her on 3/21; zhang@u.edu)
    Mr. Cass (librarian; helped me on 3/22; cass@u.edu)

Questions

Why do some teens never start drinking?
When does the average teen begin drinking?
What is considered "excessive drinking"?

Identify Keywords

Computers can search for various things, including images and even sounds, but words are the keys to a successful search when you are conducting academic research. If you have ever searched for something on the Internet, you already know something about **keywords**. They're the words that you type into the box on Google, Yahoo! Search, or whichever search engine you use. Choosing the right keywords is easy enough if you just want to know more about your favorite band's concert tour or hotels in Fort Lauderdale. You type in some relevant words—"hotels in Fort Lauderdale," for example—and away you go. But what if you want to find out whether the time of day an athlete eats carbs affects the metabolism of those carbs or whether the size of a college class affects male and female students differently? You can find valuable information on such topics almost as quickly as you can find a hotel room in Fort Lauderdale, but you will need to be more strategic. If you simply type "Does the time of day that teenagers eat carbs affect the way they use the carbs?" into a search box and hit "Search," you might get some relevant information—and you might not—or the information may be there, but it comes up 352nd in a list of 105,787 hits. There's got to be a better way.

There is. Remember, you can't talk to a search engine the way you talk to a librarian. (Well, technically you can, but search engines are a lot denser than librarians—really fast, but really dense.) You need to talk the search engine's language, and the search engine's language is made up of keywords, the words that signal the main content of a document. The same is true of the search mechanisms in databases, which researchers use to find books, articles, and other sources not available on the open Internet. (You will learn more about databases in Chapter 4.) In either case, computers, unlike librarians, don't exactly think about the questions posed to them. Instead, they look for the words you give them and try to match them up with one of two things: the text in documents such as webpages or the text in item records stored in databases. (Google does accept questions, and these questions can produce relevant information in some cases. In fact, you may start typing a question and see, below the search box, a list of search strings with your question in it appear. That's because someone already has used this question in a search. Many databases don't work this way, however, and even Google may not produce a useful list if you are asking an unusual question.)

Since questions often do not work, you need to select your keywords carefully. Keep in mind that English has a lot of **synonyms**, words that mean roughly the same thing. First, try to think of two or three words that an average person would use to refer to your topic. Next, consider the more formal language that an expert might use. Dietitians know words such as *eat* and *use*, of course, but they tend to use other terms, such as *consume* and *metabolism*, when they write articles for scholarly journals or government reports. (The term for the "insider's language" that experts use when communicating with other experts is **jargon**.) Finally, as you come across relevant sources, pay attention to the terms that appear in them. You might notice that authors tend to use *ingest* for *eat*, as well as the verb *metabolize*. Pay especially close attention to the contents sections, summaries, abstracts, and Library of Congress subject headings found in some item records. Include all of these terms—the everyday words, the jargon, and the words you come across in sources—in the section of your research log dedicated to keywords.

English also has two other kinds of *nyms* that are extremely helpful when it comes to keyword searches. **Hypernyms** are more general terms, and **hyponyms** are more specific terms. For example, as illustrated in "Example: A Research Log in Sociology," the word *youth* is a hypernym for *teenager*, and *16-year-old* is a hyponym for *teenager*. Hypernyms are especially useful when you are researching a topic on which not much research has been done. If you are looking at the ways that the rise of performance-enhancing drugs among athletes has affected the young people who look up to those players as role models, you may not find many sources on exactly this topic, but books and articles that discuss role models and young people in general might help you make an argument about how the behavior of celebrities does or does not rub off on young people; thus, you might try using the hypernym *celebrity* instead of *athlete*. Hyponyms can help you to narrow a search (or even your topic). If one of your keywords is *media*, for example, you might try substituting the hyponym *film*.

Quicktivity: Keywords, Synonyms, Hypernyms, and Hyponyms

Consider the topic you chose in Chapter 2. Brainstorm several keywords, synonyms, hypernyms, and hyponyms. Remember to mine webpages, item records, and more for keywords.

Truncate Keywords When Necessary

Words, of course, do not always appear the same way in various sources and item records. If you are looking for information about alcohol abuse and type only *alcoholism*, that word will be the only one the search engine will seek. If it comes across a document record that contains the word *alcoholics*, but not the word *alcoholism*, it will not show you that record. If a search engine could talk, it would say, "Hey, you didn't say anything about alcoholics." (Remember, computers are really fast, but they are not always very intuitive.) The trick, then, is to tell the search engine that you want all the variations of a keyword. In other words, you need to use something called **truncation**. When you truncate a word, you cut it short and replace the missing letters with a symbol, usually an asterisk (*). The search engine then will look for the letters you have provided, as well as any letters that might follow these letters. Here are some examples:

- alcohol* (alcohol, alcoholic, alcoholics, alcoholism)
- manufactur* (manufacture, manufactures, manufacturing)

Truncation is a very useful strategy, but you have to be careful when using it. If you chop off too much of a keyword, you may get a lot of **false hits**—that is, webpages or item records for sources on irrelevant topics. For example, *bull** may call up articles about bullies and bullying, but it also may give you articles about bulls! If you don't chop off enough of a keyword, you may miss relevant articles: *athletic* may call up sources on athletics and athleticism, but will not give you sources that lack *athletic*, even if they have the word *athletes*. With some practice, you can become an adept user of truncation.

Quicktivity: Truncation

Study the keywords you came up with in "Quicktivity: Keywords, Synonyms, Hypernyms, and Hyponyms." Which ones should be truncated? Write each keyword and its truncated form below it. Run a search for one of the truncated terms. Did you get any false hits? If so, try to explain why.

Identify Concept Phrases

In some cases, you may need more than keywords, particularly if the words associated with your topic are very general. Take the example of whether the size of a college class affects male and female students differently. What kinds of words would you expect to appear in webpages or articles about this topic? You might try running keyword searches for *number, students, college, men, women,* and *class*—and wind up with a lot of irrelevant sources. Here's where you have to start thinking like a search engine—or, rather, like the people who write the content in webpages, articles, and books, as well as item records. (You will learn more about item records, the summaries of basic information about sources, in the next chapter.) These people often think about subjects conceptually. In other words, instead of thinking of individual pieces—*numbers* of *students* in *college classes*—they tend to encapsulate a topic in a phrase that captures the general concept: *class size*. Often, these **concept phrases** are common within a field and point directly to a concept frequently studied in that field. Here are some more examples:

- tendency of media outlets to cover the same events in the same ways: *pack journalism*
- using techniques to soothe one's conscience when doing wrong: *defense mechanism*
- drinking too much alcohol all at once—at a party, for example: *binge drinking*

If you lack experience in the field you are exploring—that is, if you are an outsider instead of an insider—you may not be familiar with these phrases, but you can find them in various ways. First, you can be on the lookout for them when you read reference sources and webpages, just as you can look for keywords. Since the authors of some of these reference sources are experts, they probably know the phrases and will incorporate them into their articles. If you do not come across any phrases in these sources, talk to an expert in the field or a librarian. If you accurately and articulately describe the phenomenon you want to explore, one of these people probably can give you the perfect phrase that insiders use to describe this phenomenon. Keep track of these concept phrases in your research log.

Quicktivity: Concept Phrases

Check webpages, magazines, and item records for concept phrases. Consider conversations you have had with instructors and librarians, as well. Record any concept phrases you have encountered.

Combine Keywords with Boolean Operators

When conducting research on many topics, you will need to combine keywords or concept phrases to find the information you need. Take the example we examined above. You are interested not just in the general topic of *class size*, but specifically in its impact on men and women in college courses. You can combine concepts by using connecting words known as **Boolean operators**. The three main Boolean operators are *or*, *and*, and *not*.

The word *or* tells the search engine that the text or item record of a source must contain at least one of the keywords or concept phrases you list. Use *or* when you are not sure which keyword or concept phrase the author of the text or item record has used in referring to something. This technique is especially helpful when you are working with synonyms. For example, since some authors of articles about class size in college courses might use the word *university* instead of *college* or something totally different such *undergraduate classes*, you might want to search for "college or university or undergraduate" instead of just "college." In short, combining keywords or concept phrases with *or* broadens your search, giving you *more* hits than using one word or phrase by itself.

The word *and* tells the search engine that the text or item record of the source you are seeking must contain both of the keywords or concept phrases you list. For example, if you search for "class size and college," your search generally will return only sources that refer to both "class size" and "college." By using *and*, then, you are eliminating most or all of the sources that refer only to class size in K-12 schools. (Even if you use Boolean operators effectively, you occasionally will wind up with irrelevant articles. For example, a search for "class size and college" might return an article on class size in high schools if the author refers to a college teacher or to students bound for college.) In short, combining keywords or concept phrases with *and* narrows your search, giving you *fewer* hits than using one keyword or concept phrase by itself.

Finally, the word *not* tells the search engine that the text or item record must not contain a certain word or phrase. Use *not* when you want to eliminate sources that deal with an aspect of a topic that you don't want to research. The idea of weeding out some sources might seem counterproductive to some students. After all, you want to get a lot of information on your topic, right? Remember the story of the backroom at the surplus store, though. The detective wanted to see a specific receipt. What if she could turn on certain lights in that room, but leave all the receipts for unrelated items in the dark? She would greatly increase her chances of finding the receipt she wants to see in a relatively short amount of time. The Boolean operator *not* is especially helpful when the research on a certain topic has focused on a particular aspect that you are not researching. For example, perhaps much of the research on class size has focused on teaching strategies and related issues and not on learning or student achievement. Since you are not looking at this aspect of the topic, you may want to eliminate all of these sources from your search and thus save yourself the time of going through them. In short, using *not* narrows your search, giving you *fewer* hits than using a single word or phrase.

You can enclose some combined terms in parentheses to separate them from the rest of the keywords. This strategy is particularly useful when you are using *or* to search for multiple synonyms. You could combine the concept phrase of *class size* and keywords referring to college, men, and women. Using keywords, concept phrases, truncation, Boolean operators, and parentheses, we can come up with a sophisticated search string:

class size and gender and (college* or freshman or undergraduate)

This search should turn up sources that refer to class size at the college level, as well as men and women.

Quicktivity: Combining Keywords with Boolean Operators

Use the prompts below to combine keywords and concept phrases with Boolean search terms.

1 Record some synonyms and connect them with *or*.
2 Record some keywords and concept phrases and connect them with *and*.
3 Record some keywords or concept phrases that you want to eliminate from your search because they deal with an aspect of the topic you don't want to explore.
4 Put together the above lists to create at least three complete search strings.

Keep an Open Mind

Some of the best sources may not be the most appealing on first glance. Some, for example, may not seem to relate to your topic because they don't mention specific keywords you have in mind. Let's say, for example, you are looking at effective

1. The impact of a multimodal Summer Camp Training on neuropsychological functioning in **children** and adolescents with **ADHD**: An exploratory study.

Academic Journal

By: Gerber, Wolf-Dieter; Gerber-von Müller, Gabriele; Andrasik, Frank; Niederberger, Uwe; Siniatchkin, Michael; Kowalski, Jens T.; Petermann, Ulrike; Petermann, Franz. **Child** Neuropsychology. May2012, Vol. 18 Issue 3, p242-255. 14p. 3 Charts. DOI: 10.1080/09297049.2011.599115.

Subjects: CAMPS for **children**; NEUROPSYCHOLOGICAL tests for **children**; ATTENTION-deficit-disordered **children**; ATTENTION -- Testing; SOCIAL skills -- Testing; METHYLPHENIDATE; **COUNSELING**; NEUROPSYCHOLOGY; Other Individual and Family Services; Recreational (except hunting and fishing) and vacation camps

🔂 **PDF Full Text** (148KB)

Figure 3.1   Item record from *PsycINFO* (EBSCO). Source: Permission given by EBSCO*host*.

counseling or other treatment techniques for children diagnosed with ADHD and you come across the item record illustrated in Figure 3.1.

Since there's no explicit reference to counseling or treatment, some students might skim this item record and move on without locating and reading the article itself. They could be missing a very useful source, though. The "Summer Camp Training" mentioned here may involve one or more kinds of treatment, including counseling. You don't know if you don't check.

Other potentially valuable sources escape some students' attention because they don't seem specific enough. For example, let's say that you are researching the effectiveness of group therapies on African-American children with ADHD. In Figure 3.2 the title of the article seems to indicate that it deals with African-American children

Coming to Terms with ADHD: How Urban African-American Families Come to Seek Care for Their Children

Susan dosReis, Ph.D.
Matthew P. Mychailyszyn, B.A.
MaryAnne Myers, Ph.D.
Anne W. Riley, Ph.D.

Figure 3.2   Title and authors of a source. Source: Created by Michael C. Alewine.

A Novel Group Therapy for
Children with ADHD and
Severe Mood Dysregulation

James G. Waxmonsky, Fran A. Wymbs, Meghan E. Pariseau,
Peter J. Belin, Daniel A. Waschbusch, Lysett Babocsai,
Gregory A Fabiano, Opeolowa O. Akinnusi, Jenifer L. Haak,
and William E. Pelham

Figure 3.3   Title and authors of a source. Source: Created by Michael C. Alewine.

with ADHD, while the title of the article in Figure 3.3 mentions an effective group-based therapeutic approach for children with ADHD.

If you become fixated on your exact topic–the effectiveness of group therapies on African-American children with ADHD—you may ignore the second article because it does not focus on African-American children. Again, you might be skipping a useful article. Some of the general information probably applies to all children and thus could inform your thinking about your topic.

Quicktivity: Use an Open Mind to Check Out Sources

Look at a results list you got when you ran a keyword search. Click on the link to an item that does not seem directly related to your topic and spend a few minutes looking through it. Do you see anything potentially useful?

Conclusion

The strategies you have learned in this chapter are crucial ones you can use when searching the Internet or any kind of database. Once you know how to identify appropriate keywords and concept phrases, truncate terms, and connect your terms with Boolean operators, you can craft some very sophisticated search strings, the kind that will save you time and reduce the stress of a research project. You also know how to create a research log, which you now can use to record keywords, jot down the names of databases, and generally track the process of your research. When you have completed this step, you should have several sources with information related to your topic. In the next chapter, you will learn more about the wide range of sources you are going to encounter in your searching.

Steps to Success

1   Following the example from sociology in this chapter, create a research log for your research project.

2 Using what you have learned in this chapter about synonyms, hypernyms, hyponyms, truncation, and concept phrases, craft some sophisticated search strings for your topic. Record them in your research log.

3 Test three of your search strings by running searches on the Internet. Use what you have learned in this chapter to explain why the different search strings produced the results they did.

Works Cited

United States Bureau of Labor Statistics (BLS). (2015). Occupational Outlook Handbook, Retrieved from http://www.bls.gov/ooh/, accessed August 1, 2016.

4

Explore Possible Sources

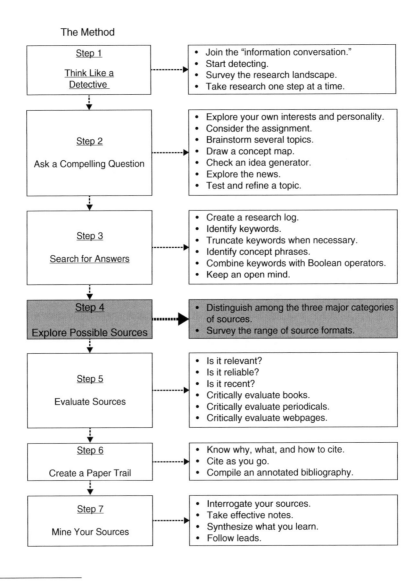

The Method

Step 1
Think Like a Detective
- Join the "information conversation."
- Start detecting.
- Survey the research landscape.
- Take research one step at a time.

Step 2
Ask a Compelling Question
- Explore your own interests and personality.
- Consider the assignment.
- Brainstorm several topics.
- Draw a concept map.
- Check an idea generator.
- Explore the news.
- Test and refine a topic.

Step 3
Search for Answers
- Create a research log.
- Identify keywords.
- Truncate keywords when necessary.
- Identify concept phrases.
- Combine keywords with Boolean operators.
- Keep an open mind.

Step 4
Explore Possible Sources
- Distinguish among the three major categories of sources.
- Survey the range of source formats.

Step 5
Evaluate Sources
- Is it relevant?
- Is it reliable?
- Is it recent?
- Critically evaluate books.
- Critically evaluate periodicals.
- Critically evaluate webpages.

Step 6
Create a Paper Trail
- Know why, what, and how to cite.
- Cite as you go.
- Compile an annotated bibliography.

Step 7
Mine Your Sources
- Interrogate your sources.
- Take effective notes.
- Synthesize what you learn.
- Follow leads.

Introduction to Information Literacy for Students, First Edition. Michael C. Alewine and Mark Canada.
© 2017 John Wiley & Sons, Ltd. Published 2017 by John Wiley & Sons, Ltd.

Chapter Summary

Take the broad view and familiarize yourself with the wide variety of sources you have available to you in your research. This chapter will introduce you to three basic categories—primary, secondary, and tertiary sources—as well as the many formats in which these kinds of sources appear: books, periodicals, webpages, and more.

Key Terms: source, primary source, interpretation, secondary source, scholar, tertiary source, media, information timeline, almanac, atlas, podcast, bibliography, citation, annotated bibliography, annotation, blog, vlog, book, CD-ROM, dictionary, encyclopedia, subject encyclopedia, government source, guide, handbook, manual, magazine, manuscript, typescript, archive, microform, microfiche, microfilm, interview, newspaper, photograph, scholarly journal, peer review, social media, trade magazine, video recording, website

Chapter Objectives

- Distinguish among primary, secondary, and tertiary sources.
- Identify and describe each format in which sources appear.
- Explain the advantages and uses of various kinds of sources.

So Many Sources ... So Little Time!

Have you ever fantasized about winning one of those shopping sprees—you know, the kind where you get two or three minutes to pick out everything you can get in a store and take it all home for free? If you're a foodie, maybe you would enjoy a spree at a gourmet shop. A techie might love the opportunity to gather goodies in a computer store—and a mechie (you know, the mechanical type, a person who likes to tinker and build) would probably prize a spree in a hardware store. If you're like a lot of people, you have even taken this fantasy to the point where you devised a strategy for your spree: a handful of spices, two armfuls of cheeses, and a whole cartful of chocolate!

Imagine, though, that you had to *do* something specific with whatever you collected on your spree: prepare a meal, for example, as the chefs on those popular cooking shows have to do, or build something from scratch. If you have, let's say, a treasure trove of power saws and routers, pneumatic nail guns, and cordless drills, but no wood or nails or screws, you won't be able to make anything.

Figure 4.1   A few kinds of sources. Source: Photo taken by Michael C. Alewine.

The same is true of a research spree. (OK, not *everyone* calls a trip to the library a *spree*, but it can be a lot like the other kinds of sprees we have described here, especially when you have chosen a topic that really appeals to you.) Since information comes in a variety of forms, you will want to be familiar with these forms and know which kinds serve which purposes. (See Figure 4.1 for images of various kinds of sources.) This chapter will introduce you to the wide variety of information tools you have at your disposal, helping you to choose the right one for any job:

1   Distinguish among the three major categories of sources.
2   Survey the range of source formats (conveniently organized here in an alphabet-
     ical list).

The second part of this book describes many of these sources in much more detail, dedicating a chapter to each major kind (reference, books, periodicals, statistics, government sources, and webpages), as well as one chapter to many other kinds of sources. Each chapter discusses strategies and tools you can use when searching for these specific kinds of sources.

Distinguish among the Three Categories of Sources

In research, as in other parts of life, a **source** is a place where you can get something. Just as oranges are sources of juice and trees are sources of lumber, books and web-pages (along with newspapers, journal articles, recordings, and many other forms) are sources of information. Since research involves finding information to increase understanding, you need to know where to find that information. In short, you need to have a firm grasp on the wide variety of information sources you have at your disposal. These sources can be organized into three categories: primary sources, secondary sources, and tertiary sources.

You can think of a **primary source** as the kind that comes first—not in terms of importance, but in terms of time in the larger scheme of things. Primary sources are like spices to a chef or wood to a carpenter. They are the raw material on which everything else depends. If you wanted to study the psychology of online dating, for example, you could investigate a variety of primary sources: profiles posted on dating sites, images of couples that you took yourself or found on the Internet, or any combination of emails, tweets, blogs, or social media posts written by men and women involved with online dating. All of these primary sources could provide you with insights into why people decide to seek romantic partners online, how they feel about the relationships that develop, whether they think this form of matchmaking is effective, and more. Although the people whose profile or blog you are reading may occasionally reflect explicitly on the psychology of online dating ("I prefer online dating because it puts personality ahead of looks"), you often will have to make your own sense of what you find. That's the nature of primary sources. The **interpretation**— that is, the sense-making—is usually up to you. You need to recognize patterns, make connections, offer explanations, draw conclusions. Like oregano or two-by-fours, primary sources need someone to make something of them—and that someone is you!

You can find numerous types of primary sources: not just images, tweets, blogs, and interviews, but also maps, statistics, audio and video recordings (including YouTube videos), newspaper articles (when they merely report the facts and do not offer interpretations), letters, diaries, novels, poems, plays, transcripts and minutes from meetings, various kinds of government documents, observations, artifacts, and more. Some of these sources are not purely raw data, since a reporter, cartographer, editor, or camera operator helped to shape or package it, but in this book we use the term *primary source* for any source that is entirely or almost entirely factual or any source that lacks explicit interpretation by an outsider.

Secondary sources come—you guessed it—second. In other words, in terms of time, they come *after* primary sources. Only after "Looking for a Soulmate" posts his online profile or tweets his ecstatic response to his first date with "Bold and Beautiful" can an outsider come along and interpret this material. **Scholars**—that is, college professors, medical researchers, some professional authors, and other people who study things and share their findings with others—often play this role, picking through primary sources, interpreting what they find, and publishing or presenting their conclusions so that others can learn from them. The places where they share their conclusions are known as secondary sources.

Like primary sources, secondary sources can appear in a variety of formats. Some of the most common are books and articles in scholarly journals. Other kinds of secondary sources include editorials and interpretive articles published in newspapers and magazines, lectures, and commentaries delivered orally on radio or television programs. In short, anything that interprets a primary source is a secondary source.

Some kinds of publications or programs can contain both primary and secondary material. For example, a news site on the Internet might contain video footage of a demonstration (primary), interviews with participants (primary), objective written accounts of the events (primary), an editorial about the meaning of the demonstration (secondary), and a recorded conversation among experts offering their ideas about why the demonstrators were involved (secondary).

Finally, **tertiary sources** provide indexing and synthesis of both primary and secondary sources. As the term indicates, they come third—that is, after both primary and secondary sources. The purpose of tertiary sources is usually to help researchers find or interpret the primary and secondary sources in a subject area. For example, a bibliography on Zionism would provide citations that researchers could use to track down books, articles, and perhaps other sources on this subject. Other examples of tertiary sources include databases, directories, and print indexes. Some kinds of sources, such as many subject encyclopedias, contain both secondary and tertiary information because they not only offer interpretation, but also feature bibliographies.

As you might have guessed, all three types of sources can prove useful to you as you conduct research on a topic. Primary sources provide raw material, secondary sources provide interpretations of the material, and tertiary sources can help you find both primary and secondary sources. Many students tend to focus on secondary sources, particularly interpretive articles published in newspapers, magazines, and scholarly journals. Although such sources are valuable and, in many cases, essential to effective research, they generally should not be the only kinds you use. Without primary sources, you probably will wind up simply repeating what others have said in their interpretations and offering little or no interpretation of your own. In short, you will be writing a kind of literature review (a kind of summary of others' research, which will be discussed in a later chapter) instead of your own interpretive study of the topic. Consumers of research—that is, readers of biographies and other studies, people who attend research conferences, and, yes, your instructors when they are reading your papers or listening to your presentations—usually want fresh interpretations, not just summaries of old research. While secondary sources can provide you with useful interpretations to inform your thinking, you usually should study some or many primary sources and draw your own conclusions about them. (Literature classes generally call on you to do this kind of work: you read some poetry, fiction, nonfiction, or drama and then, perhaps with some help from secondary sources, interpret it. Instructors in other fields often require the same kind of research, but ask you to interpret historical events, psychological phenomena, business practices, or other kinds of raw data instead of poems or plays.)

Quicktivity: Distinguish Among Primary, Secondary, and Tertiary Sources

Google your topic and study one of the webpages you find. Is this page a primary source, a secondary source, or a tertiary source? How do you know? Now try to find a different kind of source. What's the difference?

Survey the Range of Source Formats

Now that you have seen the three basic kinds of sources—primary, secondary, and tertiary sources—you are ready to get a taste of how source material is "packaged." A useful term here is **medium** (or the better-known plural form, **media**), which roughly means the form of an information source. Some common media are books, periodicals, websites, and recordings. Each of these media itself comes in different varieties: there are various kinds of books, various kinds of periodicals, and so on. In this section, we provide snapshots of many of these varieties of information sources, listing them in alphabetical order for the sake of organization.

Your selection of information sources depends on various factors. One key consideration is the **information timeline**, a way of describing the relationship between various source packages and the points in time when they cover topics. (See Figure 4.2.)

The Information Timeline

0 hours: A major event, such as a terrorist attack, takes place. Radio (NPR) and television (CNN) networks start continuous coverage within minutes of the event. News websites of all kinds also begin continuous coverage of events.

24 hours: Print newspapers, such as the *Chicago Tribune* and *The New York Times*, publish the first coverage of the event.

1 Week: National weekly news magazines, such as *Newsweek* and *Time*, begin covering the attacks, but try to capture news that has broken since the event. They also may include some commentary or stories about the larger context around the event.

1 Month: Monthly magazines, such as *Foreign Policy* and *Washington Report*, begin to provide in-depth news reports and analyses.

6 Months: Scholarly journals may publish in-depth studies of the event, aftermath, and context.

1 Year: More in-depth studies may appear in scholarly journals, and some popular books (possibly written by a news correspondent as opposed to a scholar) and government reports may begin to appear.

1+ Years: Discussion of the event may appear in scholarly books and reference sources, such as subject encyclopedias, as well as large-scale government documents, such as commission reports.

Figure 4.2 The information timeline. Source: Originally developed by UNC Libraries, http://www2.lib.unc.edu/instruct/tutorial/?section=searching. Reproduced with permission of UNC Libraries. Created by Michael C. Alewine.

Because some forms of media transmit information electronically, they need little time to reach audiences. Television news outlets, radio stations, news sites, and other kinds of websites, for example, may report on a breaking news story about a mass shooting within minutes of the event. Daily newspapers, which must be printed and delivered, take a little longer, but still generally will publish information about the event within 24 hours. Other kinds of periodicals, such as magazines and scholarly journals, are published less frequently—perhaps once a week or once a month—and thus may report on the event a week or more after the event. Finally, books and government documents tend to come even later, perhaps a year or more after the event. Each kind of information package differs not only in its timeliness, but also in the kind of approach it takes to the topic. There isn't a whole lot of time for television or radio journalists—or, for that matter, any commentators they might interview—to study a shooting before providing the early coverage of it. Authors of books and government documents, on the other hand, generally have had a chance to examine statistics, collect firsthand accounts, interview experts, and study the history of mass shootings, as well as laws and other relevant information. There is a tradeoff, however, in the area of currency. Although books and other sources on the right side generally carry more interpretation than those on the left side, they cannot be as current because they take so long to produce. While a book is in the production stage, which may take months, there may be important developments in the topic—more shootings or new laws, for example—that won't be covered in the source.

As you can see in the information timeline, sources can come with pros and cons. The same is true in other cases. Scholarly journals tend to carry more authority than popular magazines, but they usually are harder for lay readers to understand. Many manuscripts provide unique insights into a topic, but are much harder to access than other kinds of sources because they are available at only one place in the world. Amateur video footage posted on YouTube can show researchers things they can find nowhere else, but it's not always clear that it shows what it purports to show.

As you read the descriptions of various information sources below, consider their specific features, as well as their pros and cons. The knowledge you develop here can help you tremendously when it comes to choosing, evaluating, and using sources in your research.

Almanacs are compilations of various kinds of information, particularly statistics, but also brief accounts of events and more. Many contain maps and other images. Because they come out once a year, they are more current than most books, but not as current as newspapers or magazines. They can be useful sources for facts about populations, economic output, and more.

Atlases, maps, and globes are good places to go for geographical information—that is, information about the earth (and occasionally other celestial bodies)—but many also contain economic, historical, political, cultural, and demographic information, as well. Some atlases are general collections of various kinds of maps while others focus on specific topics. Examples of the latter kind include *An Atlas of Poverty in America: One Nation, Pulling Apart, 1960-2003*; *Atlas of the North American*

Indian; *The Atlas of Water: Mapping the World's Most Critical Resource*; and *The International Atlas of Mars Exploration: The First Five Decades. Volume 1: 1953 to 2003.* You often can find atlases in reference collections, but some are shelved in general collections, and some large research libraries have whole sections devoted to geographical information in the form of atlases, maps, globes, and more. You may also consider online resources like Google Earth and Google Maps to be reliable sources of geographical information.

Quicktivity: Find Maps

Google a topic that interests you—"global warming" or "ancient world," for example—and include the word "maps" in your search. Check a library's reference section for atlases related to this topic. What can you learn from maps?

Bibliographies are lists of **citations**, which are brief collections of identifying information—authors' names, titles, dates of publication, and so on—that researchers can use to find articles, books, and other sources. (Elsewhere in this book, you will learn how to use this identifying information to find sources, but you also should feel free to consult librarians when you need help.) As you may have already noticed, bibliographies—also called "references"—often appear at the ends of articles, chapters, books, master's theses, and doctoral dissertations. Bibliographies can also be found on the Web in many formats. Many researchers and faculty have created their own bibliographies (especially in their syllabi) and posted them on the Web. Many librarians also have compiled bibliographies and posted them on course-specific and subject webpages, many created with a product known as LibGuides. (See Figure 4.3.)

Bibliographies do not always appear at the ends of other works; sometimes, they stand on their own. Some even take up entire books. These traditional print bibliographies are especially useful for research in the humanities (literature and philosophy, for example) and some of the social sciences (psychology and sociology, for example). If, on the other hand, you are looking for information on a current event such as political upheaval in a particular country, then a bibliography may not always be your best source, since it may not have been compiled recently. (In such a case, you probably will be better off using something called a database, described elsewhere in this chapter.) A few examples of book-length bibliographies include *A Bibliography of Modern Arthuriana (1500–2000)*; *A Blues Bibliography*; *Books Under Fire: A Hit List of Banned and Challenged Children's Books*; *Girls are People Too! A Bibliography of Nontraditional Female Roles in Children's Books*; *The Law of the Sea: A Select Bibliography*; and *U.S. Marines in Iraq, 2004–2008: Anthology and Annotated Bibliography*. As you can see from this list, bibliographies can be very specific in terms of the subjects they cover and often are goldmines of information about other sources worth consulting.

Family Systems Bibliography

References

Chambers, M. F. (2009). Nothing is as practical as a good therapy: Bowen theory and the workplace—A personal application. *ANZJFT Australian and New Zealand Journal of Family Therapy, 30*(4), 235-246.

Coco, E. L., & Courtney, L. J. (2003). A family systems approach for preventing adolescent runaway behavior. *Family Therapy: The Journal of the California Graduate School of Family Psychology, 30*(1), 39-50.

Cook, L. (2007). Perceived conflict, sibling position, cut-off, and multigenerational transmission in the family of origin of chemically dependent persons: An application of Bowen family systems theory. *Journal of Addictions Nursing, 18*(3), 131-140.

Faber, A. J. (2004). Examining remarried couples through a Bowenian family systems lens. *Journal of Divorce & Remarriage, 40*(3-4), 121-133.

Harris, J. N., Hay, J., Kuniyuki, A., Asgari, M. M., Press, N., & Bowen, D. J. (2010). Using a family systems approach to investigate cancer risk communication within melanoma families. *Psycho-Oncology, 19*(10), 1102-1111.

Heiden Rootes, K. M., Jankowski, P. J., & Sandage, S. (2010). Bowen family systems theory and spirituality: Exploring the relationship between triangulation and religious questing. *Contemporary Family Therapy: An International Journal, 32*(2), 89-101.

Figure 4.3 Sample bibliography contained in a subject guide concerning social work theories. Source: Created by Michael C. Alewine.

Whether they appear at the ends of other works or stand on their own, bibliographies are tremendous assets to researchers because they guide them to useful sources. One especially useful form of bibliography is something called an **annotated bibliography**, which contains both citations for sources and **annotations**, or notes, indicating what researchers can expect to find in these sources.

Quicktivity: Search for Bibliographies

Visit your library's webpage and see if they have any subject guides that contain bibliographies.

Blogs, short for *weblogs*, are online sources featuring posts written by experts or laypeople about any topics. **Vlogs**, short for *video logs*, are video versions of blogs.

Books are familiar sources. A typical library contains thousands of them: children's picture books, novels, biographies, histories, self-help manuals, and many other kinds. Most have their use in academic research. Scholarly books are particularly useful, since they contain in-depth explorations of their subjects, along with bibliographies.

CD-ROMs (Compact Discs Read-Only Memory) are discs containing data. Libraries have a long history with CD-ROMs; in fact, early article databases were on disc before they went online. Even today, many specialized indexes (for items such as specific collections, newsletters, or newspapers) are still available on disc. When you ask librarians for assistance, they may direct you to these sources. Also, many federal, international, and state governments put information, especially statistical data, on disc, and libraries will usually keep these discs in special cabinets. These resources might be "library use only," so if you are a distance education student, you may have to ask a librarian to access the information that you need and send it to you.

Dictionaries, whether they appear in print or electronic format, provide spellings, pronunciations, and definitions of words. That much you probably knew. What you may not know is how much other useful information appears in a good dictionary. The entries for many words tell you something about their history—when they came into the language and where they came from, for example—as well as their specialized uses (in law or medicine, for example). Some dictionaries even offer guidance on using words, explaining whether some readers might consider certain usages incorrect. Academic libraries also contain numerous specialized dictionaries, such as legal dictionaries, medical dictionaries, and other dictionaries focusing on the **jargon**, or specialized language, used in special fields, along with dictionaries of slang, new words, and more. Examples include *Dictionary of Contemporary Slang, A Dictionary of Genetics*, the *APA Dictionary of Clinical Psychology*, and the *Dictionary of Food Science and Technology*. Most dictionaries are single volumes, but some, such as *The New Grove Dictionary of Music and Musicians*, have multiple volumes. *The Oxford English Dictionary* consists of 20 volumes containing definitions, variant spellings, sample quotations, and more for hundreds of thousands of English words, not just those in use today, but those used by speakers centuries ago. Many libraries provide electronic access to some dictionaries, while print dictionaries generally are shelved in the reference collection of a library.

Quicktivity: Use a Dictionary

Use a dictionary, such as Merriam-Webster's online dictionary (available at m-w.com) to look up one of your keywords or some jargon you encountered in a source. Record the definition. This definition may prove useful later.

Encyclopedias are like dictionaries in many respects. Usually shelved in a library's reference section, they often appear in both print and online versions, and people tend to consult them for basic factual information. Unlike dictionaries, however, encyclopedias collect information not about words, but about people, places, events, and concepts. Encyclopedia entries can be just a few paragraphs or several pages in length. These entries are typically written by experts, such university professors, librarians, and practitioners within a given profession, and these experts' names often appear along with the entries. For example, the author of an entry on a Civil War battle may have been written by a historian. Many entries feature brief bibliographies, making them invaluable sources of information when you are starting a research project. You may have heard of *Encyclopedia Britannica*, *World Book*, and other general encyclopedias, but many encyclopedias, known as **subject encyclopedias**, are more specialized. Titles and subject matter are as varied as the *American Gangsters, Then and Now: An Encyclopedia*; the *Encyclopedia of Body Image and Human Appearance*; and *The Vampire Book: The Encyclopedia of the Undead*.

Think Fast: Contents of a Subject Encyclopedia

What can you expect to find in a subject encyclopedia?

Government sources are remarkably abundant. The U.S. federal government, in fact, is the most prolific publisher in the world—and, then, of course, there is the information produced by state and local governments in the United States, as well as the federal and local governments in many other countries. Years ago, we could have said that there were literally tons of government documents, and we would not have been exaggerating. Today, much of the information produced by governments is published online. This material includes statistical information, minutes of meetings and official hearings, research studies, and much more. Some libraries, known as selective depository libraries, receive selective federal government documents, while others, known as regional depository libraries, receive copies of all federal government documents printed. Some libraries have government document librarians who deal specifically with government information, while other libraries have librarians who will help you as part of the general reference process. Print government documents are typically shelved using the SuDoc system (described later in this book), but government information can also be found on CD-ROMs and microfiche.

Quicktivity: Google "SuDoc system"

Google the keywords "SuDoc system" and see what you can find about it. How is it different from the Dewey and Library of Congress classification systems? What types of subject matter are covered in government documents?

Guides, **handbooks**, and **manuals** are specialized, practical reference sources created for use by practitioners, researchers, and students. For example, a counselor might use the *Professional Counselor's Desk Reference*. A graduate social work student, starting a significant research project, might use the *Sage Handbook of Social Work Research* or the *Handbook of Research on Electronic Surveys and Measurements*. Some researchers who work in the field carry field manuals, such the *National Wildlife Federation Field Guide to Insects and Spiders & Related Species of North America*. Guides, handbooks, and manuals are shelved in both reference and general collections, so they may or may not be available for checkout. Many are also available as e-books.

Magazines are periodicals—that is, publications that come out on a regular basis. Typically published weekly, biweekly, or monthly, they feature articles written for general audiences or readers interested in particular subjects. Some of the authors are experts, such as scientists or historians, but many are journalists who may or may not have expertise in the subjects they cover. Some magazine articles are short (a page or less); however, feature articles can be at least a few pages in length. Magazine articles may contain more information than newspaper articles, but usually lack the depth of articles found in scholarly journals or government reports. For example, an article in *Newsweek* might mention a recent study about genetically modified foods but only as brief summary. Researchers wanting more depth would need to locate the original study, which was probably published in a scholarly journal or a government document. Magazine articles can be useful sources for ideas for research topics, as they cover what is currently resonating in the news. While a lot of magazines are available in print in libraries, where they can be easily browsed, most are available online, typically through different databases. While some material in magazines is objective, other material presents opinion.

Manuscripts and **typescripts** are unpublished versions of any kind of text. (Technically, a manuscript was written by hand, and a typescript was typed.) Many poems, short stories, novels, diaries, and letters, of course, are published, but many are available only in manuscript or typescript. Researchers, particularly historians and literary scholars, sometimes visit **archives**—special collections of rare or even unique materials—to see these manuscripts and typescripts.

Microforms, including both **microfiche** and **microfilm**, are not really different kinds of sources, but just different formats for sources such as newspapers, magazines, and government documents. For the sake of convenience, though, we have listed them here separately. Microforms conserve space by collecting very small photographs of printed documents on sheets (microfiche) or film on reels (microfilm). Because the images are much too small to read with the naked eye, microforms require special reader-printers to view and print them. Many libraries also have the capability to scan these items and convert them to PDFs—useful formats for off-campus and online students. Microfilm and microfiche copies sometimes can be hard to read because of the quality of the original scan. These low-quality scans are often stamped with words such as "Best Available Copy." If you are researching children, schools, etc., in any discipline (education, psychology, social work, etc.), you may have used the ERIC online database, which indexes both ERIC documents (ED) and ERIC journals (EJ). The ERIC documents are typically found online, but many, including older ERIC documents, are not available online yet. Many libraries keep the microfiche versions of the ERIC documents; some have the complete collection from 1966 to July 2004 (ED000001 to ED483046).

Think Fast: Microforms

How do you read microforms? Can you print them? How do you get access to microfilms and microfiche if you are an online student?

Interviews allow researchers to get information directly from scholars or practitioners, such as school social workers or civil engineers. Interviews—whether conducted in person, by phone, or via email—are valuable sources because they allow you to ask very specific questions and collect exactly the information you want.

Newspapers, like magazines, are periodicals, but they generally appear more often, usually daily or weekly. Written generally by journalists, not experts, and directed at general readers, the articles tend to be brief. Newspapers present both original content and articles from national papers or news services, such as the Associated Press. A few newspapers, such as *USA Today* and *The New York Times*, have national audiences, but the vast majority are read primarily by people in a particular city or region. These local readers often will find articles about events of great national or international import, but they also expect information about local events and issues. Sometimes newspapers provide local perspectives on national stories; in the wake of a school shooting in one state, for example, a newspaper might cover strategies that local schools are using to prevent violence. Like magazines, newspapers can contain opinion pieces, as well as objective articles. They are indexed by both general databases and specialized newspaper databases. They are valuable sources for all disciplines, but especially valuable for historical research. Many libraries collect microfilm reels of newspapers going back to the 1800s, and specialized databases provide access to newspapers going back to the colonial era.

Photographs are everywhere, especially in the age of the Internet. As we discuss in Chapter 13, they can be very useful sources of information, especially if you want to include multimedia elements in your papers, presentations, and other projects. Even everyday snapshots can become historically relevant. (Just think of cell phone photos taken during the Occupy Wall Street movement.) You can find photographs on the Internet, of course, but also in a variety of print publications. Several general and specialized databases also provide access to photographs.

Podcasts are sound recordings of lectures, interviews, personal narratives, Supreme Court oral arguments, and more. They are available in a variety of formats, the most common being mp3 sound files made available via the World Wide Web. Because they are Web-based resources, you will need to evaluate the organization that is maintaining a particular recording that you want to use. (See Step 5 for guidance in evaluating sources.) There are hundreds of credible sites that provide access to podcasts, and the best way to search for them is to use a search engine, such as Google. With podcasts, be sure to listen carefully and meticulously transcribe the parts that you plan to use. Many sites, such National Public Radio, provide text transcripts of their podcasts.

Scholarly journals, like magazines, are periodicals, but both their authors and their readers are typically experts in specific disciplines such as biology and business—or even subdisciplines such as bacteriology and managerial accounting. In general, articles submitted to scholarly journals must go through something called **peer review** before they can be published; that is, one or more "peers," or fellow experts in the field, read the article to determine that the research is sound. For this reason, articles in scholarly journals generally are highly credible. Because the authors assume that their expert readers have a working knowledge of the subject matter and are familiar with the jargon of the discipline, scholarly journal articles can be very difficult for outsiders to understand. Still, because of their credibility and depth of research, these articles are very useful to researchers. When you read them, keep a subject-specific dictionary on hand. (For example, before you kick back with "Multiresidue Method for the Determination of Pharmacologically Active Substances in Egg and Honey using a Continuous Solid-phase Extraction System and Gas Chromatography-mass Spectrometry," grab a dictionary of chemical terms.)

Think Fast: Magazines and Scholarly Journals

What are some differences between a magazine and a scholarly journal?

Social media sites are interactive websites and tools used by people, governments, and organizations to communicate in both formal and informal ways. Because they can present unique content, they can be very useful, particularly as primary sources. Most lack editors, though, so use what you learn in the next chapter to evaluate them before you use them in your research.

Trade magazines, sometimes known as *trade publications*, are special kinds of magazines (although some look like newspapers). Often written by practitioners for other practitioners (and professional analysts), the articles in these periodicals provide information that readers can use to improve their products or services. For example, *Advertising Age* features articles on issues and trends in advertising written by advertising and marketing experts for other advertising and marketing experts.

Video recordings include professionally produced documentaries, as well as YouTube videos, lectures, and other recordings created by amateurs. Some libraries have extensive video collections, typically indexed in the online catalog, and many subscribe to streaming services, such as *Films for the Humanities*. Many prestigious universities, such as MIT and Stanford, make video lectures freely available on iTunes U. Regardless of the format, video recordings can be useful sources, multimedia elements in an oral report, or both.

Websites contain articles published only on the Web, along with many other types of sources described elsewhere in this chapter: images, video recordings, bibliographies, and more. It is important to distinguish between webpages designed to be open to the public in the online environment—that is, on the Web—and various kinds of proprietary material. After all, the Web is not a source, but a platform that provides access to sources. Many credible sources of information are "proprietary" in nature—meaning libraries pay a lot of money to the owners of the information to provide users with access to these sources. Even though your library makes this proprietary material—articles in scholarly journals, for example—available to you via the Web, this material itself is not the same as a webpage. For example, the article database *Academic Search Complete* is not a webpage or a series of webpages. It is a closed database that provides indexing and some full-text access to credible magazines, newspapers, and scholarly journals. Such publications generally have editors who help to ensure the information is correct and authoritative, whereas many webpages lack editors—thus the need to evaluate webpages especially carefully.

Think Fast: Articles on Webpages and Articles in Scholarly Journals

What is the difference between a webpage and a journal article made available via the Web?

Conclusion

In this chapter, you have learned about three basic kinds of sources—primary, secondary, and tertiary sources—as well as a variety of ways that source material is packaged in various formats: atlases, encyclopedias, scholarly journals, webpages, and more. As you read the second half of this book, you will find more detailed information about many of these sources. You also can find brief definitions in the glossary at the end of the book. In the next chapter, you will learn some strategies for evaluating these various sources.

Steps to Success

1   Look at the syllabi or research assignment sheets for your different courses. Do any of your instructors mention source categories, such as primary or secondary sources, or specific kinds of information sources, such as articles in scholarly journals? If so, make some notes about required sources. Why do you think your instructors limited your choice of sources in this way?

2   Visit the reference section of a library and browse the books on the shelves. Pick up five or six volumes and try to determine whether they are atlases, manuals, subject encyclopedias, or other kinds of reference sources. For each kind, record some of the pros and cons, as well as possible uses for your research project.

3   Find a tertiary source, such as a bibliography, and use it to find some secondary sources. Now, use the bibliographies in the secondary sources to find additional sources, including at least one primary source. Make a list of sources that appear potentially useful to you in your research.

4   Spend some time with a primary source you found in the activity above. Interpret one or more details. Now compare your interpretations with those you saw in a secondary source. Do you need to adjust your approach to interpretation? If so, how do you think you need to adjust it?

5   Run a search on the Web for a topic that interests you. Check out some of the pages that come up and determine whether they are webpages or other kinds of sources made available through one or more proprietary databases. How could you tell?

5

Evaluate Sources

The Method

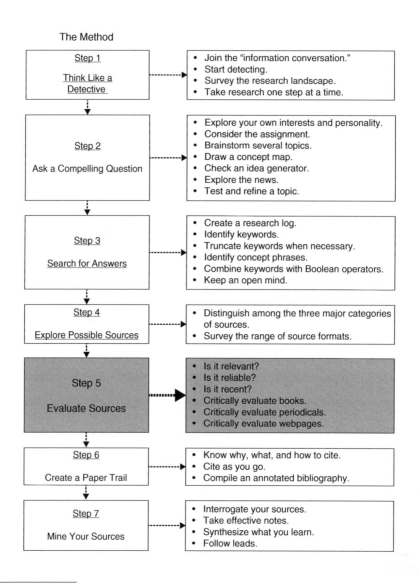

Introduction to Information Literacy for Students, First Edition. Michael C. Alewine and Mark Canada.
© 2017 John Wiley & Sons, Ltd. Published 2017 by John Wiley & Sons, Ltd.

Chapter Summary

Interrogate those sources before you start resting your case on them. Use the strategies in this chapter to evaluate them on the basis of relevance, credibility, and currency.

Key Terms: evaluation, critical thinking, relevant, credibility, credentials, academic, bias, subjective, objective, agenda, peer review, vanity press, popular books

Chapter Objectives

- Use information about relevance to select appropriate sources.
- Identify bias in a source.
- Assess an author's credentials and use them to evaluate the credibility of a source.
- Evaluate the timeliness of a source.
- Identify peculiar features of books, periodical articles, and webpages and use them to evaluate these sources.

Is It Legit—For Real?

If you're like most people, you're pretty skeptical about things, and why shouldn't you be? Much of the online world is *other*worldly, teeming with crazy urban legends, phony photos, and emails from pseudo-princes pitching obvious scams. All this fakery gave rise to the meme "seems legit," a sarcastic phrase widely applied to things clearly *not* legit-imate. In a world filled with shams and scams, hoaxes and hucksters, you need to be ready with another catch phrase: "For real?"

Think about how you apply your skepticism to your everyday life. Do you always buy a ticket to a movie without at least trying to find out something about it— especially given the costs of going to a movie these days? Probably not—you might rely on the critique of a trusted friend or relative who has already seen the film (unless it is crazy Uncle Bob, who thinks everything is art). You might watch a trailer for the film or check out some professional reviews on the Web. At any rate, you generally try to gauge the value of the movie before you spend any time or money on it. In other words, you subject it to some form of **evaluation**. You probably do the same to other things that may cost you money, time, or emotional dollars: a car, a phone, a plumber or electrician, a university, a date. It pays to take a few minutes and think critically.

The same is true when you are doing research. Now, you didn't need this book to know you shouldn't be quoting from the phony prince in a paper about investing, but you may be surprised to learn that you have to evaluate *every* source, not just the ones you encounter in the online jungle. After all, a library seems like a much safer place. Surely, if a library has it, it must be good, right? The short answer is … "kind of." Libraries do tend to collect legitimate information resources from bona fide publishers, vendors, and the like. The longer answer to the question is, well, this chapter. As you will see, there are good reasons to evaluate sources and useful strategies you can use to evaluate them.

These strategies are essential to determining which sources you should consider using, but they are not always simple to apply. Usually, there is no single factor that makes or breaks a source. Rather, you need to weigh several individual features and draw an overall conclusion. The process is both complex and essential. It involves something that educators everywhere promote as one of the most important skills in the world: **critical thinking**. When you engage in critical thinking, you think deliberately and deeply about something, not just accepting what you see or hear, but rather using your knowledge to test and question it. Many of the factors and phenomena we discuss in this chapter—credentials, bias, agenda, and more—are vital pieces of knowledge you can put to work when you think critically not just about sources you are considering in your research, but about any source of information you encounter anywhere, from salespeople to politicians to organizations. In short, whether you are exploring some mysterious scientific phenomenon for a research project or just trying to make sense of the news, critical evaluation is a crucial part of information literacy.

In this chapter, we will walk you through a series of questions you can use to evaluate sources, wherever you find them:

1 Is it relevant?
2 Is it reliable?
3 Is it recent?

We also will offer some guidance on evaluating particular kinds of sources, specifically books, periodicals, and webpages.

Is It Relevant?

A source that does not address your topic is of little use. **Relevant** sources are those that contain information directly related to whatever research question you are trying to answer. Too many students write poor essays because they "force" their sources. That is, instead of reading numerous sources and using only the relevant ones, they rely on sources that mention their topics, but do not contain detailed material that answers their research questions. An essay built on this kind of cursory research is not a coherent argument or discussion, but a hodge-podge of miscellaneous findings and observations.

Keyword searches often turn up sources that are not relevant to your topic. To check for relevance, look at item records for books and articles, as well as tables of contents (for books) and abstracts (for articles). How many of your keywords are apparent? If an item record is peppered with your keywords, it would seem to be relevant and is worth a look. If you are trying to determine if a webpage is relevant, search the document for your keywords, at least the main topic keywords. Click the Ctrl (Control) key on your keyboard (command key on an Apple keyboard) and the "F" key to create a find box, or search field, that will allow you to search an HTML page, a PDF document, or a Word document for your keywords. If these keywords appear frequently, the source would seem to be relevant.

Quicktivity: Check for Relevance

Choose one of the sources you found when you ran your searches in the previous chapter. Use what you have learned in this chapter to try to evaluate the relevance of this source.

- If the source is a book, examine the table of contents. What are the major topics covered in this book?
- If the source is an article, examine the abstract (if there is one) or read the first two paragraphs. What are the major topics covered in this article?
- If the source is a webpage, run a search for your keywords on the page. How often do they appear?

What's your verdict? Is it relevant?

Is It Reliable?

A source may be highly relevant to your topic, but lack reliability, or **credibility**. As a researcher, you want to work with credible sources because both you and your readers have good reason to believe what they say, but what makes a source credible?

One answer is **credentials**, the kinds of things that make a person authoritative. (Do you see the similar root in each word? The Latin root *cred-* means "believe" and also appears in *credence, creed* and other words.) One kind of credential is education. Logically, the more a person has studied a subject, the more he or she probably knows about it. Furthermore, to earn a degree from a reputable university, a person generally needs to pass tests, produce written or other products, sometimes even undergo oral interrogations (known by the slightly less intimidating term *oral exams*). As a result, an advanced degree is an excellent credential demonstrating a person's knowledge *of a particular subject*. (Note the words in italics. Someone with a Ph.D. in psychology is not necessarily an expert in United States economic policy or any other subject, although you may occasionally find someone cashing in on his or her degree in one subject to try to come across as credible in a different subject.) Although people with lots of formal education in a subject generally are credible, other people may be credible because they have accumulated **professional experience** through their careers. A successful CEO generally knows a thing or two about business even if he dropped out of college, and many self-taught musicians are widely respected for their knowledge of their art. Here, however, you should look for some signs that the person has achieved something notable or that the person's work has earned some kind of stamp of approval: endorsements by other experts, for example, or publication of their work by reputable presses. If someone simply claims to know a lot about a subject, but has not earned the respect of other experts or produced work worthy of publication, you should rightly wonder just how credible he or she is.

In some cases, such as breaking news events, mere exposure lends a certain amount of credibility. People who have no special education or training in earthquakes nevertheless have something worthwhile to share after they have experienced one. The same can be said of immigrants, participants in protests, victims of abuse, and other people with personal experience in events and phenomena. Think about your own experiences. They have given you some credibility in various areas—being a college athlete, perhaps, or being a single parent. Most of the time, people with personal experience are primarily describing their own thoughts or emotions; thus, their testimony, whether shared through interviews or social media or some other medium, is a kind of primary source.

To assess someone's credentials, of course, you first need to find them. If the author is an **academic**—that is, a professor or researcher associated with a college or university—you sometimes can find his or her curriculum vitae, or cv, online. A kind of resume for academics, a cv lists degrees and publications, both kinds of credentials. As you learned in Chapter 4, publishing one's research in reputable venues generally requires peer review; thus, academics with a lot of articles in respected journals or books published by top presses are credible individuals, and their publications in their fields are credible sources.

If the author is not an academic, you still can check out his or her credentials, such as experience. Often, sources include brief profiles of authors. You also can simply google the author's name to learn more about him or her, or you can check amazon.com to see if this author has written other books on the same subject. If no author is identified, try to evaluate the organization that sponsored the webpage or publication. If the organization is a well-established, widely respected entity, then the material it publishes or sponsors is probably credible. For example, many government sources (which you will study in a later chapter) often lack authors' names, but they still tend to be credible sources, as long as the sponsoring government has a reputation for objective, accurate publications. On the other hand, a website published independently by an individual who has chosen not to identify himself or herself is a source you generally should avoid. For one thing, you can't check this author's credentials. Besides, why is this author not identifying himself or herself? Is the author trying to avoid taking responsibility for the work? This kind of source is suspicious.

A second important consideration when it comes to credibility of a source is the presence or absence of **bias**—a tendency to favor something or someone over something or someone else. As a common, natural part of personality, bias is not a particularly dangerous or shameful thing. Who doesn't have a bias toward their loved ones, pets, sports teams? When you are conducting research, however, you want to find complete, balanced, accurate information, and bias is liable to get in the way. Authors who give into their bias are likely to produce **subjective** sources—that is, sources skewed by their authors' emotions or opinions. Because such sources may emphasize the facts that support one side of an argument, neglect or minimize other facts, or even fabricate material, you may not be seeing a full, accurate picture of your subject in them. They may be useful as *examples* of propaganda representing one side of an argument, but you definitely don't want to take them at face value.

Generally, the best sources are **objective**, presenting information and interpretations that have not been skewed by their authors' human emotions or preferences. Authors of these sources have weighed the evidence with little or no favoritism—it's hard to avoid favoritism entirely—and reported what the research uncovered: not just the good, but also the bad and the ugly. Often, even very carefully conducted research can produce inconclusive results. An objective source will report the actual findings of a study—even if they contradict the researcher's hypothesis—and the limitations of the study.

How can you detect bias? First, compare each source to other sources you have encountered. If one source reports information not found in any other source, the reason may be that this information is fabricated or simply cannot be verified. Second, try to determine the source's **agenda**—that is, a particular political, commercial, or other purpose, perhaps one that makes the author reluctant to share information that contradicts his or her side. Is the author affiliated with an organization that is known for taking a particular side on certain issues? Is the author trying to sell you something? Finally, look for emotionally charged language or images, tools that biased authors or designers commonly use to move their audiences. If you see any of these signs, be suspicious of this source. Set it aside and look for more objective sources.

Quicktivity: Check for Credibility

Choose one of the sources you found when you ran your searches in the previous chapter. Use what you have learned in this chapter to try to evaluate the credibility of this source.

- What are the author's credentials?
- If the author is not identified, is the publisher or sponsoring organization well-known and reputable?

- How does this source compare with others? Does it make a lot of claims not found elsewhere?
- Does this source have an agenda other than to inform? If so, what does the agenda appear to be? How can you tell?
- Note any examples of emotionally charged language or images.

What's your verdict? Is it reliable?

Insider's Tip: Vet Sources in Layers

Analysts and investigators must thoroughly examine sources—not only to extract data from them, but also to determine their credibility. It's not an easy job because we are tempted to stop questioning when we find one or two details that support our theories or when we get the information we expect to find. In this respect, we are similar to researchers in other fields.

To avoid falling into this trap, I had to learn to probe sources to uncover each layer of information. Working layer by layer, I methodically draw out details, as well as leads that can corroborate, flesh out, or challenge the information I've already collected. I have conducted many interviews this way, always asking, "What else can this source tell me?" even if the source doesn't think he or she can remember any other details. I drill down on individual facts, often until the person can provide no additional information. I then move onto the next fact and drill down again, not stopping until there is nothing else to ask. For example, if the witness says she saw a blue car parked outside a store, I might ask these questions:

Color

- What it light blue or dark blue?
- Can you compare the color to something?
- Was it all the same color?

Make, model, and year

- Did the car seem older or newer?
- Was it a sedan, an SUV, a compact?
  - What is large, medium, or small?
  - Describe the shape of the taillights.
  - Did it have a tow hitch?
- Did it have four doors or two?

Identifying marks, such as license tag or damage

- What did the license tag look like?
  - What state?
  - What color?
  - What letter and numbers?
- Did you notice any dents or other kinds of damage to the body of the car?
  - If so, where was the damage?
  - If so, what was the shape of the damage?

The same process is useful when I am examining documents, financial transactions, telephone records, and other kinds of raw data. I work layer by layer, examining associations between accounts, looking for trends and patterns in telephone calls, and drawing links between groups of people. What is normal, and what is anomalous? If someone routinely made numerous calls between 2 and 3 each afternoon, but then made no calls during that period on a certain day, what happened to break the pattern? Is this anomaly relevant to my investigation? What other information do I have or need to obtain that can help to explain the anomaly?

Just because a witness provides copious amounts of information, we cannot assume that the information is accurate. Many victims of bank robberies have stated with absolute certainty and confidence that an assailant was wearing, say, a blue baseball cap, even though video from a security camera video shows no cap. Witnesses and other sources need to be scrutinized, and their stories must be substantiated. Are there additional sources that can corroborate a witness's account? If a source cannot be validated as credible, then he or she cannot be included in our analysis, no matter how badly we want to believe the information. This can be one of the hardest parts of my job.

This cycle of exploiting and validating information can help any researcher develop a complete and accurate picture, whether the goal is to solve a crime or answer another kind of research question.

–Kerrie Harney, federal investigator

Is It Recent?

Timeliness is often a point in favor for secondary sources. The reason is simple. Because researchers build on the work done by their predecessors—standing "on the shoulders of Giants," as Isaac Newton once wrote—more recent secondary sources have an advantage over older ones. Their authors, in theory, have taken into consideration the earlier research and then added something to it. For example, someone working in the field of education today can build on the groundbreaking work of Howard Gardner, who pioneered the notion of "Multiple Intelligences." A book published before Gardner did his work would not have the benefit of this perspective. Timeliness is especially important in the fields of science and technology, where advances happen very rapidly.

If current sources are best, why do we even need the older sources? We could save a lot space in libraries if we just … . Whoa! It's easy to take timeliness too far. Older sources are valuable for two reasons. First, more recent sources do not repeat all the information presented in the older ones; thus, to get a comprehensive understanding of Gardner's work—or, for that matter, any research from any field—you need to study the original source. Second, newer research is not always an advancement on older work. Researcher B can build on the work of Researcher A and come up with an interpretation or theory that is no better than Researcher A's interpretation or theory. It might even be worse. Researchers propose ideas all the time, but often these ideas remain in competition with one another. Take psychology, where the ideas of Freud, Jung, Skinner, Erikson, Maslow, and others are all still influential—and Freud published his first book more than a century ago!

In short, you should take the publication date—or, in the case of Internet resources, the posting date—into consideration when you evaluate a source, but do not automatically dismiss older sources. Note, however, that instructors in some fields, such as nursing and computer science, may limit you to materials that were published in the last three to five years, particularly when you are looking at certain topics in which dramatic advances have occurred in the past few years.

Quicktivity: Check for Timeliness

Pick one of the sources you found when you ran your searches in the previous chapter. Use what you have learned in this chapter to assess its timeliness.

- When was the source published?
- When was the research conducted? (You may not be able to tell.)
- How important is currency in this field? (How quickly is the field evolving?)
- How does this source compare with others? Is it among the most recent, or is it relatively old?

What's your verdict? Is it recent?

Now that you have an overview of the three basic things to consider when evaluating sources—relevance, credibility, and timeliness—let's take a look at a few special considerations you should keep in mind when evaluating three major kinds of sources: books, periodicals, and websites.

Critically Evaluate Books

You can apply all that you have learned here about relevance, credibility, and timeliness to your critical evaluation of books, specifically those that serve as secondary sources. There are a few special things to keep in mind about books, though.

Unlike webpages and some other kinds of sources, many books have been evaluated for credibility even before you see them. Random House, HarperCollins, and other major mainstream publishers have their own reputations to protect. Books with misleading, inaccurate, or out-of-date information would tarnish these reputations if they published them. For this reason, manuscripts undergo a review process before these major publishers make them available to the public. Scholarly presses, such as Oxford University Press and ABC-CLIO, employ particularly stringent processes involving **peer review**, in which other members of a discipline (that is, the authors' peers) study submissions to determine if they should be published. Finally, two slightly different kinds of documents, master's theses and doctoral dissertations, though not published by mainstream publishers or scholarly presses, have a fair amount of credibility because they are written by advanced students as part of their degree programs. These students' advisors generally have guided them, perhaps reading numerous drafts along the way, and thus serve as gatekeepers overseeing the work, in fact playing a role similar to the role played by peer reviewers for scholarly presses. In fact, the authors usually have to "defend" their work before a committee of faculty experts. Some large university libraries have hard copies of theses and dissertations or provide access through an electronic database. Some authors of dissertations go on to revise and publish them as scholarly books. In such cases, it generally is better to consult the published books as the more credible sources, since the work probably has undergone revision and even more scrutiny before its publication as a book.

When you evaluate a book for credibility, check out the publisher as well as the author. If the publisher's name contains the word "University" (as in University of South Carolina Press), odds are, it is a scholarly book and thus generally credible. Some presses are scholarly, but do not have "university" in the names. Examples include ABC-CLIO, Blackwell's, CDL, Greenwood, Palgrave, Praeger, Routledge, Sage, and Wiley. Some national associations, such as the American Psychological Association and the American Sociological Association, also publish books, and they are credible, as well. For lists of scholarly presses, just google "scholarly presses." It's a little more difficult to identify reputable mainstream presses, especially if you are not familiar with the publishing industry. What you can do, though, is find the publisher's name (usually on the title page of a book, near the beginning) and then search for it on amazon.com to see what other books this company has published. If it has published a lot of books by major authors or books that have received positive reviews by reputable critics, you can consider it credible. Be wary of books published by the authors themselves or "**vanity presses**," which charge authors fees for publishing their work and generally do little or no vetting to ensure that the contents of their books are credible.

Because they serve students and professors, who often produce research as part of their jobs, academic libraries tend to have a lot of scholarly books, as well as other books published by reputatable publishers. Just because you find a book in an academic library, however, you cannot assume that it is a good source for your academic research. For one thing, many academic libraries, like public libraries, also contain **popular books**—that is, books intended for general audiences. Examples include some biographies and autobiographies, as well as books on current politics, world affairs, economic conditions, diet and nutrition, psychology, and society. Authors include celebrities, journalists, and people with experience in particular fields, such as politics or medicine. Some academic libraries even display new books in this category—best-selling novels or books of nonfiction, for example—in prominent places. Academic libraries occasionally may even have self-published books or books published by vanity presses. Because these libraries have strict and codified collection development policies, only some such books get into their collections, typically because they have some local appeal. (For example, a library might collect books dealing with local biography and history, institutional history, genealogy, and local plants and animals.) These books are typically shelved in special collections and may not even be available for checkout, but can be used.

As you can see, you have access to a variety of books—with a variety of purposes and levels of credibility—in an academic library. Scholarly books generally are the most credible, but books on history, current affairs, science, business, and other subjects written by authors with appropriate credentials and published by reputable publishers are generally fairly credible, as well. What about the rest? Do you just dismiss those? In general, you should avoid using them as secondary sources, since their authors usually lack strong credentials, or their work may not have undergone much vetting, or perhaps serious study of a subject was simply not the author's intention. As *primary* sources, however, popular books and those published by vanity presses may be very useful, since they may provide insights into the kinds of topics that are popular at a particular historical moment or the ways their authors see the world. Even fiction, which by definition is not true, can shed light on perspectives, emotions, and social conditions. Let's say you are looking at the social conditions of women in Latin America, and you decide to read some novels by Latino authors. Such books might be useful, especially if you do some additional research and find that the authors have explained that they were drawing on reality when writing their fiction. Of course, you still should clearly identify these sources as works of fiction, and you should include plenty of material from nonfiction sources, as well.

Think Fast: Library Holdings

Describe the various kinds of books stored in libraries. Which are the most credible and why?

Critically Evaluate Periodicals

You already know something about periodicals, which we covered in the previous chapters. You know, for example, that newspapers and magazines are popular sources, written for general audiences, and published with no elaborate peer review, although they often have been edited. You know, too, that scholarly journals, written by and for experts in a field, generally publish work that has undergone peer review.

Putting together these characteristics, as well as your knowledge of credibility, you can see that articles published by scholarly journals are likely to be more credible than those that appear in popular magazines. Both kinds of periodicals have an advantage over books when it comes to timeliness, since it generally takes less time to write and publish a short article than it takes to produce and publish an entire book. There are a few other things to keep in mind when you critically examine periodicals.

First, while journalists rarely have the same credentials as scholars, many develop a fair amount of expertise because they have been covering the same beat, or specific area of news, for a long time. Some of the reporters in the Washington Press Corps, for example, have been talking to people in government and studying the issues there for a long time and know things that even the scholars don't know (especially the kinds of things that go on behind the scenes and do not get published).

Second, objectivity is a longstanding principle in American journalism. For this reason, you generally can expect reputable newspapers—*The New York Times, The Washington Post, Time* magazine—to be relatively free of bias, at least in the news coverage. (Journalism, like everything else in the world, is always evolving, though, and attitudes toward objectivity are not always the same.) Whatever their policies or practices in news coverage, newspapers and magazines frequently have separate principles for what are often called editorials or opinion pieces. You might find such items useful, but know that the authors are expressing opinions, so bias is definitely present.

Finally, not all periodicals have the same principles when it comes to objectivity, fairness, or even accuracy. Some are downright disreputable. (You undoubtedly have seen a few in the supermarket checkout line.) They are intended to entertain readers and, ultimately, to make money, not to inform the public or spark productive debate.

By the way, some instructors, especially in upper-division courses, require that students use only scholarly peer-reviewed journals specific to a discipline. For example, a psychology instructor might limit students to only scholarly peer-reviewed journals published by the American Psychological Association (APA). In this situation, you can go to the APA website and pull up a list of its journals and then limit your searches in a database to the specific journal titles in this list. (See Chapter 10 for more information.) You also can ask your instructor for recommendations of journals to use.

Think Fast: Credibility of Popular Sources

What are some factors that lend some popular sources more crediblity than others?

Critically Evaluate Webpages

Since many webpages lack peer review, editors, fact-checkers, or, in some cases, even sponsors with concerns for their reputations, they call for special scrutiny when you are doing academic research. The good news is that, since there is no shortage of information on the Web, you do not need to spend hours evaluating each webpage you find. Just ask the three basic questions we have described in this chapter and then either give it a more in-depth look or just bypass it and move on to another webpage. Resist the temptation to go with the first few relevant pages featured in the results list. The most relevant, reliable, and recent sites might appear far down on the list of results, perhaps on the fifth or tenth page.

Is it relevant?

Websites rarely have item records to help you prescreen the resource, so you usually have to examine the page itself to see if it discusses your topic. As we noted above, you can simply run a search for keywords on the page, but you sometimes need to take a closer look. Let's say you are researching the current condition of the economy and you come across a page where the word *crash* appears frequently. The problem is that the page may be discussing the 1929 crash, the 1987 "Black Monday" crash, the 1992 "Black Wednesday" crash, or a dozen other historical economic and financial crises. You have to skim enough of a site's text to get a clear picture.

Is it recent?

Unlike books and articles, whose publication dates are usually easy to find, websites can be hard to evaluate when it comes to **currency**. A news article on a CNN webpage might have a clear date of publication, but many sites—even very credible ones—do not have publication dates, so look for alternative dates, such as the date when the site was last updated. Do all of the links work? If not, perhaps no one is actively monitoring and updating the site, so the information may be out of date. If a particular site lists some relevant statistical data, but the information is a few years old, you could look for the name of the source on the page and then check this source for more recent information.

Is it reliable?

A reliable source is generally free of bias and is written by authors who have the credentials and expertise to make the claims that they do. Here are a few questions to consider when evaluating the reliability of a Web source:

1   Who is sponsoring or hosting the site? Is it hosted by a credible organization such as research institute, university, or government agency?

2 What is the site's agenda—to inform you, to sell you something, to persuade you to change your mind? If you see an "About Us" section or a mission statement section, use this information to try to determine the site's agenda.

3 Does the site send up any warning flags in the areas of tone and style? Do you see any emotional language or other signs of bias? Does the site look as if it was professionally designed and edited? (Even polished webpages can lack credibility, but ones that look amateurish are somewhat more suspect than polished ones, since the latter probably have a sense of professionalism, as well as the funding to pay designers and editors.)

As you learned earlier in this book, many librarians and teachers screen websites and list timely, credible ones in Web directories, which are lists of websites related to particular topics. Since these websites already have undergone some vetting, they are likely to be credible sources. To locate a Web directory, simply google "psychology links," "sociology links," "teen suicide links," etc.

Although the Web has more than its share of shady characters, it also has some highly credible, recent sources. You may want to keep a list of sites that you find consistently reliable. The website sponsored by the Centers for Disease Control and Prevention (CDC), for example, is an excellent source for information on diabetes, child abuse, and other subjects related to health and the human body. Thomas, a site maintained by the Library of Congress, features full texts of legislative bills, laws, and policies from the United States Congress. These are but a few of the hundreds of reliable sites that are worth keeping on standby for different informational needs.

Quicktivity: "About Us"

Use the "About Us" section of a website to evaluate its credibility.

Conclusion

As you know from reading Chapter 4, libraries and the Internet have a variety of sources, from books and periodicals to webpages and video recordings and beyond, so you don't have to settle for questionable sources. As you move ahead in this textbook and in your research, remember what you learned about evaluating sources in this step. Ask the right questions, but know that source evaluation, like critical thinking, is a complex process that involves weighing various factors, not merely checking boxes. An initial quick investigation of a source is often enough to determine if it's worthy of a closer look. If something looks very promising, take more time and apply what you learned here to evaluate it. In the next step, you will learn how to cite the sources that you determine are sufficiently relevant, reliable, and recent to use in your research.

Steps to Success

1   Using what you learned in this chapter, evaluate the relevance, credibility, and timeliness of a book on your topic. Write a paragraph in which you use the books' content, the author's credentials, the absence or presence of bias, the publisher's reputation, and the publication date to make a case for using or not using this book in your research.

2   Now evaluate an article you found in a periodical, such as a newspaper or a scholarly journal. Write a paragraph in which you use the article's content, the author's credentials, the absence or presence of bias, the periodical's reputation, and the date of the issue to make a case for using or not using this article in your research.

3   Finally, evaluate a website on your topic. Write a paragraph in which you use the page's content, the author's credentials, the absence or presence of bias, the webpage's agenda, its tone and style, and the timeliness of the page to make a case for using or not using this webpage in your research.

6

Create a Paper Trail

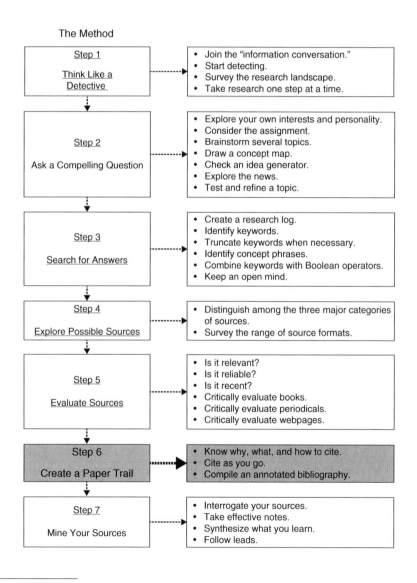

The Method

Step 1 — Think Like a Detective	• Join the "information conversation." • Start detecting. • Survey the research landscape. • Take research one step at a time.
Step 2 — Ask a Compelling Question	• Explore your own interests and personality. • Consider the assignment. • Brainstorm several topics. • Draw a concept map. • Check an idea generator. • Explore the news. • Test and refine a topic.
Step 3 — Search for Answers	• Create a research log. • Identify keywords. • Truncate keywords when necessary. • Identify concept phrases. • Combine keywords with Boolean operators. • Keep an open mind.
Step 4 — Explore Possible Sources	• Distinguish among the three major categories of sources. • Survey the range of source formats.
Step 5 — Evaluate Sources	• Is it relevant? • Is it reliable? • Is it recent? • Critically evaluate books. • Critically evaluate periodicals. • Critically evaluate webpages.
Step 6 — Create a Paper Trail	• Know why, what, and how to cite. • Cite as you go. • Compile an annotated bibliography.
Step 7 — Mine Your Sources	• Interrogate your sources. • Take effective notes. • Synthesize what you learn. • Follow leads.

Introduction to Information Literacy for Students, First Edition. Michael C. Alewine and Mark Canada.
© 2017 John Wiley & Sons, Ltd. Published 2017 by John Wiley & Sons, Ltd.

Chapter Summary

Capture key information about sources as you explore them so that you can create a paper trail, an essential element of research. When you document your sources, you not only create a record that you and others can use, but also build your credibility as a researcher.

Key Terms: documentation, citation, plagiarism, full quotation, syntax, partial quotation, paraphrase, summary, attributive phrase, parenthetical citation, footnote, superscript, endnote, references, works cited, in-text citations, annotated bibliography

Chapter Objectives

- Recognize the importance of documentation.
- Know when to cite material found in a source.
- Identify key information to include in a citation.
- Effectively incorporate source material into a project in the form of a full quotation, partial quotation, paraphrase, or summary.
- Compile a list of works cited.
- Avoid plagiarism.

The Case for Documentation

Imagine you are sitting on a jury and listening to a prosecutor argue that the defendant robbed a bank. This prosecutor delivers a long opening statement explaining exactly how the defendant supposedly planned the robbery, entered the bank in a ski mask, demanded money from the teller, stuffed several stacks of bills in a sack, and then ran out the door. After the defense attorney has delivered her opening statement, the judge asks the prosecutor to call his first witness. "Your honor," he replies, "I don't have any witnesses." The judge looks puzzled and then asks, "Well, have you entered any evidence—security camera footage, fingerprints, anything—into the record?" "No," he says, "I don't have any of that stuff, but I heard a rumor that he robbed the place." He turns to you and the rest of the jury and says, "Trust me. He did it."

What's your verdict? Chances are, you and your fellow members of the jury are not going to convict this defendant. In fact, you may be more troubled by the prosecutor than by the defendant. Who goes to trial without witnesses and verifiable evidence?

The same rules apply to research. Like the detective who has been painstakingly gathering cell phone records, eyewitness testimony, and DNA evidence, you have been combing through sources gathering evidence, but you will not have a strong case if you don't *show* this evidence or at least indicate where it can be found. In short, you would be as credible as this prosecutor—that is to say, not credible at all.

It would be nice to be able to trust everyone who tells you something, but we all know we can't. Besides, even when we are dealing with people we trust, we may find that we do not interpret evidence the same way they do. We need to know who the sources are and what exactly the evidence says so that we can evaluate them and interpret them for ourselves. In the world of research, authors make this information available to us through something called **documentation**—the topic of this chapter. Documentation involves the use of **citations**—that is, explicit references to sources—which can appear in attributive phrases, parenthetical citations, footnotes and endnotes, and lists of references and works cited.

Does all this talk of footnotes and references get your blood pumping? Of course it doesn't. Truth be told, there's nothing exciting about documentation—it's pretty dry stuff—but it's essential to successful research writing. In fact, researchers in every field would agree that it is one of the most important parts of the research process. Without it, your readers may not even know that you have *done* any research, or, worse, they may accuse you of dishonesty. There's no need to worry, though. This chapter will provide all you need to know on *why*, *when*, and *how* to document sources, along with some additional guidance on citing as you take notes and compiling annotated bibliographies:

1 Know why, when, and how to cite sources.
2 Cite as you go.
3 Compile an annotated bibliography.

When you have finished this chapter, you will be able to leave a paper trail that anyone can follow—and you will build your credibility as a sound researcher whose ideas deserve attention.

Know Why, What, and How to Cite

Documentation can look intimidating, but it really comes down to three questions:

1 Why do you need to cite sources?
2 What do you need to cite?
3 How do you cite a source?

Let's take a close look at each question.

Why do you need to cite sources?

Documentation serves a number of purposes in research. First, as suggested above, it builds your credibility as an author. Without it, a reader might suspect you of simply voicing your own unsubstantiated opinions or, worse, fabricating statistics, quotations, or other material to make up a good story or convince someone of something. *You* know you have been poring over mountains of books, studying journal articles and government documents, conducting your own interviews, and more, but how would *anyone else* know that you were doing all of this important work if you do not mention these sources in your project? Naming one's sources is so much an integral and expected part of research that scientists, historians, and other experts in various academic fields generally would pay little or no attention to secondary sources without some form of documentation. In short, presenting a research-based argument without documentation is like showing up to baseball tryouts without a glove: the insiders will not take you seriously, and you'll never get into the game.

There are other reasons for documentation. Proper citations provide authors' names, titles, dates—everything others need to find the original sources themselves. As you will see in the examples below, a good citation does not merely say that David Reynolds made some statement about Walt Whitman; rather, it tells readers exactly *where* (in what publication, for example) and *when* (in what year) he made the statement. These readers then can take this information and—using the same skills you will develop later in this book—find the source with the statement in it. This system not only proves to readers that Reynolds made the statement, since it directs them to the place where they can see it for themselves in black and white, but also allows readers to see the statement in context so that they can confirm that the author's interpretation of the source is legitimate. Furthermore, thanks to the paper trail the author has laid, readers interested in conducting their own research on this topic now can collect other information right there in the original source. Since readers of scholarly books and articles are usually researchers themselves, the presence of this source information is a tremendous aid to the research process.

Finally, documentation is just the ethically responsible thing to do. Studying reptiles, management practices, and policing trends is hard work, work that was conducted by real human beings who deserve credit for their efforts. Responsible authors give them credit through documentation.

Think Fast: The Value of Documentation

What does documentation do for a researcher? What does it do for the audience and for the authors of the original sources?

What do you need to cite?

After all this preaching about the importance of documentation, you might be surprised to learn that you don't have to cite *everything*. Expert researchers know what they need to cite and what they can simply state without crediting the source. You generally will know, too, if you keep the following rules in mind:

1 If the information you are using is a widely known fact, concept, or theory (the distance between the sun and the earth, the date of D-Day, the stages of mitosis, the concept of supply and demand, the theory of evolution, etc.), you don't need to cite it. What if you, a well-educated student, cannot, uh, exactly recite the stages of mitosis—does that mean that you have to cite this information? No, you yourself don't have to know the information. As long as it is familiar to many experts and is generally regarded as a firmly established fact, concept, or theory, you don't need to cite it. If you are unsure, check some other credible sources. If the same information appears there without citation, it's safe for you to use it without identifying the source.

2 If you are using a fact, concept, or theory that is *not* widely known by experts or an author's *interpretation* of factual information, you need to cite this material, even if you put it in your own words. If you also use exact words—even just a few—from a source, you need to enclose the borrowed words in quotation marks. (See the instructions on using partial and full quotations below.)

That's it—not all that complex, right? There will be times, probably, when you are unsure, though. When in doubt, check with your instructor or, if that's not possible, go ahead and cite it. You are much better off citing something you don't have to cite than you are if you fail to cite something you should have cited. The first kind of mistake probably will only draw a comment from your instructor or, at worst, a minor deduction. The second kind of mistake could be interpreted as plagiarism.

Technically, **plagiarism** occurs when a writer or speaker consciously and deliberately passes off something—either some words (ranging from a phrase to an entire article) or an idea—from a source as his or her own. In academic settings, plagiarism is, like cheating on an exam, a form of academic dishonesty, and the penalties are severe: an F on an assignment, an F in a course, even expulsion. Some writers and speakers do act consciously and deliberately and thus, according to this definition, are plagiarizing, but it's probably also true that many students do not know what they are doing is inappropriate. After all, that band you heard in the club last night played "Wild Horses" and never mentioned the Rolling Stones. At batting practice, your coach told you, "You can't think and hit at the same time," but didn't work Yogi Berra's name into an attributive phrase. When your choir director gave you some advice for managing your voice, she didn't give credit to the person who taught her the technique. Even your pastor, when he intoned "Pride goeth before a fall," may not have bothered to cite chapter and verse. The fact is, academic research has its own set of rules, and those rules are very clear: always give credit to your sources for exact words or ideas.

What if your mistake was an *accident*? That is, in an academic paper or presentation, you included some words from a source but forgot to enclose them in quotation marks, or you mentioned someone else's original idea but didn't know that you had to give credit to this person. Are you off the hook? After all, what you did was not conscious or deliberate, so it doesn't fit the definition of *plagiarism* above. Well, here's the thing: teachers can't read your mind or your heart. If they see that you have used words or an idea without quotation marks or a citation, they may assume that you were acting consciously and deliberately, especially if they have covered plagiarism and the proper use of sources explicitly in their syllabus, their lectures, their comments on drafts, or all three. Your innocent mistake might be interpreted as plagiarism, and you might have to face a severe penalty.

Bottom line: Know the rules for documentation and follow them religiously (but don't dis your pastor).

Think Fast: Avoiding Plagiarism

Identify two forms of plagiarism. How can you avoid each form?

Quicktivity: What Are Others Citing?

Take a close look at a paragraph in a source you have located. What has the author cited? What has he or she *not* cited? Try to explain the reasons for the different approaches to source material.

How do you cite a source?

As you can see, the necessity of documentation is common across all the academic disciplines. Chemists, economists, sociologists, art historians, and scholars of business, education, social work, nursing, and every other field routinely cite information that they take from sources. It's the way things are done here in the world of research. While you are in the world of research—in college, in graduate school, and, in many cases, in the professional world—you need to know how to document effectively and correctly.

Alas, the *how* of documentation is *not* so common across the disciplines. Many authors writing in the social sciences use a format associated with the American Psychological Association—that is, APA format. Historians tend to use something called Chicago or Turabian style. Then there's CSE (Council of Science Editors) style, along with CBE (Council of Biology Editors), MLA (Modern Language Association), ACS (American Chemical Society), and ASA (American Sociological Association) formats. You get the idea. It seems the only thing that divides human beings more than documentation is religion. As with, say, Christianity (which has thousands of denominations), all the "believers" in documentation share the same basic principles, but want things their own way when it comes to particulars.

The purpose of this chapter is not to teach you all of those particulars—or "convert" you to any particular citation style. Instead, the instructions below will guide you through four basic ways of incorporating source material into your own writing (full quotation, partial quotation, paraphrase, and summary) and four ways of identifying your sources (attributive phrase, parenthetical citation, footnotes and endnotes, and lists of references or works cited). Once you have mastered these basic principles, you can apply them in any discipline (when they are appropriate) and simply use the documentation format appropriate for that discipline. (See the list of documentation formats near the end of this chapter.)

Four Ways of Incorporating Source Material

Think about the sources you have encountered in your research. When the authors of these sources had something from another source to share with their readers, what did they do—draw an arrow to a name in the margin of the page or put the information on a sticky note? No, they *incorporated* the information into their own paragraphs. The word *incorporate* contains the Latin roots *in-* (which means, you guessed it, "in") and *corpor-* (which means—did you guess it?—"body"); thus, it literally means "in body." (If you want to see for yourself, what kind of source would you use? You got it—a reference source, specifically a dictionary, discussed in Chapter 4.) When you incorporate source material, you are bringing it into the body of your own writing; you are making it part of your own work. You can incorporate source material into a paper or presentation in one of four ways, each described below.

Full quotation: When reading a source, you may come across one or more complete sentences that are striking because of the way they are expressed; perhaps, for example, the author has used some colorful language or some inflammatory words. In such cases, you should consider using a full quotation, which is the use of one or more complete sentences from a source. You must place a full quotation within quotation marks. Do not change any of the words. If you omit words, insert some ellipsis points (…) in the spot where you omitted the words. Full quotations are especially common in research on literature, where word choice and **syntax**— that is, the way words are put together to create meaning in a sentence—are often the objects of analysis and interpretation. In other disciplines, such as psychology, full quotations are much less common.

Partial quotation: In some cases, you may want to use only part of a sentence you found in a source—perhaps just a phrase or even a single word—because only this part is colorful or inflammatory or because you wish to analyze the word choice or syntax in just this part of the sentence. As with a full quotation, you must place the exact words you use within quotation marks. Do not change any of the words that appear within the quotation marks. If you omit words in the portion you are quoting, use ellipsis points, as you would do in the case of a full quotation. Like full quotations, partial quotations are more common in literary scholarship than in research done in some other fields.

Paraphrase: Most of the time, the material you find within a source will be valuable primarily for its content, not for the way it is expressed. In such cases, you should use a paraphrase, which is the rephrasing of someone else's information in your own words. To paraphrase without plagiarizing, you must change both the words and the syntax of the original. Because you no longer are using the source's exact words, you should not use quotation marks. Remember, you don't need to cite widely known facts, concepts, or theories, but make sure to cite original interpretations.

Summary: If you come across a paragraph, a section, or even an entire chapter or article that is valuable to you for its major point and not for all the particulars, you may want to provide a summary, which is a condensed version of the original. Like a paraphrase, a summary must be in your own words and does not require quotation marks. You must cite the source unless you are summarizing widely known facts or theories.

Four Ways of Identifying Source Material

In addition to incorporating source material into your own work, you often need to identify the source, as we have explained above. Most of the time, authors do so in one or more of these four ways:

Attributive phrase: When you use an attributive phrase, you mention the source—usually at least the author's name, but also perhaps the name of the specific work where the information appears—in your own sentence. It's often a good idea to include the author's first and last names the first time you use something from the source, but you should use just the last name after the first reference.

Parenthetical citation: A second way to identify a source is to enclose source information, such as the author's name or a page number, in parentheses. The result, called a parenthetical citation, often appears at the end of the sentence in which the information appears.

Footnotes and **endnotes**: Yet another approach is to place a **superscript** number—that is, a number that appears a little higher than the rest of the text in a line—next to a word or sentence and then place the same number and the source information at the bottom, or "foot" of the page, for a footnote or near the end of the article, chapter, or book for an endnote. Word-processing programs make this process very easy. Just choose "Insert," click on "Footnote" or "Endnote," and go from there.[1]

Lists of **references** and **works cited**: Finally, most authors also list all of the sources that they cited after the text of the article, chapter, or book. Sometimes this list is called "References," and other times it is called "Works Cited." In either case, each item in the list—that is, each citation—consists of basic publication information: the author's name, the title of the source, the year it appeared, and so on.

Typically, writers use a combination of these methods: both **in-text citations** (attributive phrases, parenthetical citations, footnotes or endnotes, or some combination of the three), which let you know which specific words or sentences came from a source, and a final list (references or works cited), which presents citations of all the works cited in the text. Again, the specifics vary from discipline to discipline. Historians tend to use endnotes, for example, while psychologists use parenthetical citations.

Examples: Documenting Source Material in Literature and Psychology

Let's take a close look at the kinds of changes that take place when researchers take material from sources and use it in their own work. Below are two excerpts from different books. Under each excerpt is an example illustrating the way that a researcher might adapt the original material for use in his or her own work.

Here are some sentences as they originally appeared David S. Reynolds's book *Walt Whitman's America: A Cultural Biography*:

> The actor was Junius Brutus Booth, the clergyman Henry Ward Beecher, the singing group the Hutchinsons (see figs. 12, 20, 23, and 26). All were important elements of the performance culture Whitman loved. What they had in common, with each other and with his poetry, was a participatory spirit that permeated American life before the Civil War. Whitman's poetry was the highest flowering of that participatory culture.

---

[1] In some books, such as recent biographies, the superscript numbers do not actually appear in the text or at the back of the book, but the approach is otherwise similar. In these books, source information appears at the rear of a book along with some identifying information, such as the page and line numbers, indicating where the information appears in the book. (By the way, this note you are reading here at the bottom of the page is, as you may have already guessed, an example of a footnote. If it had appeared at the end of the chapter, it would be an endnote.)

Here are a couple of sentences showing how a researcher might capture some of Reynolds's material in the form of partial and full quotations, along with a footnote crediting the original source:

> David Reynolds refers to "a participatory spirit that permeated American life before the Civil War." Reynolds says, "Whitman's poetry was the highest flowering of that participatory culture."[1]

Finally, here is a breakdown, showing each component of the new version:

David Reynolds refers to (attributive phrase)
"a participatory spirit that permeated American life before the Civil War." (partial quotation)
Reynolds says (attributive phrase)
"Whitman's poetry was the highest flowering of that participatory culture." (full quotation)

Here is another passage, this one from *Willpower: Rediscovering the Greatest Human Strength*, a book by Roy Baumeister and John Tierney:

> All in all, these findings point toward the remarkable benefits of exercising willpower. Without realizing it, people gained a wide array of benefits in areas of their lives that have nothing to do with the specific exercises they were performing. And the lab tests provided an explanation: their willpower gradually got stronger, so it was less mentally depleted. Focusing on one specific form of self-control could yield much larger benefits, just as self-experimenters from Ben Franklin to David Blaine had maintained…. As long as you were motivated to do some kind of exercise, your overall willpower could improve, at least over the course of the experiment.

Here are two sentences illustrating how a researcher might use this material:

> Citing both the findings of psychological studies and the results of less formal experiments, Baumeister and Tierney (2011) note that willpower exercises can help people strengthen their resolve to do things. They explain that exercise in one aspect of life can bring positive outcomes to a completely different part of life.

Here is a breakdown:

Citing both the findings of psychological studies and the results of less formal experiments (summary)
Baumeister and Tierney … note that (attributive phrase)

[1] David Reynolds, *Walt Whitman's America* (New York: Knopf, 1995), 154–155.

(2011) (parenthetical citation)

willpower exercises can help people strengthen their resolve to do things (summary)

They explain that (attributive phrase)

exercise in one aspect of life can bring positive outcomes to a completely different part of life (paraphrase)

Reference

Baumeister, R. F., & Tierney, J. (2011). *Willpower: Rediscovering the greatest human strength*. New York, NY, US: Penguin Press. (entry in APA list of references)

Cite As You Go

Many students wait until they have completed their research and even written one or more drafts before they start documenting the source material they used. If you have ever taken this approach, you probably know the problems that come with it. Maybe you forgot where you pulled some information. Maybe you remembered where you got it, but then couldn't find the source in the library or on the Web. Maybe you can't even remember whether you found a particular idea in a source or came up with it yourself. (This last problem is probably the worst. Since it would be extremely difficult to retrace all of your steps in the research process, you may never be able to determine whether the idea appeared in a source you were using, but you shouldn't leave out a citation because, if it did appear in a source, someone might accuse you of plagiarism. Your only choice might be to abandon the idea!)

A much, much better approach to documentation is to cite source material *during* the research process. As you take notes on sources, as you will learn to do in the next chapter, use what you learn in this chapter to cite everything along the way. Use this simple system:

1 Begin reading (or watching or listening to) the source. If you come across something useful—an enlightening interpretation, for example—record it in your notes as a full quotation, partial quotation, paraphrase, or summary. Include a page number if the source has page numbers.
2 Before you go back to the source to read, watch, or listen some more, *immediately* record a citation for the source and place it in a list of references.
3 Continue working your way through the source, recording useful information as you come across it. You will have to repeat No. 1, but you don't need to repeat No. 2, since you already have recorded a citation for the source.

Use this process for every piece of information you pull from a source. When it comes time to write your paper (or blog or presentation or whatever), you may not need to cite some of this information because it is a fact or a widely known concept, and you may not need page numbers, since some citation styles don't require them, but knowing exactly where you found something may prove very useful to you if you need to go back to it—to check the accuracy of your transcription, for example, or to see the information in context.

If this strategy is so great, why don't more people use it? You probably can guess why:

1   It takes time.
2   It's tedious.
3   It often requires extra work (since you almost certainly will not use everything you cite in your notes, you don't need to cite facts, and you may not need page numbers even for some of the information you do cite).

Still, the time you spend, the tedious tasks you complete, and the extra work you do will pay huge dividends in the end. You will be able to find what you need, cite it properly, and spend much less time on your in-text citations and lists of references or works cited at the drafting stage. There's one more huge advantage that probably will become obvious only after you have completed your current project. If you decide to explore a similar topic—as researchers often do—in another project, such as a senior capstone paper or a master's thesis, you will be able to go directly to the pages where you found your information, even years later, and you already will have much of your documentation complete.

Insider's Tip: Cite As You Go

When I am doing research or even just taking notes on something I have read or watched so that I can refer to them later, I always cite as I go. I also always enclose exact words in quotation marks. Now, I take a lot of notes—thousands of pages of notes. (Thanks, Mom, for insisting that I learn to touch-type all those years ago.) All that citing and quoting is time-consuming, and I never seem to have enough time in my life, but I make a habit of this practice for two reasons. First, I always know where I found the material, so I can cite it if I publish something containing it or, even if I don't use it, I can find it again if I want to verify it or see other information in the source. Second, I never have to worry that I will unknowingly pull some exact words from a source out of my notes and put them straight into something I am writing for publication, leaving myself open to accusations of plagiarism.

–Mark

Compile an Annotated Bibliography

You remember **annotated bibliographies**, right? As you learned in Chapter 4, these tertiary sources consist of citations of sources, along with annotations, which capture key details about the sources. Since many instructors assign annotated bibliographies, it's a good idea to learn not only how to find them, but also how to write them. Creating the citations is relatively simple: consult the guidelines for the documentation format that your instructor requires (Chicago, APA, MLA, etc.) and follow the instructions and examples. Writing the annotations requires a bit more work, but you can apply what you learned about writing summaries in this chapter. Remember, a summary is similar to a paraphrase because you should be using your words, not the exact words of the source, but it is different because you also should be condensing the information. Note only the most important aspects of the source and capture them in as few words as possible. If the source contains a thesis, paraphrase it and touch on the ways the author has supported this thesis. Check with your instructor to see if he or she wants you to evaluate the source. If so, you should consider the quality of the argument, narrative, explanation, or description in the source. You also might want to use what you learned about evaluating sources in Chapter 5. For example, if the source assesses the success of "No Child Left Behind," has the author been unbiased? Does he or she have appropriate credentials? Write a summary that you would want to have if you were considering consulting this source.

Conclusion

Now you know the whys, whats, and hows of documentation. That is, you know the reasons for citing sources, the kinds of information you need to cite, and the mechanics both of incorporating source material into sentences (through full quotations, partial quotations, paraphrases, and summaries) and of citing it in various ways (in attributive phrases, parenthetical citations, footnotes or endnotes, and lists of references or works cited). You also have learned the value of citing as you go. Finally, you have seen how you can use what you have learned in this chapter and the previous chapter to write annotations for annotated bibliographies. In the next chapter, you will learn a useful technique for recording what you learn from your sources.

Documentation Formats

APA (American Psychological Association)

Fields: Criminal justice, education, psychology, and sociology (although some sociology courses require ASA style)

Help guides: *Publication Manual of the American Psychological Association*, 6th Edition (check your library's online catalog); Purdue OWL: APA Style (available online).

Chicago (or Turabian)

Fields: History and others
Help guides: *The Chicago Manual of Style*, 16th Edition (check your library's online catalog); Purdue OWL: Chicago Manual of Style (available online).

MLA (Modern Language Association)

Fields: English and others
Help guides: *MLA Handbook for Writers of Research Papers*, 8th Edition (check your library's online catalog); Purdue OWL: MLA Style (available online).

There are many other citation styles that can be used in the different disciplines. To see a list, google the phrase "complete discipline listing" and look for a site sponsored by the Purdue Online Writing Lab (Purdue OWL). Even this list is not complete. There are even more citation styles, including some peculiar to specific publishers.

Steps to Success

1 Begin reading a source you found using the searching techniques you learned in Chapter 3. Use what you have learned in this chapter to turn a few relevant details from this source into one full quotation, one partial quotation, one paraphrase, and one summary. Try to be strategic, using quotations for sentences that contain colorful or inflammatory wording, paraphrases for material important purely for its content, and summaries for material that you want to condense.
2 Look back at your response to No. 1. Explain why you quoted, paraphrased, and summarized what you did.
3 Practice citing your quotations, paraphrase, and summary in at least two citation formats, such as Chicago and APA.

7

Mine Your Sources

The Method

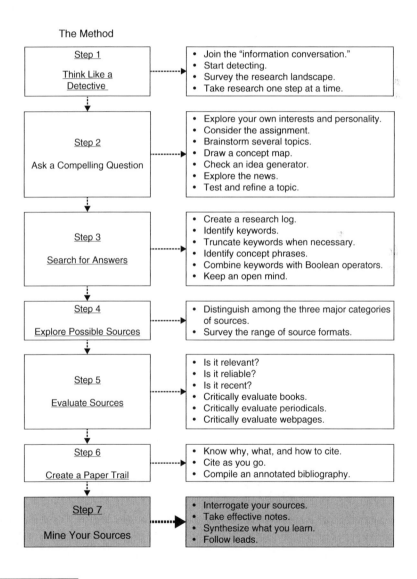

Introduction to Information Literacy for Students, First Edition. Michael C. Alewine and Mark Canada.
© 2017 John Wiley & Sons, Ltd. Published 2017 by John Wiley & Sons, Ltd.

Chapter Summary

Mine the sources you have found, evaluated, and documented to draw out the kind of detailed, insightful material that will make an effective paper or presentation. In this chapter, you will learn to interrogate your sources, take effective notes, and synthesize source material and your own ideas.

Key Terms: synthesize, interrogate, thesis, hypothesis, *post hoc* fallacy, analogy, correlation, reflection, scientific report, abstract, introduction, methods, results, discussion, conclusion, references

Chapter Objectives

- Identify key parts of sources.
- Interrogate sources.
- Take effective notes.
- Synthesize source material and your own observations and ideas.
- Use sources to find other sources.

Getting the Most from Your Sources

As you have seen in the preceding chapters, the right tools and strategies can take you far in a research project, helping you to collect a lot of relevant, credible sources you can use to answer your research question and understand your topic. Once you have all those books, articles, webpages, interviews, artifacts, recordings, and other sources, what do you do with them? Your situation is a lot like that of a detective who has spent months investigating a crime. He has used his detective powers to find revealing printed and electronic documents (like your books, articles, and webpages), to identify informants (like your interview subjects), to accumulate physical evidence (like your artifacts), and to secure images from security cameras (like your recordings). He is well on his way to solving the crime, but he hasn't proven anything yet. In fact, he may not even fully *understand* what happened. Having all that evidence is only part of the process; now he has to mine it for answers, and that means studying it very closely, recording what he finds, and putting it together with his own understanding of crime and criminals.

Detectives appreciate the importance of mining their evidence for answers. As a researcher, you will be much more successful if you appreciate the value of drawing out key information from your sources and using it, along with information from other sources and your own experience, to answer your research question and shed new light on your topic. Remember, your goal is not merely to *assemble* statistics, images, and quotations into a kind of laundry list, but to **synthesize** this information—that is, to use all of it together to construct something meaningful, something that leads to a better understanding of your topic for both you and your audience.

Just as there are strategies for finding, evaluating, and documenting sources, there are techniques you can use to mine those sources for information. In this chapter, we will take you through each of these strategies:

1 Interrogate your sources, studying them carefully to understand their thesis or hypothesis, reasons, and evidence.
2 Take effective notes, which you later can use to draft your project.
3 Follow leads.
4 Synthesize all that you have learned from sources, as well as what you know from your own experience, and begin to craft a meaningful answer to your research question.

This step in the research process is the culmination of all of your work crafting a research question and then finding, exploring, evaluating, and documenting sources. You can make the most of all this work by using the strategies in this chapter to turn research into answers.

Think Fast: Assembly vs. Synthesis

What is the difference between assembling bits of information and synthesizing them?

Interrogate Your Sources

The Citation Project shows that most students from colleges and universities all over the United States typically look at only the first 3-4 pages of any given source. On one level, this phenomenon is understandable. Many students—and, for that matter, many professionals—have plenty to keep them busy: work, family obligations, community projects, entertainment, social media, and more. Still, when you read only the first 3-4 pages of a source, you definitely are missing something—namely the remaining 10, 15, or 20 pages, which probably contain a lot of useful facts and ideas. In fact, in many sources, the first few pages contain the thesis and background information—both important and useful—but little or none of the "meat"—that is, the supporting evidence and explanation that flesh out the argument. The same is true of other kinds of sources: interviews, documentaries, and more. Remember, the writers of many of these sources are doing the same thing your instructors are asking you to do: examine evidence (in the form of statistics, observable behavior, natural phenomena, images, music, movies, plays, or text), draw conclusions, and share those conclusions. To understand their conclusions, evaluate their validity, and begin drawing your own conclusions, you have to study the sources completely and deeply. In other words, you need to **interrogate** them, asking question after question about their conclusions, as well as the evidence and reasoning behind those conclusions.

Begin by identifying the source's **thesis**—that is, the main point or set of points the writer or presenter is trying to make—or, in the case of many scientific reports, the **hypothesis**—that is, the idea that one or more scientists are testing by conducting an experiment or studying data. For example, a historian may wish to argue that a particular incident helped to shape a larger movement, such as the temperance movement in the United States in the nineteenth century or the civil rights movement in the mid-twentieth century. A chemist, on the other hand, may want to test the effect of one substance on another in a particular environment, hypothesizing that there will or will not be a certain kind of effect. Historians and other writers in the humanities tend to state their theses in the form of a single sentence—or perhaps two or three sentences—early in their essays or books, sometimes at the end of the introduction, whereas scientists, who generally follow a more prescribed format, typically state their hypotheses in sections clearly labeled "Introduction." As you read an essay or report, jot down this main idea. When you are reading a scientific report, make a note of the results of the experiment, as well. You will find this information in a section conveniently labeled "Results." (Scientists tend to be more direct than researchers in the humanities, at least when it comes to their research reports.)

As you study the rest of the source, study the author's process and reasoning. How did he or she come to conclusions or set up an experiment? Does everything make sense, or do you see things that could have skewed results or led to a questionable conclusion? For example, if a team of social scientists are studying the role of a drug-prevention program, but examine only programs in rural schools, how are their findings limited? If an art historian makes a case for an evolution of a painter's style, has she considered a sufficient number of paintings? Whatever the subject, be especially critical—not necessarily negative, but critical as in being a critical thinker—when it comes to conclusions about causes and effects. It's easy to fall into what is known as the ***post hoc* fallacy**—that is, to assume that A caused Z just because A came before Z. (The Latin phrase *post hoc* means "after the fact.") Cause is extremely difficult, often impossible, to prove, particularly outside a lab, where experimenters can control the variables—that is, the factors that may shape a phenomenon or an event. In anthropology, history, literature, criminal justice, education, economics, and other fields, researchers have little or no control over variables in the real world and have to use a lot of evidence and reason—sometimes with help from **analogy**, a comparison that may help to make their case—to show that A (and not B, C, D, or many other factors) really did cause Z, that it wasn't a common factor that caused both A and Z or that Z just happened on its own. Researchers, particularly in the sciences, often distinguish between cause and **correlation**, which involves two or more events that happen together, but are not necessarily linked through cause and effect.

Now that you know how to interrogate sources, you know one of the best (and best-kept) secrets to success in research. As the evidence from the Citation Project shows, many students do not know this secret. You do. Furthermore, once you start applying this secret to your research, you will find that it not only makes better research papers, but also actually makes them easier to write.

Think Fast: Interrogating a Source

What does it mean to "interrogate" a source? What kinds of questions should you ask of it?

Take Effective Notes

Taking notes, of course, is a way to record information you find in sources so that you can refer to it later. Taking notes *strategically* is much more: it's an invaluable aid to your thinking. As you have seen, mining sources effectively involves interrogating them and synthesizing the information you find in them, along with your own ideas, to create something original and meaningful. Strategic note-taking helps you with both interrogation and synthesis.

The first thing you will want to do is put away your highlighter. Save it for studying your textbooks (although note-taking is often better for studying, as well). Reading sources with a highlighter in hand makes some sense, since it allows you to mark key passages; the problem, however, is that there isn't much you can do with the passages you have highlighted. You have a paper to write or a presentation to prepare, and there are those highlighted passages, just sitting there. You need something that helps you to interrogate and synthesize your source material, and strategic note-taking is that something.

One old-school note-taking method is to handwrite notes on cards, which you then can arrange and rearrange in various orders to try to discover the best organizational scheme. This book's method calls for a different kind of note-taking, the kind done on a computer. Digital notes have some important advantages over handwritten notes. Perhaps the most important is that digital notes can be easily and quickly searched. When you have taken a lot of notes and can't remember where you defined *amygdala*, you will be able to find your definition a whole lot faster if you can run a search for the word instead of rummaging through pages or flipping through notecards. Digital notes can save you time in other respects, as well. If you can touch-type, you probably can type faster than you can write. If the source is itself digital, you might be able copy and paste sentences from it and not have to type much at all (but remember to type the quotation marks around the passages you paste into your document, as well as a citation and page number). Finally, you won't have to retype any quotations or other material that you are going to use in their entirety in your first draft because you can simply copy them and paste them right into your first draft.

Begin your computer outline by typing five headings: "Introduction," "Background," "Supporting Evidence," "Conclusion," and "Miscellaneous." As you learn more about your topic in your research, you can add additional headings, as well as subheadings, but these basic headings at least give you some places to start putting your notes as you study your sources. If you are using Microsoft Word, you can select "Outline" under "View" in the menu and be able to move these headings, along with anything you add later, simply by clicking and dragging whatever you want to move. You can drag pieces of your outline up and down to rearrange them; you also can drag them to the left to "promote" them—making a subheading a heading, for example— or to the right to "demote" them. (You also might try taking notes in an app, such as Evernote," but it may be harder to move things in some apps.) Organizing notes in an electronic format is at least a little easier than arranging notecards and infinitely easier than working with highlighted passages, which you cannot move without a pair of scissors.

Now that you know an effective strategy for *how* to record notes, let's consider *what* you should include in them. You already know that an author's thesis or hypothesis is important, as is the reasoning underpinning it. What else should you record in your outline? Pay close attention to examples and explanations, which can be very useful to you as a researcher. Remember, your goal is to use facts and interpretations you find in sources, along with your own observations and ideas, to understand something. Anything in a source is fair game, even if it is not directly related to the author's thesis—even if it contradicts an author's thesis! You may see something that did not occur or matter to the author. Reflect on anything that strikes you. Pause from time to time and recall your own thesis or hypothesis. What possible connections do you see? What might a little incident that an author mentioned in passing reveal about the phenomenon that you are studying?

When you come across a fact, explanation, or anything else that seems worth recording in your notes, use this simple two-step process to begin synthesizing and interrogating:

1   Decide where this piece of information belongs on your outline. If it's a useful piece of background information—a definition or some context, for example— put it in that section. If it helps to support the point you wish to make, put it in the "Supporting Evidence" section. If you are not sure where to put it, just stick in the "Miscellaneous" section. (This section is sometimes a good place to store anecdotes and other tidbits that you might use when you are trying to craft an engaging introduction or a satisfying conclusion.) As you record more and more notes, look for similarities among your pieces of information, add subheadings that capture these similarities, and group similar details together under these headings. Whenever you get to a point where you have more than five details under a single heading or subheading, look for ways to divide up these details, again putting similar details together under an appropriate subheading (or sub-subheading or

sub-sub-subheading). As you make decisions about where details belong, you have to think very carefully about how they all fit together. In short, the very process of organizing your facts, interpretations, and other pieces of information in an outline is forcing you to begin the process of synthesis.

2 Once you know where a piece of information goes, type it, along with a citation. Finally, add at least one sentence of **reflection**—that is, some kind of thought about this fact or interpretation. For example, you might ask a question about it, challenge it, comment on it, or connect it to something else you have learned about your topic. This extra sentence can help you interrogate the source or synthesize this information and other information.

This process takes time, but it's time well spent. In fact, it's some of the most valuable time you will spend on your entire research project because it helps you make the crucial transition from simply finding information to *using* it to create understanding.

Example: Note-taking in Education

Let's look at how the process of note-taking might play out in a research project. Imagine that you are preparing a vlog proposing ways that colleges can help students succeed in their academic work. You head to the library, and a librarian at the reference desk steers you toward a book called *Emotional Intelligence*, written by Daniel Goleman. Some students would either (a) skip this book because the title contains nothing about *student success*; (b) find it on the shelf, flip through it, but discard it because, on first glance, the material seems to focus on parts of the brain, psychological phenomena, empathy, family relationships, and other subjects, but not *student success*; (c) read the first few pages and give up on it because the author does not explicitly lay out the keys to *student success*; or (d) read a lot of the book, but draw little from it because (you guessed it) it doesn't seem to say much about *student success*. These students, as you can see, have become fixated on *student success* and want to find sources that offer up little packages of information that they unwrap and then assemble in their papers.

You're different. You know that conducting research—*real research*—is not about assembling packaged components, but about building something original and meaningful, something that leads to a better understanding of a topic, not just for you, but also for your readers. You know that reading this source carefully just might leave you with the kind of understanding that can lead you to new insights into student success. As you read the author's evidence and explanations and reflect on your experience in school, as well as information in other sources you have read, you start to see connections between the material in this source and your own project. For example, you come across this state-ment in Chapter 2: "All impulse is a feeling bursting to express itself in action. Those who are at the mercy of impulse, who lack self-control, suffer a moral deficiency. The ability to control impulse is the base of will and character." The author is connecting impulse to morality, not a focus of your research, but you notice that he also refers to self-control. You recall from another source you read that self-control plays a role in student success. Now, thanks to this source, you see that lack of self-control has its basis in a psychological phenomenon dealing with impulse. Are some students more susceptible to impulses and thus more likely to struggle with the self-control they need to succeed in school? If so, could an intervention that helps these students control impulses lead to greater student success?

Look back over the process described in the previous paragraph. Follow-ing this process, you have gone from "impulse" to (ta-da!) *student success*. The work you had to do was harder than finding an article about student success and just summarizing it, but the results are more impressive (because you have *synthesized* material) and potentially more valuable (because you have made a connection that others may not have yet made). You are doing *real research*!

Quicktivity: Connect Details

Focus on a small part of a source—a few minutes from the heart of a documen-tary or a paragraph from the body of a journal article. Identify one thing—a fact, an interpretation, an explanation—that does not seem to be directly related to your topic. Now try to connect it to something else you have read, seen, heard, or experienced. If necessary, make a leap. You have nothing to lose: think creatively and imaginatively. Make a note of any connections you can make.

Example: Note-taking in Biology

In your research, you often will come across information that does not seem directly related to your angle on your topic. Of course, you can't record all of this information. There just aren't enough hours in the day. Still, don't be too picky. Perhaps you have noticed that little factoids sometimes stick in your brain whether you write them down or not. Later, as you are thinking about your topic or working on a draft, some thought you're having will be somehow related to one of these factoids and—presto!—the factoid pops into your brain. The problem is, if you never wrote down the factoid, you may not remember enough details to use it, and you may not be able to find it because you don't have a citation for it.

If writing down everything is impractical, but leaving out some factoids is risky, what is a researcher to do? First, "zoom out" a little when taking notes; that is, don't neglect anything that is not directly related to your topic. If you are focusing on one issue regarding stem cells, at least jot down the other major ones. You might refer to them in an introduction or a conclusion. Second, pay close attention to colorful quotations and details, illuminating analogies, striking statistics, and interesting anecdotes. These little bits of information can go a long way toward making your writing engaging and compelling. For example, an analogy between stem cells and something more familiar to non-experts might help your readers understand a basic concept in the background section of your paper or speech. As always, make sure to enclose exact words in quotation marks and to record a citation, as well as the location of this detail within the source.

Follow Leads

Like any good detective, a good researcher knows how to follow leads, or bits of information that lead to other, perhaps more useful information. Take words, for example. If FBI agents combing through a suspect's email correspondence keep coming across references to "*pontifex maximus*," "*genius*," and "*dominus et deus*," they would want to follow these words to more information—first, probably, by looking them up in English and Latin dictionaries or encyclopedias (where they would learn that they all have to do with a religion of ancient Rome). This information may help them to craft a psychological profile of the suspect or divine his or her motivation. Similarly, as a researcher, you will want to pay attention to words and phrases you encounter in your sources—specifically ones that appear in the theses and hypotheses, as well as any that might be unfamiliar to you. Look them up in an appropriate reference source, such as a dictionary, if necessary, but also use them when you perform keyword searches.

One excellent source of leads is the list of references, notes, or works cited that generally appears at the end of article, chapter, or book. (Just think of the guy who tells the detective that he heard a woman say something about the suspect. The guy is like a source leading you to another source: the woman who apparently mentioned the suspect.) The citations in these source lists are terrific leads. For one thing, they save you a lot of keyword searching because you can use the specific information in them to find the source or, if it is not in your library or available online, order it through document delivery (which will be covered in the chapter on books). Furthermore, because authors cite only sources that have some connection to their topic, you have reason to believe that they are relevant to your topic (although some probably will be more relevant than others). Finally, the authors of the sources you study already have screened the sources they cite, so these sources are probably credible. If they weren't, a careful researcher generally would not use them, at least not without noting anything questionable about them.

Look for other leads, as well. For example, the authors of scholarly sources almost always will refer, either in the citations or in the text itself, to other researchers working in this field. You can use what you know about keyword searches, specifically author searches, to try to find books, articles, webpages, or other sources written by these researchers. (Some of these sources may be mentioned in the list of references, notes, or works cited, but many will not be if the author of the source in front of you did not refer to those specific sources in his or her own work.) You also can search for these authors' names on the Web and email them to set up an interview.

Some sources refer not only to people, but also to government agencies or organizations, such as the Centers for Disease Control and Prevention or the American Civil Liberties Union. Google the names of these agencies and organizations, and you almost certainly will find even more information, perhaps reports or editorials posted online, as well as contact information, which you can use to ask questions or set up interviews. Some sources may mention relevant places, such as museums, galleries, or archives. These places are also worth checking out for the same reasons: they may have experts you could interview, artifacts you could study, and bibliographies you could use to find additional sources.

Pay attention to any graphics you come across in your sources. Graphics, charts, and diagrams may contain very useful statistics and other information. You will want to record anything potentially useful in your notes, of course, but also make a point of checking out the source of this information if it came from somewhere else. For example, many business articles cite statistics from government reports; you could follow this lead—that is, the citation that accompanies the graphic—to find the original report, which may have even more statistics you can use.

Finally, sources can lead you to ideas for ways to present or capture your information in your final product. In some cases, you might simply insert a table or an image from a source right into your own paper, poster, or presentation (taking care to cite it, of course), but it's often even better to adapt the material and ideas you find in sources—thus, for example, creating your own graphics from statistics you found in sources or even conducting your own experiments, surveys, or observations. In general, the more original material you present in your research, the better.

Quicktivity: Follow a Lead

Identify a keyword, citation, person, organization, or place in one of your sources. Use what you learned about searching in Chapter 3 to find a relevant source.

Example: Scientific Report

Understanding the parts of a source can help you to mine it. Dissecting all of the many different sources is outside the scope of this book, but it's worth taking a close look at one very common kind. A **scientific report**, sometimes known as a lab report, typically reports on a specific experiment or group of experiments and is very common in both the natural sciences, such as chemistry and physics, and the social sciences, such as psychology and sociology. With some exceptions, scientific reports contain seven parts:

Abstract: This summary of the report is a useful key to the topic explored, as well as the findings of the authors. Often reading the abstract can help you decide whether a scientific report is sufficiently relevant to your topic and worthy of your time.

Introduction: Because this section typically contains a brief literature review connecting the authors' original research with previous research, it can give you a sense of what research already has been done on this topic, as well as some of the notable researchers and relevant theories. These details can be useful leads for you.

Methods: This section, which describes what was actually done in the experiment, provides information (about instruments, sample size, procedures, and so on) that other researchers can use to replicate the experiment. You may want to use this information to design your own research study.

Results: Look here for selected results from the study, mainly those that correspond to specific hypotheses or research questions. The authors will take various data (not necessarily everything that they recorded) and present them in the form of tables, charts, and text. Use the findings described in the "Results" section to deepen your understanding of the topic. Keep in mind what you learned about timeliness in Chapter 5. It can sometimes take years to have original research published, so the publication date is not necessarily descriptive in terms of when the actual research was carried out. In other words, a 2015 article may be reporting data from a study that was actually carried out in 2008.

Discussion: See this section for the authors' remarks on the significance of their results, even if these results do not substantiate the hypothesis or research question. You also may find additional discussion of other studies or relevant theories that correspond with the findings. Because this section sometimes addresses possible directions for future research, it is a good place to look for research questions that you could try to answer in a project of your own.

Conclusion: Because it typically summarizes the experiment and findings, you may want to read this section, along with the abstract, before you read the entire report. That way, you will have a general sense of the purpose and results of the experiment.

References: See this list of relevant sources for some ideas of other sources that might provide you with additional information on your topic.

Some scientific reports contain appendices—that is, collections of additional information such as lists of survey questions used in the experiment. Like the "Methods" section, an appendix may give you ideas you could use to devise your own experiment.

Conclusion

You will know when you are truly mining your sources—and so will your classmates and professors. You will be able to have interesting, meaningful conversations with your instructors and fellow students about your topic right off the top of your head. You will be able to recall examples, make connections, and cite evidence. You will start to feel like an expert in your topic, and indeed you really are becoming one. Giving oral presentations will be much easier than it used to be because you will be able to think on your feet. You will be a more confident student with much more to offer the field you are studying. Other students and even professors—no joke—will start to consult you because you really know what you have been researching. This kind of knowledge means more than good grades. It can mean securing a spot in graduate school or landing a great job. Most important, it is the essence of learning—not just personal learning, but the learning that humanity uses to achieve progress in science, technology, the arts, politics, business, and education. It is what allows us to make a better world.

Steps to Success

1 Choose one of the articles or books you located in your research process. Use what you have learned in this chapter to begin mining it for information that can deepen your understanding of your topic. Take notes that include not only phrases and sentences from the source (along with citations), but also your reflections on this source material, such as questions and interpretations.

2 Review any other notes you have taken for your project, along with your own observations and ideas. How do particular facts, anecdotes, statistics, conclusions, or ideas in the source you are reading confirm, contradict, or amplify the information from other sources and your own experience? When you see connections, type your thoughts on these connections, either after the source material or on separate lines in your outline.

3 Skim your entire outline, considering the arrangement of your points as you go. When it makes sense, rearrange, promote, and demote your various points. Add new headings or subheadings as necessary. Now read your outline again. Have you begun synthesizing information so that you are saying something new about this topic? If not, what else could you change or add?

Part II

Types of Sources

8

Reference

Types of Sources

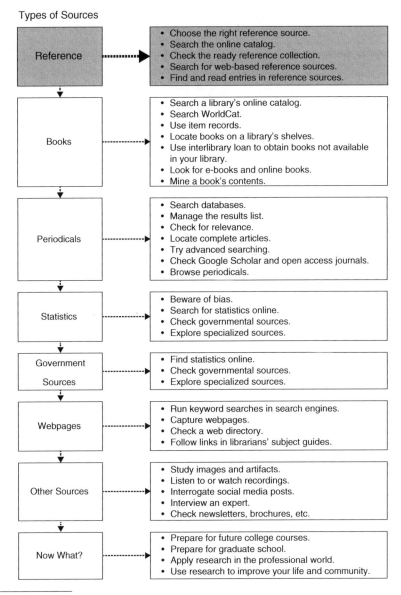

Reference	• Choose the right reference source. • Search the online catalog. • Check the ready reference collection. • Search for web-based reference sources. • Find and read entries in reference sources.
Books	• Search a library's online catalog. • Search WorldCat. • Use item records. • Locate books on a library's shelves. • Use interlibrary loan to obtain books not available in your library. • Look for e-books and online books. • Mine a book's contents.
Periodicals	• Search databases. • Manage the results list. • Check for relevance. • Locate complete articles. • Try advanced searching. • Check Google Scholar and open access journals. • Browse periodicals.
Statistics	• Beware of bias. • Search for statistics online. • Check governmental sources. • Explore specialized sources.
Government Sources	• Find statistics online. • Check governmental sources. • Explore specialized sources.
Webpages	• Run keyword searches in search engines. • Capture webpages. • Check a web directory. • Follow links in librarians' subject guides.
Other Sources	• Study images and artifacts. • Listen to or watch recordings. • Interrogate social media posts. • Interview an expert. • Check newsletters, brochures, etc.
Now What?	• Prepare for future college courses. • Prepare for graduate school. • Apply research in the professional world. • Use research to improve your life and community.

Introduction to Information Literacy for Students, First Edition. Michael C. Alewine and Mark Canada.
© 2017 John Wiley & Sons, Ltd. Published 2017 by John Wiley & Sons, Ltd.

Chapter Summary

Start building a strong foundation for your research with reference sources. Printed and online subject encyclopedias are ideal starting points for research because their entries feature concise overviews of subjects, definitions of terms, and, best of all, bibliographies that can lead you to other credible sources. These invaluable resources also can help researchers as they continue to refine their topics.

Key Terms: reference sources, reference collection, almanac, atlas, bibliography, biographical dictionary, directory, encyclopedia, guide, handbook, subject encyclopedia, electronic resources, ready reference collection, online reference sources, Wikipedia, entry, index

Chapter Objectives

* Identify various types of reference sources.
* Locate specific reference sources.
* Mine reference sources for information, including titles of other relevant sources.

Start in the Right Place

Let's say your teacher has asked you to prepare a brief report on recent trends in the development of "early college" programs in the United States. What do you do?

A *Google "early college."* That's not a bad thought, and you might find some useful information. Then again, you might not. The problem, as you will see in the chapter on Internet sources, is that no one is organizing all the material on the Web or even checking to make sure it is all accurate. For these reasons, you might waste a lot of time wading through websites about specific early colleges or, even worse, locate inaccurate, incomplete, or biased material on the Web and then unknowingly include this information in your report.

B *Consult a book on early colleges.* This is another good idea, even better than the first one, but it also has downsides. For one thing, because books often take a long time to write, edit, and publish, the information in them is usually several months old or older, so they are not ideal sources on recent trends.

C *Consult a journal article.* Journals are also great sources, which may prove very useful later in your research process, but they tend to be very specific and may not contain the basic factual information you need when you are getting started.

D *Head to the reference section of the library.* Jackpot!

While all of these sources are useful (and will get their own chapters in this book), reference sources are often the best place to *start* your research. Whether you are exploring trends in "early college" programs, identifying various kinds of heavy artillery or psychological defense mechanisms, determining the etymological roots of a word, or tracking down a fact about any one of millions of people, places, or things, the reference section of a library (or its online companion) often can provide you with credible, easy-to-find information in a matter of minutes. It also can serve you all the way through the rest of the research process, from fleshing out points with additional facts to checking the accuracy of your information.

This chapter will walk you through five strategies for using reference sources in your research:

1   Choose the right reference source.
2   Search the online catalog.
3   Check the ready reference collection.
4   Search for Web-based reference sources.
5   Find and read entries in reference sources.

You also will learn how exactly to use the information you find in reference sources when you are creating your final product.

Let's get started looking at ways to get started!

Choose the Right Reference Source

If you didn't know the meaning of the word *reference*, what would you do? If you were studying with some friends, you might simply ask somebody. If, on the other hand, you were studying alone (or with some buddies with limited vocabularies), you probably would consult a dictionary. If you have ever done this, you already have used a type of reference source. You may be familiar with other kinds of reference sources, such as atlases, directories, encyclopedias, guides, and handbooks. As you will see later in this chapter, each of these different types has a different purpose or use.

Reference sources are, generally speaking, collections of vast amounts of factual information—terms, dates, people, and other facts, as well as historical or theoretical overviews. You usually can find hundreds or even thousands of these sources in libraries' **reference collections**, where they generally are organized by call numbers, just as the books in the general collections are. Because they need to be there for anyone who might need them, reference sources are not supposed to leave the library. Although you can't check them out, you can photocopy pages from them. Many of these same sources are also available in electronic format, and you can search them by using a library's databases or by visiting them on the Web. In recent years, some academic libraries have repurposed some reference space for use as an "information commons," which may contain various technology workstations arranged in such a way to support student collaboration. For this reason, some reference collections are smaller, and many of their items are now shelved in general collections and so are available for checkout. As always, a good starting place when beginning a research project is the reference desk, where reference librarians can guide you to appropriate reference sources, no matter where they are located.

Reference sources are ideal starting points for students and even, in many cases, for experienced researchers because they contain succinct entries (ranging from one or two paragraphs to several pages) written for non-experts, along with bibliographies that can lead researchers to other good sources. In short, reference sources allow you to go directly to credible, relevant information, often written in an accessible style and presented in a concise and organized format. Instead of spending two hours stumbling blindly through questionable and incomplete websites, lengthy books, and narrow discussions in journal articles, you can spend 30 minutes finding exactly what you need—all highly credible—in a reference source. Sounds like a good deal, right?

Think Fast: The Value of Reference Sources

Describe at least two uses for reference sources.

How do you know which of the many references sources in a library or online are best for your project? The answer has to do with the kind of information you need. Let's return to the sample topic of "early college" programs. Do you need an explanation of these programs with information on what they are, where they are available, when students can begin them, and so on? You probably want to check an encyclopedia of some sort. Do you want to find the names of some organizations that study or support "early college" programs? Check out a directory. Perhaps you already have found some sources on the subject, and you come across an unfamiliar term or place. In that case, it sounds as if a dictionary or an atlas is the reference source you need. The box on the opposite page contains a brief description, along with several examples, of each kind of reference source.

When choosing a reference source, keep one more thing in mind. While all are generally credible, some are more specialized than others. Take encyclopedias, for example. Some, such as *Encyclopedia Britannica* and *World Book*, are general encyclopedias with entries on thousands of people, species, monuments, philosophies, religions, countries, languages, and more. Similarly, a standard dictionary, such as *The Merriam-Webster Dictionary* or *The American Heritage College Dictionary*, has all the common words—and plenty of uncommon words!—in the English language. Because general encyclopedias and dictionaries have to cover so much ground, they often cannot go into a great deal of depth, and they may leave out a lot of highly specialized concepts or words.

If you want more depth or more breadth, you will want to consult one or more subject encyclopedias. As the name suggests, subject encyclopedias focus on particular subjects, such as religion, popular music, movies, medicine, or American history.

Some of these encyclopedias are extremely specialized. For example, in addition to an encyclopedia of language in general, you can find an encyclopedia of the English language and even a book—a really, really thick one, in fact—on English syntax. In general, the more specialized the reference source, the more details you can expect to find, and the more items in that field you can find. If, for example, you look up Edgar Allan Poe in a general encyclopedia, you might find an entry a half-page long with the basics of his birth and death dates, place of birth, and notable poems and short stories. If you look up Poe in *The Dictionary of Literary Biography*, on the other hand, you will find three separate entries—one that focuses on Poe as a writer of fiction and poetry, one that treats him as a writer of science fiction, and another that highlights his work as a journalist—and each of these entries would be packed with several pages of information. But wait—there's more! You could even find an encyclopedia that focuses exclusively on Poe; here you would see hundreds of entries on individual poems and stories, as well as family members, magazines he edited, writers who influenced him, and more. Here are two examples:

Frank, Frederick S., and Tony Magistrale. *The Poe Encyclopedia*. Westport: Greenwood Press, 1997. Print.

Sova, Dawn B. *Critical Companion to Edgar Allan Poe*: A *Literary Reference to His Life and Work*. New York: Facts on File, 2007. Print.

As you can see, subject encyclopedias are often the best reference sources, since they tend to have in-depth discussions of a large number of subjects within a given field.

Types of Reference Sources

Each type of reference has a different set of strengths and weaknesses. You wouldn't look for an overview of the Vietnam War by looking in a directory of U.S. manufacturers, right? A historical dictionary or an encyclopedia would be better choices, and the best choice probably would be a subject encyclopedia such as, say, *The Encyclopedia of the Vietnam War: A Political, Social, and Military History*. Here are some common types of reference sources, along with examples:

- **Almanacs** are annual publications typically featuring summaries of the year's events, as well as thousands of facts about the modern world, such as population statistics. Examples include the *Information Please Almanac* and the *World Almanac and Book of Facts*.
- **Atlases** contain maps showing political boundaries, population densities, geographic formations such as mountain ranges, and more. Historical atlases show the world as it stood in previous eras. (Since political boundaries and other geographical details have changed over the centuries,

historical atlases are invaluable sources on some historical topics.) Examples include *Goode's World Atlas*, the *New Historical Atlas of the World*, *The New Penguin Atlas of Ancient History*, and *The Routledge Atlas of the Arab-Israeli Conflict*.

- **Bibliographies** contain citations for sources on a particular topic and are useful for tracking down additional information. Examples include the *Bibliography of Bioethics*, the *Bibliography on Holocaust Literature*, and the *Bibliography on Future Trends in Terrorism*.

- **Biographical dictionaries** feature long or short profiles of notable modern or historical figures. Some cover a wide variety of individuals, while others focus on a particular subject such as popular music or science. These reference sources are especially useful when you are looking for lesser-known figures, who generally do not have individual entries in general encyclopedias. Examples include *American National Biography*, *Current Biography*, *Who's Who in America*, the *Biographical Dictionary of Modern American Educators*, and *Notable Women in the American Theatre: A Biographical Dictionary*.

- **Dictionaries** typically contain information about words. Standard dictionaries feature spellings, pronunciations, definitions, and etymologies, along with information about part of speech, various forms of words, and, in many cases, synonyms and usage. Specialized dictionaries provide similar information for a narrower selection of words, such as jargon or slang words. Examples include *Merriam-Webster's Collegiate Dictionary*, *The Oxford English Dictionary* (which, because it provides archaic spellings and definitions of English words as they were used hundreds of years ago, is an essential source for understanding some old works of English and American literature), *The Harvard Dictionary of Music*, *The New Partridge Dictionary of Slang and Unconventional English*, and *Mosby's Dictionary of Medicine, Nursing & Health Professions*.

- **Directories** contain contact information, such as addresses and URLs, for associations, organizations, corporations, and the like. Examples include *The Directory of Business Information Resources*, *Federal Regulatory Directory*, *Health Care Careers Directory*, and *The United States Government Internet Directory*.

- **Encyclopedias** contain definitions, descriptions, explanations, and other basic information about a wide range of subjects in the arts, business, education, history, sciences, and more. Examples include *Encyclopedia Americana*, *Encyclopedia Britannica*, and *World Book*.

- **Guides** and **handbooks** often contain how-to information for citing sources, writing letters, punctuating sentences, and the like. Examples include *The Chicago Manual of Style*, the *MLA Handbook for Writers of Research Papers*, and *Emily Post's Etiquette*.

- **Subject encyclopedias**, like general encyclopedias, contain basic information, but focus on particular fields, such as business, education, medicine, and politics or even narrower topics within these fields, such as international relations or school counseling. Examples include *Great Physicists: The Life and Times of Leading Physicists from Galileo to Hawking*, *The Encyclopedia of Serial Killers*, *Encyclopedia of Global Warming & Climate Change*, *Encyclopedia of Urban Legends*, *Franklin D. Roosevelt: His Life and Times: An Encyclopedic View*, and the *Encyclopedia of Video Games: The Culture, Technology, and Art of Gaming*.
- *Other reference sources* include *CQ Researcher* and *Opposing Viewpoints*. *CQ Researcher* contains extensive reference entries providing overviews of topics, background, different points of view, relevant legislation, timelines, bibliographies, and links to other useful sources of information. *Opposing Viewpoints* provides reference entries, viewpoint essays, scholarly articles, magazine articles, and statistical information (especially in the online version). If you are not familiar with the various issues surrounding a topic, either *CQ Researcher* or *Opposing Viewpoints* is a great place to start. These sources are still available in print format; however, more and more libraries are providing electronic access, which includes more dynamic content.

Search the Online Catalog

The number of reference sources that have been published—even the number in a typical academic library—is dizzying. The box above lists just a fraction of these sources. How can you find one relevant to your topic?

Start with the library's online catalog. Does the "Advanced Search" page allow you to limit to reference sources? If so, you could type in some keywords, such as *water* or *Islam*, and choose "reference" so that you will get only reference items on these subjects. The online catalog may index electronic reference sources along with print resources. In case it does not, you also should check the library's home page to see if it contains links to **electronic resources**, *e-references*, *e-resources*, or *research guides*. These links may lead you to all-inclusive guides to electronic reference sources (both proprietary and those that are freely available). Click on any such links you see and look for electronic reference sources, such as *Oxford Reference Online*, *Sage E-reference*, or the hundreds of freely available online reference sources (discussed below). If you have any trouble browsing or searching for electronic reference sources, contact the reference desk. Let the librarian on duty know what your topic is. He or she may be able to suggest a few good reference works or help you run some searches.

Check the Ready Reference Collection

While you are at the reference desk soaking up all that free assistance from a friendly librarian, have a look at the **ready reference collection**, which is usually found very close to the reference librarian's station, often right behind the desk. This collection consists of several frequently used reference sources, such as a current almanac, an atlas, a dictionary, a thesaurus, and various publication and citation guides such as *The Chicago Manual of Style*. Just ask for the one you want.

Quicktivity: Find Reference Sources

Use the tips above to locate at least two reference sources related to your topic. Try to find one very specific reference source. Record the citations in your research log.

Search for Online Reference Sources

There are a host of freely available **online reference sources** on the Web, including some that you might not even think of as reference sources (such as bartleby.com, imdb.com, weather.com, and others). Some, such as Merriam-Webster's online dictionary, are highly credible because they are managed by well-established companies (which have an interest in protecting their reputations) and contain material written and edited by experts. Others contain material written by amateurs with no specialized training or experience and edited by, well, maybe nobody. Which sounds like the better choice? You got it. The former are just as good as printed reference materials you find in a library's reference section while the latter may be good—or may be bad or sometimes good and sometimes bad. You just don't know. Use what you learned in Chapter 5 about evaluating sources to determine which online reference sources are good choices.

While we're on the subject of online reference sources, it's time to say something about the elephant in the room: **Wikipedia**. Almost any search of the Web will pull up a relevant Wikipedia entry. You will have many instructors who simply tell you "do not use Wikipedia," but you may also have a few instructors who do allow its use. Remember, you must follow the parameters set by each individual instructor. In any case, there are some very good reasons to be cautious about Wikipedia: the lack of credentials for many authors, as well as the absence of a thorough editing process. Some Wikipedia entries actually are written and maintained by experts, but that is not always readily apparent from the entries themselves. For these reasons, you should be very wary of the text in Wikipedia entries.

Think Fast: Compare Reference Sources

What makes some reference sources more credible than others?

Find and Study Entries in Reference Sources

Once you have located a print or electronic reference source, you need to find the specific definition, statistics, overview, or whatever it is that you want to read. This information is often organized into **entries**—that is, sections of text typically ranging from a few words to several pages. (See Figure 8.1.) Each entry is on a fairly narrow subject, such as President Obama, global warming, Pythagorean theorem, Tourette syndrome, or rap music. In the case of print reference sources, entries often appear in alphabetical order. If so, you can look up your subject in the source just as you would do in a dictionary. If the source has a different organizational scheme—by broader subject area, for example—or if you look for your entry and cannot find it, try looking up your subject in the **index**, which is an alphabetical list of topics in a book. There you may find a page number where relevant information is located. For example, let's say you need to read up on desert winds. You have found a subject encyclopedia on meteorology, but you can't find an entry on desert winds. You can check the book's index, where you probably will find a reference to desert winds or winds. You then could look at the page listed and find the information you need.

Planking

Planking is a phenomenon in which people make themselves rigid (like a wooden plank) and then lie face down in unexpected places, such as on guard rails, railroad tracks, the roof a tall building, etc.—seemingly perfectly balanced on just one part of the body (typically the stomach). These events are usually photographed or videoed and then disseminated via social media. There has been controversy associated with planking, as some of the locations have been very dangerous. Numerous injuries and at least one death have been reported.

References:

"Australia Man Plunges to 'Planking' Death" (2011). NBCNews. http://www.nbcnews.com/id/43036847/ns/world_news-asia_ pacific/t/australia-man-plunges-planking-death/#.VbFcEdjbLDQ "

"The Lying Down Game: How to Play." (2009). *The Telegraph*. http://www. telegraph.co.uk/news/6162412/The-lying-down-game-how-to-play.html

See also **Lying Down Game**

Figure 8.1   Sample unsigned brief reference entry. Source: Created by Michael C. Alewine.

Information literacy **4** 392-439

   ACRL **4** 395-397

   bias **4** 399

   defined **4** 392-393

   research (see Research Literacy)

   teaching methods **4** 415-422

   and World Wide Web **7** 19-22

Information technology **5** 112-199

Figure 8.2 Sample index page from a multivolume reference set. Source: Created by Michael C. Alewine.

By the way, you may notice that some print reference sources are not single books, but multi-volume sets. The index to these sets often appears in the final volume, but be careful. If the volumes are organized according to subject, each volume might have a separate index. Note that the term "cumulative index" means that the index covers the entire set of volumes. In a cumulative index, you typically will see a volume number (perhaps in bold), as well as a page number or range of page numbers. Related topics might be slightly indented underneath the main entry. (See Figure 8.2.)

In the case of electronic reference sources, you can simply run a keyword search as you would on a Web search engine. Running a keyword search in an electronic reference source is every bit as simple as googling something on the Internet, but using an electronic reference source has one enormous advantage: everything you find will generally be the most accurate, authoritative, and credible information available anywhere, whereas the material you find on the Web may or may not be credible—and, since you probably are not yet an expert on the topic, you won't know the good from the bad.

Of course, once you have found an appropriate reference source and then located a relevant entry within the source, you need to read the entry. As you read it, take notes on key concepts, names, dates, and the like. Also, take advantage of the overview to get a sense of any central issues and debates related to this subject. This information may help you begin to develop some research questions. Remember to use any cross-references or bibliographical notes to find other relevant information. Cross-references will direct you to other entries in the reference source. For example, in an entry on Carl Jung in a subject encyclopedia on psychology, you might find a cross-reference to Sigmund Freud. Bibliographies, which often appear at the ends of entries, feature titles of other relevant, credible sources. For example, an entry on El Greco in an encyclopedia of art might list titles of biographies of the painter, as well as critical studies of his work.

For the sake of brevity or simplicity, some reference sources may use abbreviations and notations instead of complete words and explanations. This is especially true of highly specialized reference sources such as *The Oxford English Dictionary*. If you come across an abbreviation or symbol you don't understand, check the introductory material or the table of contents. A good reference source typically contains a key to abbreviations and symbols. As always, if you need help, see the reference librarian on duty.

Quicktivity: Explore a Reference Source

Look up a relevant person, place, or thing in a reference source you located for the last Quicktivity. If necessary, use the index for the source. Skim the entry and follow a cross-reference if you see one. If you see any abbreviations or symbols, look them up in the source's explanatory matter, probably located at the front of the book.

When is it OK to use a reference source when doing research? Unless your instructor explicitly forbids it (because he or she simply wants your own opinion, for example), it's always fine to *consult* a reference source and take notes on definitions, basic facts, and so on. This information may never make it into your paper in the form of a quotation or even a paraphrase, but it may help you understand a topic or develop a research question. If you do use any of this information, you must decide whether to cite it. Remember, as you learned in Chapter 6, you do not need to cite factual material that is widely known by experts (and maybe by many other people, as well); thus, since reference sources tend to summarize facts and widely accepted concepts or theories, you won't need to cite much of what you find in these sources. For example, you might use a subject encyclopedia to find the distance between Cuba and the United States, some basic tenets of Buddhism, the parts of the water cycle, or the meaning of the phrase "trickle-down theory." You don't need to cite these basic facts and concepts. In some cases, however, you should cite material you find in reference sources because it involves some interpretation or painstaking research. Of course, you always need to place exact words from sources in quotation marks. If you do wind up citing a reference source, you should consult the citation guidelines for the format you are using (APA, MLA, etc.). In many cases, you will need to check to see if the entry in the book is "signed," meaning an author is identified, such as in the example below. (See Figure 8.3.)

When citing signed reference sources (as when you cite anthologies, collections of essays, or edited books with different authors of each chapter), you often need to include the entry author, the entry title, and the inclusive pages, along with the standard publication information, such as the name of the publisher and the date of publication. Below is an example of a citation for an entry in a reference encyclopedia:

Metherd, Molly. "The Latin American Diaspora." *Cultural History of Reading*. Eds. Gabrielle Watling and Sara E. Quay. Westport, Conn.: Greenwood Press, 2009. 46–58. Print.

Poor Richard's Almanack

In an age of almanacs, Benjamin Franklin's Poor Richard's Almanack was the greatest book of its kind. By no means an invention of Franklin, almanacs had been appearing in the American colonies since at least the 1640s and were a common, profitable source of income for colonial printers. Franklin's brother James had come out with a Rhode Island almanac "By Poor Robin" for 1728, and Franklin himself had published almanacs by John Jerman and Thomas Godfrey in 1730. When he conceived of his own version, Franklin elected to write the material himself rather than pay the high cost of hiring a philomath. He wrote behind the guise of a persona, Poor Richard, who explains in the first volume that he has begun to write almanacs to satisfy a wife tired of watching him "do nothing but gaze at the Stars" (1185). Franklin also hit on another idea. Recognizing his almanac's potential for "conveying Instruction among the common People, who bought scarce any other Books," he filled the empty spaces in his tables with witty sayings (1397). Both ideas turned out to be strokes of genius. The first edition of his debut almanac, printed in long primer on 6.3 x 3.9-inch leaves, sold out in a month, and he came out with two additional editions. Sales of later almanacs, which he sent to shops from New England to Charleston, later reached about 10,000. In 1740, Franklin came out with a "Pocket Almanack," printed in Caslon brevier on 1.2 x 2.8-inch leaves, and continued this successful small version in different form in ensuing years. The importance of Franklin's almanac, however, goes well beyond its popularity. As Richard E. Amacher explains, it not only increased Franklin's own fame and financial security, but gave rise to imitators among almanac makers in both England and the colonies (133).

"No other almanac," Amacher notes, "has ever been so famous or influential" (134). The sayings, which Franklin collected in an essay called "The Way to Wealth" and published in the 1758 edition of the almanac, turned out to be especially noteworthy. Also known as "Father Abraham's Speech," this essay went through more than 70 editions between 1757 and 1890 and has been called "probably the most printed and translated work in all American literature'" (qtd. in Amacher 135). Poor Richard's Almanack continued to appear until the nineteenth century, though Franklin's active involvement in its composition ended after the 1758 edition.

Mark Canada

See also ALMANACS; BENJAMIN FRANKLIN.

References

Amacher, Richard E. "Benjamin Franklin." The Dictionary of Literary Biography. American Colonial Writers, 1606-1734. Ed. Emory Elliott. Vol. 24. Detroit: Gale, 1984. 125-147.

Franklin, Benjamin. Writings. New York: Library of America, 1987.

For Further Reading

Green, James N. "English Books and Printing in the Age of Franklin." A History of the Book in America. Ed. David D. Hall. Vol. 1. Cambridge: Cambridge University Press, 2000. 248-298.

Miller, C. William. Benjamin Franklin's Philadelphia Printing. Philadelphia: American Philosophical Society, 1974.

Tebbel, John. A History of Book Publishing in the United States. Vol. 1. New York: R.R. Bowker, 1972.

Figure 8.3 Sample signed reference entry. Source: Created by Mark Canada and Michael C. Alewine.

Some instructors may frown on a paper that cites only reference sources. That may be because the writer is needlessly citing factual information, but it may also be because the instructor wants you to study nuanced, interpretive discussions of a topic, not just basic background information. Remember, we said that reference sources were great places to *start* your research, not that you should *stop* with them.

Conclusion

In this chapter, you have learned about the ideal place to begin your research on any topic under the sun: reference sources. As you have seen, reference sources come in both print versions—found in libraries' reference collections—and electronic versions, often available through libraries' websites or on the Web. These sources, which come in a number of varieties ranging from atlases to encyclopedias, provide basic factual information and overviews to help provide researchers with a foundation on any topic, as well as the kind of information that can point to research questions. You also learned how to locate these sources, find relevant entries within them, and read and use the contents of these entries.

Steps to Success

1 Choose a subject you are studying in one of your courses—perhaps something you may need to discuss in a paper or simply something about which you would like to learn more. Locate at least three different kinds of reference sources, including at least one printed source and one credible electronic source, on this subject. For example, you might look up Rome in an online atlas, a printed almanac, and an electronic subject encyclopedia on the ancient world available through your library's databases.

2 Find the relevant entries and study them, taking notes as you go. Compare the information in the entries in these various reference sources. Does each have a different kind of information? What parallels do you notice?

3 Use the bibliography in one of these entries to find additional information on the same subject.

9

Books

Types of Sources

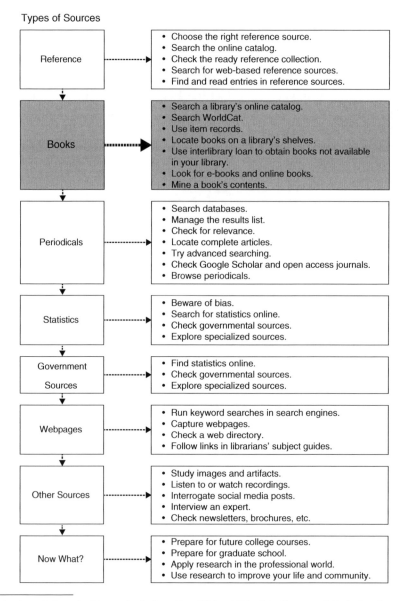

Introduction to Information Literacy for Students, First Edition. Michael C. Alewine and Mark Canada.
© 2017 John Wiley & Sons, Ltd. Published 2017 by John Wiley & Sons, Ltd.

Chapter Summary

Hit the books and discover in-depth studies featuring countless facts and interpretations that can enrich your understanding of many topics. In this chapter,
you will learn how to locate books, in both print and electronic formats, and
mine them for useful information, including citations of other sources that can
inform your research.

Key Terms: catalog, keyword search, author search, title search, subject search,
federated search, advanced search, WorldCat, item record, Library of Congress
Classification system, Dewey Decimal Classification system, interlibrary loan,
document delivery, e-book, online book, table of contents, index

Chapter Objectives

- Use keywords and other search terms in an online catalog to identify call
  numbers for books.
- Use call numbers to locate books on library shelves.
- Browse library shelves to identify other relevant books.
- Use a table of contents and an index to mine the contents of a book.
- Tap a book's bibliography to identify other useful sources.

Books: More Than Mere Life-changers

Books spark the imagination. They take us to worlds that no longer exist and others
that are far, far away. They record our shared history (or rewrite that history and
spark new debates). They ask questions about who we are, what we do, and why we
do it. Henry David Thoreau, who wrote a few books and read a lot more, said, "How
many a man has dated a new era in his life from the reading of a book!"

If books can broaden our minds, touch our hearts, and inspire our souls, they
also can help us reach more immediate ends by informing our research. As you will
recall from your reading in the previous chapter, we had you begin your research
with reference sources, such as subject encyclopedias. If this step went well, you now
have a handle on some relevant terms, know some background on your topic, and
have a list of other sources you can explore. You have dipped your toe in the pool;
now it's time to plunge into the deep end. It's time to begin your research in earnest.

For a variety of reasons, books are your logical next step. For one thing, because of
their length, they generally provide more detail than other sources, such as journal
articles or websites. In fact, they provide so much detail that they can be intimidating,

but don't worry. This chapter will show you how to get just what you need from a book in minimal time or, in some cases, how to read some books meticulously and compile a wealth of useful material for your research needs. Much of the value in this detail lies in the context it provides. Often, the author of a book explores a very narrow topic, but surrounds his or her investigation of this topic with history, statistics, images, observations by others, and more. A book about beach erosion on North Carolina's Outer Banks, for example, might recount the history of beach erosion over decades or even millennia, compare various instances of beach erosion in Florida and Maine and other locales, describe various types and subtypes of erosion, and illustrate the history, instances, and types with photographs, illustrations, and graphs. In short, a book often provides a "bird's-eye view" of a topic, not just a microscopic view of its intricate details. (The microscopic view is what you will find in journal articles, as you will see in the next chapter.) Often, a scholarly book has a wealth of intricate details, too, and ideally these details will be organized logically into chapters, explained clearly in sentences and paragraphs, and carefully documented with bibliographies, endnotes, footnotes, or references. Excellent sources in their own right, books also can lead you to other useful sources. As you will see, they usually contain extensive bibliographies that list dozens or even hundreds of other relevant, credible sources on the same topic. In the end, one book often will provide you with as much useful information as several periodical articles. In many cases, though, you do not have to read a book in its entirety—more on that later.

As is true with all aspects of research, you will be more productive if you proceed with some strategies. Here are the key ones for using books:

1　Search a library's online catalog.
2　Search WorldCat.
3　Use item records.
4　Locate books on a library's shelves.
5　Use interlibrary loan to obtain books not available in your library.
6　Look for e-books and online books.
7　Mine a book's contents.

You remember Chapter 3: Search for Answers, right? Before you begin exploring the world of books, return to the research log you set up when you read that chapter. It will be a great resource as you use this chapter to investigate books.

Search a Library's Online Catalog

Do the words "card catalog" mean anything to you? Believe it or not, instead of inputting information about books into computers, library staffs once used 3-by-5 cards, each containing information about an author, a book, or a subject. To find a book, library patrons had to flip through the cards, which were arranged alphabetically in wooden cases with many small drawers. (See Figure 9.1.) While this system

Figure 9.1   A card catalog. Source: Permission given by Creative Commons, https://www.flickr.com/photos/mamsy/4175783446/sizes/o/in/photostream/ Used under CC-BY-SA 2.0 https://creativecommons.org/licenses/by/2.0/.

may seem somewhat antiquated to many people today, it was actually fairly efficient– and no one ever worried if the Internet was up or down!

Today we use an electronic version, typically called the online or library **catalog**, which can be searched in the library or from a networked computer anywhere in the world. (See Figure 9.2.) The box for a basic search of this online catalog often appears on the main page of a library's website. You also may see a link to a page where you can perform an advanced search. Some libraries have links labeled "Library Catalog" or "Search for Books and more ...," while others have something like "Search for Articles, Books, and more ..." (There is an important difference, which this chapter will discuss.) With very few exceptions, online catalogs are freely available on the Web. No login is required, although most catalogs allow affiliated people, such as college students, to create accounts within the catalog systems so that they can save records, keep their search histories, export citations (lists of books), and more. An online catalog provides you with lists of items after you complete searches with the keywords, concept phrases, truncation technique, and Boolean operators you learned to use in Chapter 3. It also will provide you with the call number and status so that you can locate each book in the library.

You can perform many kinds of searches in a library catalog, but the most common are **keyword**, **author**, and **title searches**. This chapter uses screen captures

Figure 9.2   A student searching a library's online catalog. Source: Photo taken by Christopher W. Bowyer; permission given by Christopher W. Bowyer.

from a number of libraries around the United States so that you can see the similarities and differences among those catalogs' interfaces. Although they sometimes look slightly different, these catalogs generally work in the same way. For this reason, you should have little trouble using just about any library catalog, even if you have never seen it.

Keyword searches

The default setting in most catalogs is the **keyword search**, since the most common operation, particularly in academic libraries, is searching for materials by keyword—that is, by topic. (See Figure 9.3.) As you learned in Chapter 3, you can combine keywords with Boolean operators, such as *or* and *and*. Otherwise, avoid using groups

Keyword Search	▼

domestic abuse and prevention

Submit

Figure 9.3   Basic keyword search. Source: Created by Michael C. Alewine.

of words unless you are searching for a concept phrase, such as "women in combat" or "war on drugs." As you may have noticed, you can use long strings of words, even questions, in Google searches, but some library catalogs will not "understand" a search with anything other than keywords, concept phrases, and Boolean operators. For example, a typical college library contains dozens or even hundreds of books that describe the federal legislative system in the United States; however, if you type "How does a bill become a law?" in the keyword box for the library's online catalog, you probably won't see the results for all or even any of them.

Quicktivity: Search an Online Catalog

Consult your research log and take a look at the search terms you created with your keywords, concept phrases, truncation, and Boolean operators. Try using these search terms now in your library's catalog. Record the call numbers for several books you find. If you are working on your own computer, you can simply copy them and paste them directly into your research log. (You will learn more about call numbers later in this chapter.)

Author searches

In some cases, you will have more than just some keywords to conduct a search. For example, you may have come across the names of some experts when you were looking through subject encyclopedias. In such cases, you can conduct an **author search** in the library's online catalog. Remember to set the search type as "Author." Traditionally, an author search should consist of a last name, followed by a first name; however, many catalogs allow users to search for authors in a variety of ways—with no commas, for example, or with first names followed by last names, which is more of a natural-language search. (See Figure 9.4 and Figure 9.5.) You can search if you have

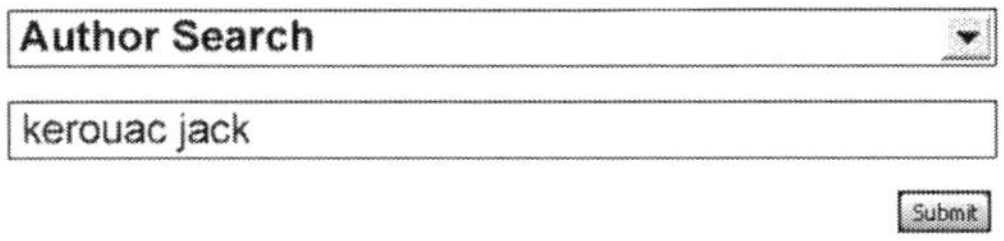

Figure 9.4 Author search (last name first). Source: Created by Michael C. Alewine.

Figure 9.5 Author search (natural language). Source: Created by Michael C. Alewine.

Figure 9.6   Title search. Source: Created by Michael C. Alewine.

only an author's last name, but the results may include several false hits, particularly if the last name is a common one such as Anderson or Jones.

Title searches

Use a **title search** when you have a book's exact title or at least the first few words. Set the search type to "Title" and type all the words you know in the title. (See Figure 9.6.) Keep in mind that many items in a library have the same or similar titles. If you conduct a title search for "*harry potter*," you may come up with many items, including both books and videos. You would be better off using the complete title of the specific item, such as "*harry potter and the deathly hallows*." You may still end up with both books and videos, but at least you have narrowed it down. Most catalogs also allow researchers to search by phrase using quotation marks. This approach can reduce the number of unrelated results.

Subject searches

Although they are not as common as keyword, author, and title searches, you ought to know something about **subject searches**, as well. Typically, the subjects in these searches are tied to specific Library of Congress subject headings, which employ a controlled vocabulary that would not be obvious to most people. For that reason, subject searches generally are not as useful as keyword searches (unless you happen to be a professional library cataloger). Let's say you wanted to learn about the death of Anne Boleyn, one of the wives of King Henry VIII of England. What would you have to type in a subject search box? Go ahead and think about it. Take your best shot. Are you ready? Think you got it? Did you come up with "*Anne Boleyn, Queen, consort of Henry VIII, King of England, 1507-1536* – death and burial"? No? Then you probably can see why subject searches are generally not as useful as keyword searches. A keyword search for the two obvious words connected with a Boolean operator, "Boleyn and death," would turn up the same item as this very specific subject heading—and require a whole lot less expertise in arcane subject headings. (If you did guess the exact subject heading, you either are a born librarian or you must have the *Library of Congress Subject Headings*—all five volumes—at your bedside for casual reading.) Subject headings can be very useful, though, when you come across them in item records, as you will see later in this chapter.

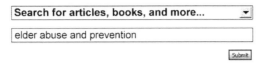

Figure 9.7 Federated search. Source: Created by Michael C. Alewine.

Federated searches

Some library search engines allow you to conduct something called a **federated search**, which allows you to search for keywords found in the item records of not only books, but also periodicals and other sources. (See Figure 9.7.) It sounds like a time-saver, right? It can be, but it also can cost you time if it forces you to wade through a lot of unrelated material before you locate what you are actually seeking. For example, if you know the title of a book and want to see if a library has it, you may have to sort through reviews of that book and periodical articles with similar titles, whereas a title search in a regular online catalog would turn up only books in the library's collection.

Quicktivity: Use Author and Title Searches

Check your research log. Conduct searches for authors and titles listed there. Record the call numbers in your research log.

Advanced searches

Keyword, author, title, and subject searches are all possible through libraries' basic search functions, which are often the defaults on their websites. Much of the time, however, you will want to choose "**Advanced Search**," which is different from the basic search in two respects. First, an advanced search typically has three search fields instead of one, and you will be able to designate a kind of search—keyword or author, for example—for each field. (See Figure 9.8.) Second, you can set limits such as date

All Fields ▼	reading or literacy	AND ▼
All Fields ▼	children	AND ▼
All Fields ▼	development	AND ▼
All Fields ▼	parents	Add a row

Figure 9.8 Advanced search. Source: Created by Michael C. Alewine.

range, material type, and even multiple libraries (if your library is part of a multiple library system or consortium).

Say, for example, you remember seeing a how-to DVD on cabinet construction at a particular library, and you remember that it looked fairly new. If you run a basic keyword search for "cabinets," you may get a long list of books and videos about kitchen cabinets, as well as governmental cabinets, produced over the last century and more. With an advanced search, you could limit the results to videorecordings produced in the last five years and stored at a particular library. Thanks to these limits, you now probably will have to wade through only a few results instead of dozens; this advanced search might even take you right to the one title you had in mind.

Quicktivity: Use Limits to Narrow a Search

Visit the "Advanced Search" screen on your library's online catalog and conduct some searches by using limits. For example, you might try limiting the dates to pull up only books published in the last five years. Record the limits you used, as well as the call numbers, in your research log.

Search WorldCat

Searching for books in your own library's catalog makes perfect sense, but you don't have to limit yourself. Many libraries also allow you to use a catalog called **WorldCat** (which is also freely available on the Web via the Online Computer Library Center, or OCLC, at oclc.org). As the name implies, WorldCat allows you to find books in libraries all over the world, although typically it is set to provide results from specific geographic areas. Even more sophisticated than many individual catalogs, WorldCat has advanced functionality that may prove useful to you. (See Figure 9.9.) If you need something fast, it will let you know what books are available in other libraries, so you can drive there and pick up what you need. (Don't have time to drive from Minnesota to Miami to pick up that book about the Florida Everglades? Don't sweat it. Interlibrary loan allows you to get the book without leaving town—more on that later.)

Quicktivity: Use WorldCat to Expand Your Searching

Check your research log for any books you have not been able to locate in your academic library. Run a title search in WorldCat to find these books. Record the author, publisher, publication date, and call number for each book in your research log. If you don't have any notes on books you could not find, run a keyword search in WorldCat to locate relevant books and jot down their publication information.

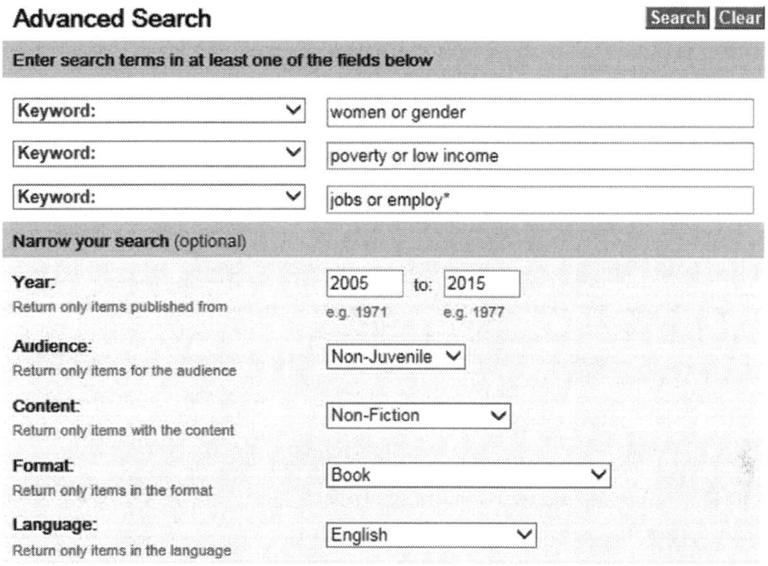

Figure 9.9 WorldCat advanced search (Web version). Source: Permission given by OCLC. © 2016 OCLC Online Computer Library Center, Inc. Reproduced with permission of OCLC. WorldCat is a registered trademark/service mark of OCLC.

Use Item Records

OK, you have dutifully typed your keywords and Boolean operators—or an author's name or a title—into a catalog search box and submitted your search. What comes next? You will see a list of results similar to the list you would see in an online Web search. Look over the titles and click on the title of one that looks relevant. The next thing you will see is something called the **item record** (see Figure 9.10). That's kind of a dull name for something that is a goldmine of information—if you know how to read it. The item record contains the basic things you might expect: the author's name, the title of the book, the name of the publisher, the date of publication, and the call number. For your purposes, the call number will be the most important information you will need to find the book in the library; however, you first need to decide if the book is worth tracking down. Before you head off to the stacks, check the date. Is the book sufficiently current for your needs? Item records also often contain detailed information about contents. Check this information to see if the book contains the kind of information you need. Before you leave the computer, you may want to check one more thing. Remember those Library of Congress subject headings? We said subject searching is generally not very useful for most of us because we don't have them memorized and can't guess them—but what if someone gave you the subject heading for exactly what you needed? That heading would be like a secret password—the "Open Sesame" of the library world—that would give you access to one or more books on your topic. Well, the item record contains that secret password. Near the bottom of every item record will appear one or more subject

Author: Silver, Lauren J.

Title: System Kids: Adolescent Mothers and the Politics of Regulation

Publisher: Chapel Hill [North Carolina]: The University of North Carolina Press, [2015]

LOCATION	CALL #	STATUS
General Stacks	HQ759.4 .S537 2015	AVAILABLE

Description: x, 198 pages; 22 cm

Bibliography: Includes bibliographical references (pages 177-189) and index

Contents: The want to see you fail: dilemmas in child welfare -- Playing case manager: work life in a culture of fear -- The better places don't want teen moms: invisible lives, hidden program spaces -- The real responsibility is on you! the self-sufficiency trap -- I am young. I'm not dumb; and I'm not anxious: identity performances as service negotiation -- The program allowed me to get pregnant: everyday resistance, dignity, and fleeting collectives -- Conclusion: Moving from disconnected systems to communities of care

Subject Teenage mothers -- United States

Child welfare -- United States

Aid to families with dependent children programs -- United States

Maternal and infant welfare -- United States

ISBN 9781469622590 paperback alkaline paper
1469622599 paperback alkaline paper
9781469622606 electronic book
OCLC # 886880982

Figure 9.10   Item record for a book. Source: Created by Michael C. Alewine.

headings for that book. Click one of the headings, and you will see other books with the same subject heading. In other words, these subject headings in the item record provide a gateway to many other sources, for which you don't have to conduct separate keyword, author, or title searches. For this reason, subject headings in item records are terrific time-savers. Before you head to the stacks, use the subject headings in the item records to make a list of several books that you can then retrieve from the shelves.

Quicktivity: Use Subject Headings to Find Additional Sources

Study the item records for several books you have located by conducting keyword, author, or title searches in your library's online catalog. Click on the subject headings and record the authors, titles, and call numbers of other useful books you find.

Locate Books on Library Shelves

Once you have some call numbers, you can locate the books in the library's stacks. Each book has a unique call number, but books on similar topics have similar call numbers. Academic librarians—that is, the librarians at colleges and universities— usually use the **Library of Congress Classification (LCC) system**, in which the first letter or letters refer to the general subject area of the book. The letter B, for example, comes first in the call numbers of books about philosophy or religion, and the letters QM come first in the call numbers of books about human anatomy. The remaining numbers and letters correspond to more specific aspects of a book.

A – General Works
B – Philosophy, Psychology, Religion
C – Auxiliary Sciences of History
D – World History and History of Europe, Asia, Africa, Australia, New Zealand, Etc.
E – History of the Americas
F – History of the Americas
G – Geography, Anthropology, and Recreation
H – Social Sciences
J – Political Science
K – Law
L – Education
M – Music and Books on Music
N – Fine Arts
P – Language and Literature
Q – Science
R – Medicine
S – Agriculture
T – Technology
U – Military Science
V – Naval Science
Z – Bibliography, Library Science, Information Resources (General)

Public libraries, such as the one you might have in your hometown, often use the older **Dewey Decimal Classification (DCC) system**, in which a single—though possibly long—number refers to the subject area of a nonfiction book; sometimes letters also accompany this number.

000 – Computer Science, Library and Information Science & General Work
100 – Philosophy and Psychology
200 – Religion
300 – Social Sciences
400 – Language
500 – Science
600 – Technology
700 – Arts
800 – Literature
900 – History, Geography & Biography

A call number serves as a kind of "address" for each book. Once you locate the record for a book in an online catalog, you can use the call number to walk right to the shelf where the book with this call number is located.

While you are in the shelves, do a little browsing. After all, an item record can provide you with only so much information. Catalogers do not include every subtopic from a book in its record. For example, a keyword search in the catalog using "dogfish," a type of shark, will not provide a result for *The Book of Sharks*, by Richard Ellis, because the term "dogfish" is not in the catalog record. Since many books will not come up in your results, browsing the titles of the books on the shelves can sometimes provide you with a hidden gem. Now, you probably don't want to begin wandering aimlessly through a library's stacks looking at bindings, unless you have a lot of curiosity and a lot of time. Rather, after you have used the catalog to identify some potentially useful books, use the call numbers to locate them and then look at the books to the left and the right of them. Hey, if the rules permit it, grab a chair or sit on the floor and spend some time picking books off the shelves and thumbing through them. By the way, many online catalogs are set up for electronic browsing. When you use these catalogs, you can click on a call number, see the call numbers of nearby books, and click on them to see their item records.

Example: Anatomy of a Call Number

E457 .W597 2009 (Library of Congress system)
E – indicates that the subject is United States History
457 – indicates that this is a biography (or other personal paper) by or about Abraham Lincoln
W597 – indicates the author's last name, which for this particular title is White
2009 – indicates the year of publication

Quicktivity: Visit the Stacks

Use the call numbers you have recorded to track down the books in your library. Note in your research log which books you check out.

Use Interlibrary Loan

Many people are accustomed to ordering items from amazon.com or another retailer and having the items delivered to them. Did you know you could do the same thing with a library? The process is called "**interlibrary loan**," or "**document delivery**," and it's available from many public and academic libraries, usually at little or no charge to you. If you come across the title of a book in a subject encyclopedia, a book's bibliography, WorldCat, or the Internet and cannot find it in your local library's catalog, check with your library to see if you can order it through interlibrary loan, which libraries use to share their books, book chapters, journal articles, and even videos and reels of microfilm. In the case of chapters or articles, many libraries will send electronic versions as email attachments to your library, which will in turn make them available to you. If you begin your research sufficiently early—several weeks before your deadline, that is—the libraries with the materials you want will have time to send them to your local library so that you can use them.

Quicktivity: Use Interlibrary Loan to Order Books

Go to the WorldCat search page and conduct some keyword, author, or title searches. Record the authors, titles, publication dates, and call numbers for books that appear to be relevant and credible. Go to your library's screen for interlibrary loan and request these books.

Look for E-books and Online Books

Some libraries have hundreds or even thousands of books that are not on their shelves. These books, known as **e-books**, contain the same kinds of useful material found in physical books: context, images, statistics, indexes, and more. In fact, most e-books are simply electronic versions of books that have been published as physical books. An item record for an e-book usually will have a link that will take you to a screen where you can start reading or browsing the book. Navigating an e-book may be a little trickier than turning the pages of a physical book, but e-books have one very useful advantage for researchers. You can search them! Instead of looking for keywords in an index, you can type in the keywords and then look at all the hits. Again, remember to take notes on pages and citations.

Just as you have to purchase books from Barnes and Noble or amazon.com, libraries generally purchase the books—both the physical books and the e-books—in their collections, but there are also many books that are available for free on the Internet. Many of these **online books** are classic works of literature available from university websites. The University of Virginia, for instance, provides free access to novels and stories by Joseph Conrad, James Fenimore Cooper, Stephen Crane, Frederick Douglass, Mary Shelley, Harriet Beecher Stowe, Mark Twain, and many other writers. Similar online text resources include Project Gutenberg, bartleby.com, and author sites for Edgar Allan Poe, Walt Whitman, and other writers. Some of these sites even feature secondary sources, such as biographical works.

Another source of free online books is Google Books, which features scanned pages of numerous books about a variety of topics. You can run searches within Google Books, but you also may stumble on some Google books when you are doing

Web research. (See Chapter 13 for guidance on conducting research online.) Many books available through Google Books are complete, but be alert because some books are available only in part. You might find a paragraph with some very valuable material, begin reading, and then find that the next page is not available. Don't despair! Chances are, you still can get your hands—or at least your eyes—on that book by ordering it through interlibrary loan.

Mine a Book's Contents

No matter how you found it (through a library's online catalog, WorldCat, or Google Books), how you got it (by visiting a library's shelves, ordering it through interlibrary loan, or pulling it up online), or what its format is (print or electronic), you eventually need to determine if each book you have found is something you want to explore for your research. With the right strategy, you usually can make this decision in two minutes or less.

1 Skim over the **table of contents** or list of chapters or sections near the beginning. Do the chapter titles refer to the kinds of things you want to learn, or are they approaching your topic from an angle not useful to you? For example, you may have tracked down a book about teenage drinking for a paper on binge drinking in high school. If all of the chapter titles refer to aspects of college—"Alcohol and the College Athlete," "Fraternity Hazing Rituals," and "Drinking in the Residence Hall," for example—you probably want to bypass it.
2 If the table of contents passes the test for relevance, skim a few paragraphs from some different chapters. Is the content substantive—that is, does it consist of statistics, historical context, expert observations, anecdotes, and other materials that will help you to understand the topic? Has the author cited his or her sources with parenthetical citations, footnotes, or endnotes? Is the language accessible, written for someone with your level of knowledge about the topic? If the answers to all of these questions is "yes," the book is worth more investigation.

You can use this same method for each book you find, perhaps ultimately accumulating a half-dozen or more books you can spend much more time exploring.

The next thing to do, when you have the time, is to begin applying what you learned in Chapter 7 to mine the contents of this book. If it appears really substantive, credible, and accessible, you should plan to read substantial parts of it or even the whole thing. Doing so is really time-consuming, of course, but, when it comes to developing a thorough and nuanced understanding of a topic, there's simply no substitute for reading a really good book by an expert. As you already know, it's important to take lots of notes—also a time-consuming but invaluable strategy. Remember to use what you learned in Chapter 6 and cite as you go.

You don't have time to read every book you pull from the library's shelves. There just aren't enough hours in the day. In some cases, you will want to mine books for specific pieces of information. For example, a book on high school drinking may have some statistics on the numbers of high school students who have participated in alcohol-induced violent behavior. You don't have to read the entire book to get this information, but how do you find it? The table of contents or a list of charts near the front of the book may lead you to the right part of the book, or you can check the **index** at the end. Look up a keyword or phrase—"violence," for example— in this index and see if it appears with page numbers. If at first you don't succeed, try some other keywords: "fighting," "rape," "assault," "sexual assault," etc. Turn to the appropriate pages and take notes, citing as you go.

Finally, make sure to check the book's bibliography, sometimes called "For Further Reading" or "Selected Reading," for other sources on this topic. Make a list of sources that look promising and use what you have learned in this chapter and will learn in other chapters to track down these sources. For example, once you have a book's title, you can use a title search in a catalog to get its call number and then find it on the library's shelves.

Quicktivity: Use a Table of Contents and an Index

Use the table of contents and the index for each book you have located to determine its value. Begin taking notes on it.

Conclusion

In this chapter you have learned about the value of books in research, and you learned how to run searches in library catalogs and WorldCat, read item records, find books on shelves, secure books through interlibrary loan, work with e-books and online books, and use indexes and other tools to mine the contents of a book. When you have mastered these skills, you have come a long way toward your goal of becoming an efficient researcher, but there are many more resources you will want to be able to tap. In the next chapter, you will learn how to find and use periodicals.

Steps to Success

1 Take the books that were listed in the bibliographies of the reference sources and see if you can locate them by author or title in your library (remember, you may have to request them via interlibrary loan).
2 Take the first main keyword that describes your topic and add it to another keyword using *and*. Record the number of results. Add an additional keyword using *and*, and then record the number of results after that (example: *cell phones and driving and teenagers*).

3   Look at the item records for some of your most relevant results—do you see any subject headings or keywords in the records that you can use to help you expand your searches? Record those in your log. Rerun your searches.

4   Physically locate your books in the library (you will need the call number for each item). Look at the tables of contents and the index sections—does each item provide information about your topic? Record all important information for each source that you plan to use, such as author, title, and publication information. Later, you will need to make sure that you record all page numbers of any ideas or information that you plan to use in your research project.

5   Look at the bibliographies of the books that you plan to use—are there any books listed that you would like to explore?

10

Periodicals

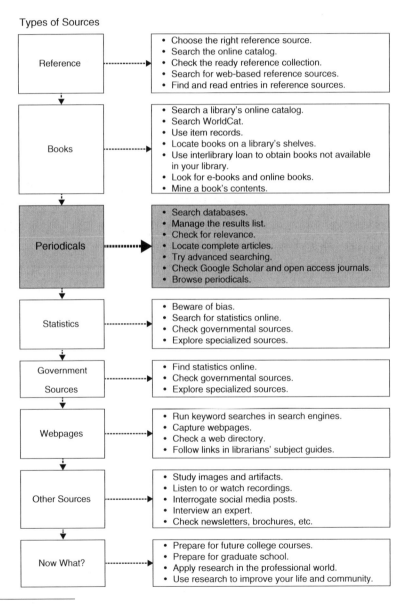

Types of Sources

| Reference | • Choose the right reference source.
• Search the online catalog.
• Check the ready reference collection.
• Search for web-based reference sources.
• Find and read entries in reference sources. |

| Books | • Search a library's online catalog.
• Search WorldCat.
• Use item records.
• Locate books on a library's shelves.
• Use interlibrary loan to obtain books not available in your library.
• Look for e-books and online books.
• Mine a book's contents. |

| Periodicals | • Search databases.
• Manage the results list.
• Check for relevance.
• Locate complete articles.
• Try advanced searching.
• Check Google Scholar and open access journals.
• Browse periodicals. |

| Statistics | • Beware of bias.
• Search for statistics online.
• Check governmental sources.
• Explore specialized sources. |

| Government Sources | • Find statistics online.
• Check governmental sources.
• Explore specialized sources. |

| Webpages | • Run keyword searches in search engines.
• Capture webpages.
• Check a web directory.
• Follow links in librarians' subject guides. |

| Other Sources | • Study images and artifacts.
• Listen to or watch recordings.
• Interrogate social media posts.
• Interview an expert.
• Check newsletters, brochures, etc. |

| Now What? | • Prepare for future college courses.
• Prepare for graduate school.
• Apply research in the professional world.
• Use research to improve your life and community. |

Introduction to Information Literacy for Students, First Edition. Michael C. Alewine and Mark Canada.
© 2017 John Wiley & Sons, Ltd. Published 2017 by John Wiley & Sons, Ltd.

Chapter Summary

Deepen your understanding of a topic by delving into periodicals. Some of the most common and important of sources, articles in periodicals also can be hard to locate if you don't know how to navigate databases and journal finders. In this chapter, you will learn exactly the strategies you need to get to these articles, evaluate them, and use them in your research.

Key Terms: access, authentication, federated search, full text, Google Scholar, lay readers, limits, newspapers, open access journals, periodicals, popular magazines, results list, scholarly journals, trade magazines

Chapter Objectives

- Distinguish among popular magazines, trade magazines, and scholarly periodicals.
- Use databases strategically to locate articles in periodicals.
- Distinguish between federated searches and searches of specific databases.
- Secure articles by locating full texts of them online, finding hard copies or microforms, or ordering them through document delivery.
- Browse periodicals to learn about fields and identify possible research topics.

Periodicals: Something for Everyone

You probably have spent some time flipping through the channels on cable TV. There's something for just about everybody, right? Sports freaks have ESPN in all its iterations, and movie buffs can curl up on the couch for a night with everyone from Cary Grant to Jennifer Lawrence. Then there are the news programs, the home shows, the shopping shows, the game shows, the cartoons, and more. (Often, we might feel like Bruce Springsteen, who sang decades ago that there were "57 Channels and Nothin' On." Today, it sometimes seems like 5700 channels and nothin' on—but that's another discussion.) Cable TV, in short, is the a-la-carte approach to television: you don't have to settle for shows designed for general audiences, but can choose exactly what you want—if you can find it.

Long before cable TV or even broadcast TV, periodicals provided readers with the same kind of specialized news and entertainment. In the nineteenth century, Americans could choose from a variety of publications, including fashion magazines, literary magazines, children's magazines, and more. Today, the selection is mind-boggling. Just take a look at a magazine stand in a major city or even just the shelves in a drugstore, and you will see scores of magazines focusing on food, fitness, crafts, sports, the outdoors, and more. On the Web, you can find thousands—yes, thousands—more: magazines and journals on everything from archery, beading, and chemistry to Xbox, yoga, and zoology.

Along with these specialized magazines, you can find many publications of more general interest, not just magazines and journals, but also national and local newspapers. All of these publications are forms of **periodicals**, which are collections of articles (and usually images) and appear periodically—that is, on a regular basis. Many newspapers are published every day, and magazines and journals may come out weekly, monthly, quarterly, or less often. As you will see in this chapter, the very nature of periodicals makes them valuable sources of information for researchers. Because they come out more frequently than books, they tend to have more up-to-date information in them. Also, since the articles are relatively short—at least when compared with books—they can be very focused. Indeed, highly specialized publications are likely to carry articles very closely related to your own narrow topics.

This chapter will not attempt the Herculean task of introducing every periodical or even every database, but it *will* provide the strategies you need to find just about any article in just about any database, along with some tips for finding articles through other means:

1   Search databases.
2   Manage the results list.
3   Check for relevance.
4   Locate complete articles.
5   Try advanced searching.
6   Check Google Scholar and open access journals
7   Browse periodicals

First, however, we need to take a closer look at some of the basics of periodicals, which are perhaps the most complex of all the sources you will encounter in your research.

Think Fast: Form and Advantages of Periodicals

How is a periodical different from a book? What are some good reasons to explore periodicals in your research?

Insider's Tip: A Journal for Just About Anything

I'll never forget the first trip I took through the periodicals section of a major university library. I was a graduate student in English at the University of North Carolina at Chapel Hill, and for some reason—I don't remember why—I was strolling through the shelves of journals there. These shelves held hundreds of current issues of journals, but I remember only one: a periodical that focused on—are you ready for this?—ancient coins.

Remember, periodicals by definition come out regularly. That means that the editors of this journal were producing, on a regular basis, new information about ancient coins. Now, they couldn't have been announcing the production of new ancient coins, of course, the way a magazine about modern coin collecting would, and they would not keep publishing the same information we already have about ancient coins—there's no point in that. Rather, scholars were (and still are) publishing new information about old coins. As you read earlier in this textbook, that's how scholarship works: experts study the evidence, some of it newly discovered evidence but much of it the same evidence already available, and come to new interpretations that extend our understanding of a particular field, including the field of numismatics (the study of coins).

The ubiquity of highly specialized periodicals is good news for you and other researchers. After all, if there is enough research to fill a periodical specializing in ancient coins, chances are there also is enough research on your topic to provide you with evidence and insights you can use to increase your understanding of this topic.

–Mark

The Basics—Not So Basic

Dealing with periodicals can be tricky because they often have, well, issues. (Who said researchers don't have a sense of humor?) For starters, they don't all come out with the same frequency. While many newspapers are "dailies," some come out weekly. Many magazines and journals appear less frequently—perhaps once a month, a few times a year, or even once every two to three years. Some journals do not come out until they have enough content for a complete issue, and some (education-related journals are notorious for this) even change their publication frequency every few years; they might go from 9 issues a year to 8 to 11 and back again. Then there are the special issues and supplements. *Time*, for example, frequently publishes publications focusing on specific subjects, such as the Beatles or technology or the Pope, that are not part of its regular publication schedule.

Another tricky aspect of periodicals is that their contents differ dramatically. Remember (from Chapter 4) that **newspapers** usually carry a wide variety of articles intended to inform and entertain general audiences. They also focus on the latest *news*, not events from a week or more ago. As we noted at the beginning of this chapter, many popular **magazines** are much more specialized, but they still target lay readers—that is, people who have no special training or education in the subject matter. **Trade magazines**, on the other hand, are aimed at professionals from specific fields. Publications such as *The American Nurse, Global Trade Review, Columbia Journalism Review, Hotel Business, Travel Weekly*, and *Funworld* (for people in the amusement park industry—alas, not librarians and English professors) help executives, practitioners, and others in nursing, finance, tourism, and other fields keep up with trends, relevant legislation, best practices, and other information aimed to help them succeed. Because they feature glossy pages, relatively short articles, and plenty of color photographs, trade magazines look much like popular magazines. **Scholarly journals** are, like trade magazines, aimed at insiders, but they tend to be more, well, scholarly. In this case, the insiders are primarily college professors and others who conduct research in fields such as nutritional biochemistry, social psychology, and elementary education. Many of the articles are arguments—not the trash-talking kind, but rather the kind in which a writer offers a reasoned interpretation of evidence, attempting to explain a scientific phenomenon, for example, or a historical event. Writers of these articles generally identify their sources with various kinds of citations, such as endnotes. Because their purpose is information and not entertainment (and, truthfully, perhaps also because they don't have large audiences or budgets), many scholarly journals are not feasts for the eyes. Instead of glossy pages and color pictures, you often will see page after page of text and, in some cases, diagrams and charts. In short, if *The Journal of Biomedical Informatics* doesn't get you with its title, it probably isn't going to grab you with its appearance. Finally, two other kinds of periodicals found in libraries are annual reviews and various organizational reports, although you probably will not spend much or any time with these kinds of sources for most of your research unless you are working in a few specific fields.

Think Fast: Types of Periodicals

Describe the similarities and differences among newspapers, popular magazines, trade magazines, and scholarly journals.

With the exception of librarians, most people don't think much about **access** to periodicals—that is, the ability to see the information in them. After all, what could be easier than plunking down a few bucks for a copy of *Us* or *GQ* at the supermarket checkout? For libraries, however, access to periodicals doesn't come cheap. Most periodicals cost money and lots of it; in fact, many periodicals charge libraries much more than they charge individuals. For example, a journal that costs one of your instructors $35 a year to subscribe to might cost a library $2,500 a year. Since libraries subscribe to hundreds or even thousands of journals, cost is a serious consideration. For this reason, most university libraries cannot afford to provide students with "direct access" to every journal article they might want for their research (although document delivery can provide them with indirect access, as we will discuss later in this chapter). Depending on the college or university you are attending, your access will vary. Large universities with a lot of professors doing a lot of research, for example, generally provide access to many more journals than community colleges or small liberal arts colleges.

Think Fast: Access to Periodicals

Why don't academic libraries provide you with access to all periodicals?

Because periodicals and databases are businesses, owners control access to them. (It's hard to make money from something available for free. That's why music companies hate file sharing.) The money that you—and, in the case of public institutions, states—pay to universities helps cover the costs of periodicals and databases; thus, thanks to something called IP range authentication, you typically will not have to log into databases when you are on campus. It's a different story when you are off campus, though. Off campus, where most people are not students and thus don't have rights to use the periodicals the universities are paying for, odds are you will have to log in using a username and password that are specific to you, generally the same ones that you use to log into other things on campus. This system helps ensure that only students and others associated with the university have access to the periodicals. Public libraries may provide a general password, which they may change every six months or so, for users to secure access to databases when they are away from the library.

Quicktivity: Obtain Off-campus Access

Check with your university library to see what is necessary for off-campus access. Even if you have no immediate plans to use databases off campus, you never know when you will need to do so. Set up an account, activate it, and test it. Make sure that you note the username and password for future use and do not share this information with anyone else. Remember, if you use article databases unethically, you can lose your access privileges.

Then there are the limitations imposed by copyright. During the course of your research, you may find that an issue of a periodical contains all of the articles originally published in that issue, except for the specific article that you want. Thanks to copyright law, individual ownership of articles does not allow for widespread online dissemination via databases. (See *New York Times Co. v. Tasini*, 533 U.S. 483, 2001.)

Don't let these complexities deter you from using periodicals. After all, these sources—particularly scholarly journals—are extremely useful for researchers. Besides, with a little practice, you will become adept at locating articles in periodicals, and the process generally will be about as simple as locating books on the shelves—except that you often won't have to leave your computer to read the articles you find. One constant is that, when it comes to locating periodicals, there is no better source for help than a librarian—and at some libraries, there are even personnel who specialize in helping students with periodicals.

Search Databases

Back in the day (actually not that long ago), researchers searched for periodicals using print indexes—that is, books listing thousands of articles, arranged by topic. Some libraries had several sets of these indexes. Researchers could use the citations in these indexes to try to track down the hard copies of the periodicals on shelves or had to wait days or even weeks for periodicals to show up in the mail via interlibrary loan. Some libraries still have print indexes available, but most students prefer electronic indexes, or article **databases**, which provide not only the necessary citations, but also abstracts and, in many cases, access to the full texts of the articles. Databases are generally available in your library—in a physical sense—through computer terminals, and they are also generally available virtually to you at home via the Internet. For most researchers nowadays, then, the first thing to do to find articles in periodicals is to run one or more searches in databases.

Of course, you already know quite a bit about running searches, thanks to the information on keywords, Boolean operators, and more in Chapter 3. Designers of library websites have tried to make searching databases easy by placing keyword search boxes in prominent places on their home pages. Often, these boxes allow you to conduct federated searches, allowing you to search not only for articles, but also for books and other sources—as you learned in the previous chapter. In other cases, typing a keyword in a box might turn up only books or only journals. The problem is that librarians haven't agreed on any specific labels for the various kinds of searches they allow on their websites. (For example, many do not use the term "federated search.") Instead, you will find a variety of labels: "articles," "databases," "eJournals," "e-resources," "electronic resources," "everything," "find articles and more," "journals & periodicals," "online resources," "research," "research guides," "subject guides"— and this is by no means a complete list. Sometimes you can't even tell what you are searching—just articles? articles and books? articles, books, and websites? For this reason, you will want to take your time with your library's webpage. Find out how information is organized on the page and see where the different links take you.

Once you know what's what, you can decide whether to conduct a federated search or a more specialized search for just articles in periodicals. If you decide to go with the latter (because you want the most recent information, for example), look for either an alphabetical list of periodical databases or subject pages where several relevant resources, including periodical databases, are located. Both have their advantages and disadvantages. An alphabetical list is good for getting quick access to a specific resource. For example, let's say that you need to bring a current news article to your next class; an alphabetical list will take you right to the database

Figure 10.1 EBSCO*host*'s Social Work Abstracts (advanced search). Source: EBSCO. Reproduced with permission of EBSCO.

Newspaper Source or *The New York Times* online. The downside of the alphabetical list is that a complete list of all databases that your library provides access to can be overwhelming. Furthermore, you won't be able to see several databases for the same subject at once and choose among them. Subject lists, on the other hand, allow you to see similar databases grouped together. For example, you can see a list of databases indexing periodicals carrying articles on geology; thus, you could choose one, run some searches, choose another, run more searches, and so on. Since databases do not always index the same periodicals, you sometimes may want to take this approach, since searching only one database may mean that you are missing several relevant articles. One downside of a subject page is that you may not readily see general databases that could be very useful. For example, if you need a few articles on fracking, a general database such as *Academic Search Complete* might be easier to use than a subject-specific database requiring a higher level of disciplinary knowledge. Whichever list you use, look for database descriptions, which can help you determine the subject coverage for each database. Once you find a useful subject page, you may want to bookmark it so that you can return to it quickly as necessary.

As you run searches in different databases, keep in mind that the functions and interfaces generally will be very similar. Take, for example, an advanced search in *Social Work Abstracts* (EBSCO*host*) and another advanced search in a different database—say, *Social Services Abstracts* (ProQuest). (See Figure 10.1 and Figure 10.2.) Although they are different databases owned by different companies,

Advanced Search Command Line   Thesaurus   Field codes   Search tips

child abuse   in   Anywhere

AND ▾   prevent*   OR   interven*   in   Anywhere

AND ▾   ethnic*   OR   cultur*   in   Anywhere

⊕ Add a row   ⊖ Remove a row

Limit to: ☐ Peer reviewed ❶

Publication date: All dates ▾

Search   Clear form

Figure 10.2 ProQuest's Social Services Abstracts (advanced search). Source: ProQuest. Reproduced with permission of ProQuest.

they look and act alike. That's because the people who design databases do so in consultation with librarians, and there is competition among these publishers and vendors. Each wants its products to be as user-friendly to researchers as possible. The winner in this competition is you because, once you learn to search one database, you can search just about any other. Sure, each will have a slightly different look, maybe a few different bells and whistles, as well, but you rarely will have to start from scratch because you have learned the basic features standard to most or all of them: keywords, Boolean operators, truncation limits, and basic and advanced modes of searching.

Quicktivity: Explore a Library's Website

Find your library's website and identify the following:

1 Where are the article databases listed?
2 How are they organized—alphabetically by title, by subject, by something else?
3 Are there easy or quick searches (federated searches) where you can search multiple databases?
4 How can you get help? Is there an "Ask-A-Librarian" feature?

Manage the Results List

Whether you are doing a federated search or searching in a database that indexes only articles in periodicals, you eventually will come to a **results list**, similar to the kind of results list you would encounter when searching for books. As a default, there will be a certain number of results (typically 10-25) per page. This default, along with other default settings, is set by the library. Most databases allow the user to alter this number. How much information is contained in the results list for each search is also determined by each individual library. Look for an "Options" or "Settings" link to see what you can alter to make the list more appealing to you. One suggestion is to make the results list provide as much information as possible; in particular, consider including abstracts if they are available. (See Figure 10.3.) That way, you do not have to click into each item record. Depending on the database, as well as the individual preferences of your library, you may see icons indicating direct full-text access, such as HTML (plain text), linked full text (which can be in a variety of formats), and pdf.

As you go through the results, you can select (usually with a checkbox or a folder icon next to each item in the results list) individual records that you want to save and email to yourself or to other members of a group. As you select items, they are saved to a temporary folder. When you are done, you can simply email the citations

1. **Gender Pay** Gap and **Employment** Sector: Sources of Earnings Disparities in
the United States, 1970-2010.

Academic
Journal

By: Mandel, Hadas; Semyonov, Moshe. Demography. Oct2014, Vol. 51 Issue 5, p1597-1618. 22p. 7 Charts. Abstract: Using data from the IPUMS-USA, the present research focuses on trends in the **gender** earnings gap in the United States between 1970 and 2010. The major goal of this article is to understand the sources of the convergence in men's and **women's** earnings in the public and private sectors as well as the stagnation of this trend in the new millennium. For this purpose, we delineate temporal changes in the role played by major sources of the gap. Several components are identified: the portion of the gap attributed to **gender** differences in human-capital resources; labor supply; sociodemographic attributes; occupational segregation; and the unexplained portion of the gap. The findings reveal a substantial reduction in the gross **gender** earnings gap in both sectors of the economy. Most of the decline is attributed to the reduction in the unexplained portion of the gap, implying a significant decline in economic **discrimination** against **women**. In contrast to **discrimination**, the role played by human capital and personal attributes in explaining the **gender pay** gap is relatively small in both sectors. Differences between the two sectors are not only in the size and pace of the reduction but also in the significance of the two major sources of the gap. Working hours have become the most important factor with respect to **gender pay** inequality in both sectors, although much more dominantly in the private sector. The declining **gender** segregation may explain the decreased impact of occupations on the **gender pay** gap in the private sector. In the public sector, by contrast, **gender** segregation still accounts for a substantial portion of the gap. The findings are discussed in light of the theoretical literature on sources of **gender** economic inequality and in light of the recent stagnation of the trend. [ABSTRACT FROM AUTHOR] DOI: 10.1007/s13524-014-0320-y. *(AN: 99008130),* Database: Business Source Complete

Subjects: PAY equity; RESEARCH; **WAGES -- Women**; WAGES -- Men; PUBLIC sector; PRIVATE sector; UNITED States; **GENDER** inequality; SEX **discrimination** -- Economic aspects; **GENDER** differences (Sociology) -- Economic aspects; ECONOMIC aspects

Show all 7 images

PDF Full Text (696KB)

Figure 10.3   EBSCO*host*'s results list (detailed view). Source: EBSCO. Reproduced with permission of EBSCO.

and available full-text articles to yourself or someone else. It's a good idea to create an account with the publisher or vendor if possible. That way, if you are conducting a significant amount of research, you can create folders to save individual sets of results for each assignment. (This approach is similar to creating a research log.) You also can save your searches, some of which may involve multiple databases, multiple keywords, and multiple limits. By saving your searches, you can rerun them periodically, which should produce some new results over time as new sources are published. Many database accounts allow you to create various types of alerts that will let you know when new relevant articles are published. It's like having your own personal librarian reading articles and texting you when something good appears.

Clicking on a title in a results list typically will take you to an item record, which may include an abstract and related subject headings. When you get this far, you are ready for the next part of the process: checking for relevance.

Quicktivity: Explore an Item Record

Use one of your keywords from your research log to run a search in a federated search box or a box for an article database. Click on one of the article links that appear and study the item record. What kinds of information does it contain?

Prevention of Human Trafficking for Labor Exploitation: The Role of Corporations.

Authors: Jägers, Nicola[1]
Rijken, Conny[2]

Source: Journal of International **Human** Rights. Winter2014, Vol. 12 Issue 1, p47-73. 27p.

Document Type: Article

Subject Terms: *HUMAN trafficking -- Prevention
*EXPLOITATION of humans
*HUMAN trafficking victims
*HUMAN rights
*JUS cogens (International law)
*SLAVERY -- Law & legislation

Abstract: The article discusses the **role** of **corporations** in preventing **human trafficking** for **labor exploitation**. Topics discussed include an analysis of the United Nations Protect-Respect-Remedy (PRR) Framework and the Guiding Principles on Business and **Human** Rights in relation to **human trafficking**, the three P paradigm in preventing **human trafficking**, namely, prosecution and **prevention** of **human trafficking** and the protection of victims, and the concept of the jus cogens prohibition of slavery.

Figure 10.4 Item record for an article from *Academic Search Complete* (EBSCO*host*). Source: EBSCO. Reproduced with permission of EBSCO.

Check for Relevance

In Chapter 5, you learned about evaluating sources for a number of things, including relevance. You can use the item record to do cursory analyses of articles to evaluate their relevance for your research topic. (See Figure 10.4.) Start with the abstract, which should summarize the article, giving you a sense of the topics covered in it. If the article describes an empirical study, you also should get a sense of the methodology. You also may want to glance at any subject terms, since they can give you some idea of the contents of the article. Check the document type, as well. If it is some kind of review, such as a book review, it probably will not provide the kind of in-depth information you need, or it will provide secondhand information (although it may lead you to a good book on your topic). Even the title of the journal may be revealing. For example, if you want to focus on self-image among college students and the article appears in something with the words *child psychology* in the title, you may want to skip this article.

Locate the Complete Article

Once you have run one or more searches and identified some articles that appear to be relevant, the final part of the process is to locate the complete article. This final task can be a piece of cake—or something less appetizing. It all depends on the availability and accessibility of the periodical. Let's walk through the various possibilities, from best to worst (but not impossible).

- *Piece of cake*: Many articles are available in "**full text**" via the database itself. In other words, when you arrive at the item record, you will see a link to the entire text of the article (often with graphics, as well) either as a pdf (essentially one or more images of the actual pages of the article) or as html text (the words all laid out, but not in exactly the same format as they appear on the pages of the periodical). The former provides a more realistic experience of reading the original periodical, while the latter may be easier to search. The latter may or may not indicate page breaks, so you may not be able to be as precise with your documentation. As you may have guessed, having access to full text via the database is the best of all possible worlds when it comes to retrieving articles you want to read.
- *Tasty muffin*: Some periodicals are available for free online; thus, if the article you want is not available in full text via the database itself, you may be able to google the title of the article and find it on the Web. If it doesn't appear, try googling the name of the periodical and then using the citation you found in the item record to follow the links on the periodical's webpage until you arrive at the article. Many periodicals are not available this way, but it may be worth a try.
- *Vegemite (an acquired taste)*: If the article is not available in one of these first two ways, you are going to have to work a little harder. In some cases, the item you want will be available not through the database where you found it, but through another database. In these situations, you can use a **link resolver** to try to get to the article through this second database (and thus avoid doing a whole new search in that database). Link resolvers, like search interfaces, vary from library to library. Even large libraries with big budgets do not have the perfect link resolver—it does not exist. A link resolver is a specialized database that connects researchers with library periodical holdings, no matter where those periodicals are available. It even shows print holdings. If there is no full text available for an article you find via a database, you probably would see a link that allows you to use the link resolver to search for the full text. This link may go by a variety of different names or even symbols: "Check for full-text availability," "Links," and so on. The link resolver will then give you a range of options. If your library provides access to the specific journal or article that you are seeking, then there should be a direct link to it or a link to an online journal, where you then have to search by citation or browse by date, **volume number**, and **issue number**. (Typically, the volume number corresponds with the year in the periodical's run, and the issue number indicates the number of that issue in the given year. For example, if a periodical began publication in 1993, all the issues from 1994 would have "2" for the volume number. The first issue in 1994 would be Volume 2, Issue 1, the second issue in the same year would be Volume 2, Issue 2, and so on.) If the full text is available, then you will be able to save, print, or email it. You have to be

careful because link resolvers sometimes contain bad or outdated information; for this reason, it may look as if an article is going to be available and then "Wham!" you are disappointed because it's not. (Who can help you? Yep, you got it: your friendly librarian.) Sometimes, link resolvers will take you to the library's online catalog, which you can use to search for the periodical by title. If you find it, you will need the citation (from the database where you found it listed) to track down the correct issue and the appropriate page range.

- *Soup crackers*: Some periodicals are available online through subscription. While they may be linked through a specific database, it is sometimes easier to locate them via the link resolver, which takes all subscriptions that a particular library has and organizes them by title and subject. You can both browse and search periodicals without necessarily having to go through a database first. In such cases, you will see a link to the appropriate database or in many cases to the direct online subscription that your library has. Pay close attention to the dates of coverage, which can vary from database to database. (See Figure 10.5.)
- *Soup crackers (but stored in the basement)*: Sometimes you may have to go "old school"—that is, visit the periodicals section of the library and track down the hard copy or microform version of a periodical. The link resolver may point you there with a phrase such as "Library Print Holdings." (See Figure 10.5.) Use the information you find, as well as the citation, to find the article.
- *Soup crackers (available only by mail order)*: Finally, in some cases, your library may not provide access to an article in any of these ways, but don't despair. Most university libraries, as well as many public libraries, will enable you to get your hands—or your eyes—on this article, usually for free, through interlibrary loan. In other words, you tell the library what you want, by providing the basic citation information, and a member of the library's staff will order a hard copy or

American Biology Teacher

Academic OneFile   2006 - 2013

Academic Search Complete   2005 - 2011

Direct Subscriptions   2010 to present

Education Research Complete   2005 - 2011

JSTOR Life Sciences Archive Collection   1938 - 2011

Library Print Holdings

Resource Type: Journal
ISSN: 0002-7685 Online ISSN: 1938-4211
Publisher: University of California Press
Subject: Sciences -- Biology and Life Sciences; Education -- Teaching and Curriculum

Figure 10.5   EBSCO*host*'s A to Z link resolver record for *American Biology Teacher*. Source: EBSCO. Reproduced with permission of EBSCO.

electronic version of the article from another library that does have access to it (because this other library subscribes to the periodical) and have it delivered to your library. In many cases, the link resolver will take you directly to a Web form, where you can input the citation information (author, title, journal title, volume number, issue number, etc.) to order the item. Document delivery services will usually provide you with a transaction number. You will want to record this number in your research log so that, if you have questions, you can share it with library staff, who can in turn use it to check on your request.

Regardless of which means you have to use, you generally can get the article you need.

Try Advanced Searching

By now, having read Chapter 3 and much of this chapter, you should be able to run a basic keyword search in a federated search engine or a particular database, such as *Academic Search Complete* or *PsycINFO*. This basic search typically involves a single box, where you type keywords and, if you like, one or more of the Boolean operators covered in Chapter 3. In some cases, though, you may want to conduct an advanced search, one that involves more than one search box and various ways to limit the kind of search for each box. (See Figure 10.6.) Sometimes, in fact, the default for a search on a library's webpage will be the advanced search (and, in other cases, it will be a basic search). This advanced search is useful because it allows you to experiment with various sets of keywords and find what works and what does not. Technically, you could do basically the same thing with a basic search (with one search field), but you would have to construct something that looks a little like a math equation:

(child abuse) and (prevent* or interven*) and (ethnic* or cultur*)

Comparing the two makes the advanced search all the more appealing, doesn't it?

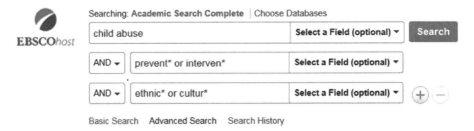

Figure 10.6 EBSCO*host*'s Academic Search Complete (advanced search). Source: EBSCO. Reproduced with permission of EBSCO.

> ### Quicktivity: Search General and Subject-specific Databases
>
> Take your keywords and complete an advanced search in both a general database and a subject-specific database. How many results did you get in each database? Do you see any of the same titles?

"No Limits" might be an appealing slogan for a sporting goods company or a self-help seminar, but it wouldn't do for databases. When it comes to running keyword and other kinds of searches in databases, **limits**—restrictions that you can place on a search—can be very good things. They help you trim your results to something more manageable and relevant. After all, it's more efficient to go through a relatively small number of results tied closely to your topic than tens of thousands of results, most of which have very little to do with your topic. If you wanted thousands of results for every search, you could just google everything and forget about periodicals and databases—not a good idea. Even a well-crafted search with appropriate limits may turn up some sources you don't want to use, but limits can keep the number of these sources way down. Of course, you could take limits too far, so to speak. (Some students, after learning about limits and truncation, set every possible limit and truncate every word—and then wind up with very few or no results.) Your choices for advanced search limits will vary a little by database. Here are some common fields you can limit:

- *Subject*: If you search multiple keywords and get too many irrelevant results, take one of the main concepts and limit it to be found within one of the given subject headings. Be careful, though. Limiting all of the words to subject searches may give you too few results. (See Figure 10.7.)
- *Publication date*: As you learned in Chapter 5, recent sources sometimes are better choices for research, particularly in the sciences, because they present new findings not included in older articles. Limiting by publication date can help you identify only recent articles, but you can use this approach to isolate articles from

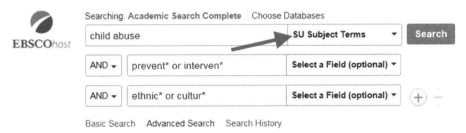

Figure 10.7 EBSCO*host*'s Academic Search Complete (advanced search). Source: EBSCO. Reproduced with permission of EBSCO.

any date range or even those published on a specific date. For example, if you wanted to see immediate reactions to landmark events, such as the initial moon landing, you could limit results to those published the following day—in this case, July 21, 1969.

- *Document type*: In some cases, you may want to search for only specific kinds of sources, such as books, book reviews, conference proceedings, dissertations, editorials, magazines, maps, newspapers, pamphlets, reports, even images or videos. Limiting by document type helps you weed out other kinds of sources.

- *Peer review*: Similarly, you sometimes may want to focus on sources that have undergone peer review, so you will want to use this limit. (See Chapter 4 for more on peer review.) Indeed, some instructors require students to use only peer-reviewed sources.

- *Audience*: Some databases allow you to limit results to those with specific audiences, such as the general public, students, practitioners, professionals, researchers, and so on. These limits can be particularly useful to graduate students who want to make sure that the results they find are in line with their level of academic discourse.

- *Full text*: This limit looks very appealing because it saves you having to mess around with link resolvers, bound periodicals, or document delivery. If you have a pressing need—for articles to bring with you to class in an hour, for example—you might use this limit, but otherwise you generally should avoid it. Why? Limits can be good things when they help you weed out sources that are not relevant, that are too old, that lack sufficient credibility, and so on, but weeding out perfectly relevant, recent, and credible sources just because they are not available in full text ultimately can hurt you. For one thing, you are liable to miss very important sources with crucial findings and thus misunderstand one or more aspects of your topic. Furthermore, you actually might make more work for yourself. In the short term, considering only full-text sources will save you having to go outside the database for sources; however, if you find insufficient information, you might have to start your searching all over or, even worse, you might spend hours trying to squeeze meaningful conclusions out of insufficient evidence.

- *Language of publication*: Depending on the database and even the topic, many results will be in other languages. If this becomes a problem, then you can limit specifically to sources written in a language you can read.

- *Methodology*: Some databases, such as *PsycINFO*, allow you to limit results to empirical and other types of research articles, such as clinical case studies, longitudinal studies, field studies, literature reviews, meta-analyses, qualitative and quantitative studies, and more. If you are in a database that does not allow for this type of limit, you can first limit to scholarly sources and then use keywords such as *method*, *results*, or *discussion* to identify empirical research articles or other kinds of keywords for other kinds of sources.

- *Age groups*: In educational, psychological, and other databases, a useful limit is age range or level. For example, in *ERIC*, you can limit to different grade ranges such as birth to kindergarten, elementary, middle grades, or secondary or even to specific grades (e.g., grade 3, grade 7, etc.). There are also limits for childhood, infancy, school age, adolescence, middle age, and so forth. Furthermore, you can use more general keywords such as *child**, *teen**, *juvenile*, *minor*, *aged*, or *elderly*.

- *Other limits*: Some business databases allow you to limit results in various other ways—by company name, for example, or NAICS/industry code.

Many limits can also be set in the results list. For example, you can limit to subject headings, thesaurus terms, date ranges, geographical limits, document types, and more. In science databases, you can typically limit to many various disciplines or sub-disciplines.

Think Fast: Limits

How should you approach setting limits in your initial search? What purpose does setting limits serve?

Quicktivity: Create a Database Account

Set up an account in a database. Practice emailing yourself citations and saving searches. Set up an alert.

Check Google Scholar and Open Access Journals

Google Scholar, a tool that has become very popular with students and faculty alike, allows you to locate scholarly materials that are freely available on the Web. The upside of Google Scholar is that you can quickly locate useful, relevant materials without having to use sophisticated search techniques or controlled vocabulary. The downside is that you get a lot of results that are not relevant and also a number of results that will ask you for a fee. (You probably will be better off going through document delivery, which generally is free.)

Many libraries link some of their databases, such as *JSTOR* and *Project Muse*, as well as direct subscriptions to online journals, with Google Scholar, so if you are on campus you can access a number of these materials. Some libraries have also set it so that you can log into Google Scholar from off campus and access all proprietary materials that they subscribe to that are indexed by Google Scholar. Many journals you find just sitting on the Web can be a prepublication (an author's draft prior to publication or a post-publication, which has corrections made to the original published version). Be careful with these versions, since material in them may vary from the published version, which is the official version of the source. It's easy to fall in love with Google Scholar, but you will want to keep its limitations in mind.

Plenty of scholarly journals are legally available online and go through the same rigorous peer-review process as any other journal. They typically go by the name **open access journals**. Most libraries will include many of these publications in their online catalogs or provide access through their link resolvers. Sites such as the Directory of Open Access Journals (DOAJ) and the Open Access Journals Search Engine (OAJSE) provide free access to thousands of scholarly journals. There are many other sites, especially in the sciences, which provide access to open access journals. Many new journals are specifically launched as open access journals.

Think Fast: Journals on the Web

What is the potential difference between a journal you find through Google Scholar and an open access journal you find on the Web?

Browse Periodicals

Searching online databases can be a little tricky, but there is a certain satisfaction that comes with knowing the ins and outs, along with the ecstatic reward of finding just the right result. The perfect article—credible, comprehensive, right on topic—is, after all, a rare find. Still, there's something to be said for browsing—that is, poking around in the stacks of periodicals, loose or bound, with tangible pages you can turn. (See Figure 10.8.) Of course, it's not the most efficient way to locate specific articles on a topic. After all, you could spend hundreds of hours paging through random periodicals and *never* come to an article on your topic. The point of browsing, though, is not to locate that perfect article, but to broaden your view, develop a sense of context, expand your sense of a field, and give yourself a chance to stumble on something fascinating, maybe even something that would make a great topic for a research project. Remember, you don't know what you don't know. You don't even have to thumb through hard copies to browse periodicals. Most databases have electronic lists of all publications that are indexed in a given database; thus, by following the links in these lists, you can browse issues electronically.

You can even browse strategically. To get a peek at the trends, issues, and inside dope in a particular field you are studying or might want to study—anthropology, hospitality and tourism, public administration, physics, whatever—spend a few hours browsing trade magazines and scholarly journals. If you spend enough time with these periodicals, you are likely to come away with a new appreciation of the field, a sense of whether you would enjoy working in it, and some questions you might want to ask of people already in the field. Another approach to browsing is to

Figure 10.8 Student browsing bound periodicals. Source: Photo taken by Christopher W. Bowyer; permission given by Christopher W. Bowyer.

wander through some popular magazines, especially those with broad subject matter: *Time, Newsweek, National Geographic,* and *Smithsonian* all cover a wide variety of topics, exposing you to lots of people, places, events, and ideas that might lead to productive research projects.

Think Fast: Searching vs. Browsing

What is the difference between searching for specific articles and browsing periodicals? What are the advantages and disadvantages of each?

Conclusion

This chapter has introduced you to some of the trials and treasures of periodicals. For a variety of reasons, including the expense of subscribing to them (for libraries anyway) and the complexity of getting to the articles you want, scholarly journals and other kinds of periodicals are among the most challenging kinds of sources to work with in the research process, but they are well worth the effort. In fact, they are crucial for serious researchers. Once you have mastered the three steps described in this chapter—locating a citation in a general or subject-specific database, evaluating it, and tracking down the article itself—you will have little trouble finding and securing what you need in periodicals. You will have taken a huge step forward in becoming a master researcher.

Steps to Success

1   Complete a Google image search for "reader's guide to periodical literature" and take a look at some of the images that show this print index and what the pages and records look like. (Does seeing these citations make you nostalgic for the good old days?) Now, do a keyword search in a database such as Academic Search Complete. What similarities do you see in the information in the print index and the information in the database's item record?
2   Visit your library's website and look for one or more search boxes. Try to determine whether a box allows you to conduct a federated search or a search in a selected database. If you encounter both kinds of boxes, conduct the same keyword search in each. How do the results differ? After comparing the results, jot down some of the advantages and disadvantages of each kind of search.
3   Set aside two hours to browse periodicals, either physically or electronically, and take notes on the experience. What did you learn? What surprised you? What questions would you like to ask people in this field? What kinds of ideas or phenomena might make for an interesting research project?
4   Using the steps described in this chapter, identify, evaluate, and try to secure five articles on a specific topic. Now, reflect on your experience. How many articles were available in full text? How did you try to secure the ones that were not? What challenges did you face, and how did you overcome these challenges?

11

Statistics

Types of Sources

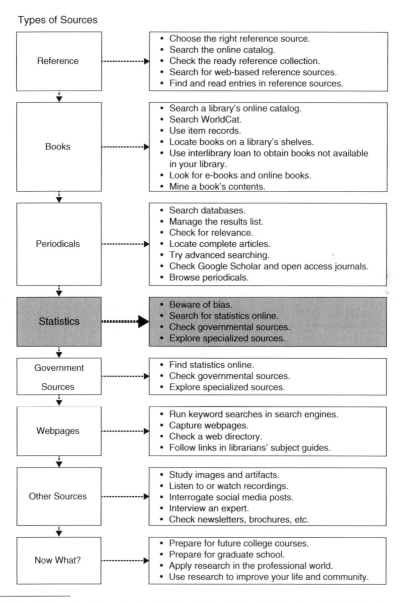

Introduction to Information Literacy for Students, First Edition. Michael C. Alewine and Mark Canada.
© 2017 John Wiley & Sons, Ltd. Published 2017 by John Wiley & Sons, Ltd.

Chapter Summary

Play the numbers game to your advantage by tapping some statistical sources. Statistics on populations, sales, construction, energy, and countless other things can provide you with useful insights into a large variety of topics. In this chapter, you will learn about various kinds of statistics, as well as leading sources where you can find them.

Key Terms: statistics, demographics

Chapter Objectives

- Explain pitfalls in research on statistics.
- Identify leading sources of government statistics.
- Identify other leading sources of statistics.
- Discriminate among various sources of statistics.

The Numbers Game

In his 2001 book, *Damned Lies and Statistics: Untangling Numbers from the Media, Politicians, and Activists*, Joel Best warns readers that bad **statistics**–that is, numbers of people or products, sizes of cities, rates of changes, and the like—come from all corners of society—conservative, liberal, government, and non-governmental sources—but he also concedes that we need statistics. As academic researchers, you probably will need them from time to time, as well. In some fields, such as economics and political science, they are central to many kinds of research. In others, such as music and theatre, they play a lesser role, but they can be useful in any field. (You can bet that managers of concert halls and theatres care a great deal about at least one form of statistics: gate receipts!) Remember, too, that research is not something people only do for classes or in jobs. If you become active in your community or the world, you probably will need to track down statistics related to employment, health, recreation, or other fields. Knowing how to find statistics, in short, can be a useful skill.

Knowing how to read, compile, and use statistics is another matter, one much too large for us to cover in depth in this book. Instead, this chapter will offer a few general observations and suggestions and then walk you through three approaches you can take to finding statistics in your research:

1 Find statistics online.
2 Check governmental sources.
3 Explore specialized sources.

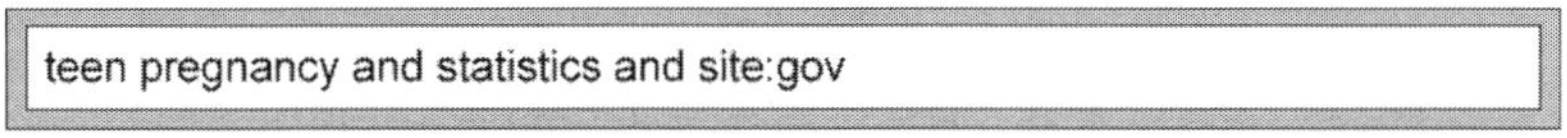

teen pregnancy and statistics and site:gov

Figure 11.1 Internet search limiting to government sites only. Source: Created by Michael C. Alewine.

As you work through these strategies, you will find that that there are a *lot* of statistics out there.

Since people can choose statistics strategically to support their own positions (or even just make them up), you need to be careful about the ones you use. Remember what you have learned about evaluating sources and use it to evaluate the sources of statistics. If a source looks questionable, look for a more credible one.

Find Statistics Online

While there are many great print sources, including government documents, for statistical data, the most current data usually are going to be found online. You can locate these statistics the same ways you locate other kinds of information on the Internet. Start with a search engine, such as Google. Limit to government sites first by using *site:gov*. (See Figure 11.1.)

If you want to check the accuracy of the data being quoted by a website or if you want to see if more "current" data are available, search for the "original" source of the data—in the example below (see Figure 11.2) that is the National Center for Health Statistics, which is an entity of the Centers for Disease Control and Prevention. The original source should be your goal—thus the importance of starting early—so that you can follow paper trails (using what you have learned about documentation and searches) to original sources.

Quicktivity: Google Government Statistics

Use the process described above to find some online sources of government statistics. Identify the sources. Consider any problems with these statistics.

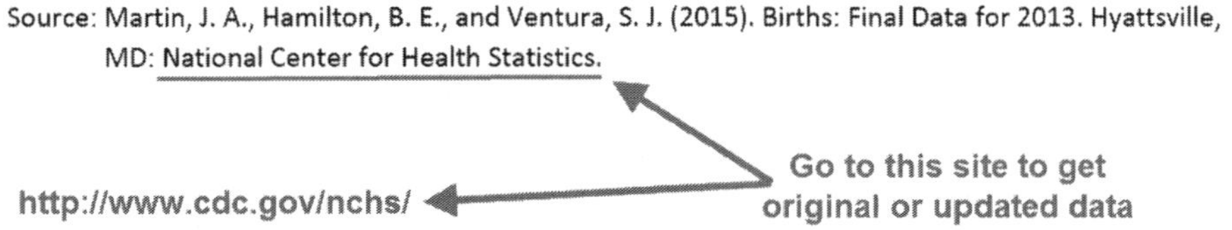

Source: Martin, J. A., Hamilton, B. E., and Ventura, S. J. (2015). Births: Final Data for 2013. Hyattsville, MD: National Center for Health Statistics.

http://www.cdc.gov/nchs/

Go to this site to get original or updated data

Figure 11.2 Sample source note from a website. Source: Created by Michael C. Alewine.

Check Government Sources

As you may have gathered from the previous section, where we encouraged you to use "site:gov" in your Web searches, some of the best sources of statistics are government entities at various levels. Not all government statistics are online, though, so you will want to be familiar with other places you can find them. Even ones that are online are easier to find if you know the exact names of the sources. Let's take a close look at several specific sources and repositories of local, state, national, and international statistics.

Depending on what you need, probably the best source for local statistical data (especially **demographics**, which deal with race, ethnicity, income, and other aspects of people and groups of people) is the U.S. Census. Search *American Factfinder* and select "Community Facts." Simply enter the name or zip code of the location for which you want data, and you will be presented with several data sets, including information about business, economics, education, employment, families, housing, population, race, and so forth. Other local data may be available from chambers of commerce, town and county government sites, local school district sites, and state entities. If there is a library, college, or university in the local area you are researching, local professors and researchers who work there may have created specialized documents with the kind of data you want. For example, a professor might receive a grant to study the local health, poverty, education, or crime. Try searching the catalogs for these local libraries to see if such geographic-specific reports are available.

Most states have some form of data center, accessible through state government entities or online portals. To get to this data center, try googling "statistics and data and" the name of the state. This approach will give you access to statistical data portals covering a wide range of subject matter. Also, universities, especially flagship universities, may have specific research institutes that look at various state issues and collect data. Finally, the Census offers "State and County Quickfacts."

When it comes to national statistics, the good news is the United States government makes them readily available via USA.gov, a one-stop shop for all federal data, but the bad news is the quantity can be overwhelming. The site, while enormous, will attempt to guide you where you need to be. Another useful feature is the availability of historical data going back several years for various topics. This is not a site for the impatient. Set aside some time to explore it, run searches, study the results, and make notes in your research log. If you spend enough time, it probably will be time well spent.

You may consult foreign governments for international statistics, but the U.S. Census Bureau also publishes a great deal of statistical data, especially economic statistics, about other countries and our dealings with them. The online *CIA World Factbook* is a great source for all types of information about different countries. The *Europa World Year Book* is also very useful if your library has it, although it is a very expensive two-volume set. The United Nations provides hundreds of useful data sets with demographic information, as well as statistics on economic and social conditions, health, and more. Specific international organizations, such as Amnesty International and the World Health Organization, also publish international statistics.

Quicktivity: Find a State's Data Center

Search online for your state's data center. What kind of data sets does it present? How might this information be useful to you in your research (or someone else doing a different kind of research)?

Explore Specialized Sources

Historical statistics are plentiful in both print and online formats. If you start with a Web search for "historical statistics," you will find several sites, including guides created by various libraries. Older editions of the *Statistical Abstract of the United States*, which ceased publication in 2012, are routinely saved by libraries and are a great source of historical statistical data. Older editions are still available via the vendor ProQuest, and your library may provide access. The *Statistical Abstract* site (at census.gov) provides links to historical data going back as far as 1871. Furthermore, if you check the reference and general collections of almost any academic library, you often can find a variety of historical statistical data sources dealing with general or very specific subject matter. Two worth noting are the multivolume *Historical Abstracts of the United States: Earliest Times to the Present* and *International Historical Statistics*, a multivolume set divided according to geographic area. Both are available electronically.

Another approach to locating statistics is to consider the field. As we noted above, statistics are particularly central to certain fields, so it's no surprise that these fields have numerous sources for data specific to them. For example, business students need a whole host of statistical information throughout their college careers, whether they are studying accounting, finance, management, marketing, or another business-related discipline. Business students can use proprietary databases, as well as freely available government statistics online, to find industry information, key ratios, and other kinds of statistical information. The U.S. Bureau of Economic Analysis is one of the best sources of both national and international economic and business statistics, including current data on consumer spending and the Gross National Product (GDP). The U.S. Census also publishes data on business and economics. The U.S. Bureau of Labor Statistics is the best place for current information on employment. Trade.gov has foreign trade information, and the United Nations, World Bank, and World Trade Organization all publish this kind of data, as well.

Crime statistics are often of interest to political scientists, experts in criminal justice, and other researchers and practitioners. The Bureau of Justice Statistics provides a wide range of statistical data on crime and punishment, health of prisoners, arrest-related deaths, and more. The Federal Bureau of Investigation (FBI) maintains Uniform Crime Reporting, another source of useful data. Each state has its own state police or other investigative entity, which provides local crime data. Some nonprofit organizations, such as Amnesty International and the Death Penalty Information Center, publish statistics on prison conditions, capital punishment, and other specific aspects of criminal justice.

A variety of sources offer statistical information on social conditions. The World Bank, for example, provides a number of data sets on gender equity, organized by country and topic. The Organization for Economic Co-operation and Development (OECD) provides statistics related to the economic and social conditions of women around the world. The U.S. Department of Labor maintains a set of data concerning women in the workforce. The National Center for Educational Statistics, the CDC, the U.S. Census Bureau, and the Bureau of Labor Statistics provide information related to education, health, housing, and work.

When it comes to health, the CDC's National Center for Health Statistics is the premier source of data. Here you can find numbers related to how we live, what diseases we live with and die from, and how social conditions affect our health. Specific topics for which you can find statistics include diabetes, firearms, heart disease, infectious diseases, cancer, suicide, dental care, even teens and texting while driving. The CDC also has a FastStats page organized in alphabetical order by topic. The World Health Organization (WHO) provides a number of data sets concerning health-related topics, organized by country and region. Finally, the National Institutes of Health (NIH) National Library of Medicine provides links to hundreds of health-related statistical sources.

Quicktivity: Explore Historical Statistics

Consider some statistics relevant to your research. Use what you have learned about historical statistics to find some statistics on your topic from various periods of history. Do you see any notable trends?

Conclusion

There is no shortage of statistical data, particularly in the areas of demographics, business, crime, and health, and much of it comes from government sources that are available online or in print. Fairly simple Web searches will turn up many major sources of data, but always check the source. You also can explore specific sources, such as the American FactFinder and *CIA World Factbook* for general statistics or other kinds of sources, such as the *Statistical Abstract of the United States* and Uniform Crime Reporting, for historical statistics or statistics from a particular field.

Once you arrive at a website or a printed statistical source, it takes careful consideration and navigation to locate stats that are truly relevant to your research topic. In the next chapter, you will learn even more about government sources, which are good for more than statistics.

Steps to Success

1   Identify a very specific statistic related to your topic—the amount of oil the United States imported from Angola in 2013, for example—and use what you have learned in this chapter to try to find this statistic. Record the steps you took, as well any lessons you took from this exercise.
2   Brainstorm a list of fairly common statistics related to your topic, such as the population of the United States or the unemployment rate in France. Look up these statistics in three sources. What do you notice? Are there any differences? If so, how might you explain the differences?
3   Use what you have learned about keyword searches to google a statistic. When you go to the page containing the statistic, try to determine the source. Did the sponsor of this webpage generate the statistic, or did it come from a different source? How can you tell? If it came from a different source, try to find the original source.
4   Plunge into a couple of statistical sources related to your topic, such as the CDC's National Center for Health Statistics, and just roam around. What do you notice? How might some casual exploration of such sources help generate or narrow research topics?

12

Government Sources

Types of Sources

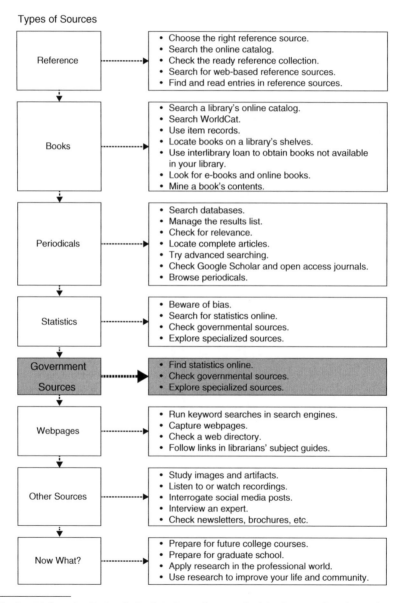

Introduction to Information Literacy for Students, First Edition. Michael C. Alewine and Mark Canada.
© 2017 John Wiley & Sons, Ltd. Published 2017 by John Wiley & Sons, Ltd.

Chapter Summary

Ask what your government can do for you. One answer is "Help you with your research." State and national governments, along with related organizations, produce a vast amount of information. In this chapter, we will explore the various forms, strengths, and limitations of government sources and examine strategies for locating them.

Key Terms: government sources, federal depository library, Superintendent of Documents (SuDocs) Classification system, Federal Digital System (FDsys)

Chapter Objectives

- Explain the role of government entities in producing and disseminating information.
- Identify bias in government sources.
- Use various strategies to identify government sources relevant to your research.

The World's Most Prolific Publisher

The U.S. government has taken its share of hits from conspiracy theorists and other suspicious folks—about JFK's assassination, Area 51, and any number of other subjects—and, who knows, maybe some of these people are right, but it's hard to imagine that what the federal government is hiding amounts to even a tiny fraction of what it *is* telling us. By law, each of the thousands of bureaus, committees, divisions, offices, subcommittees, and task forces within the federal government must keep records and make most of these records—with exceptions for those that might compromise national security—freely available. That's just the beginning. The federal government also produces countless publications with information about the economy, health, education, and other topics. In a typical year, the Bureau of Labor Statistics, U.S. Census Bureau, Government Printing Office, National Technical Information Service, and Federal Register, along with many other departments and agencies, produce tens of thousands of documents and reports. (Is it any wonder the U.S. government is the most prolific publisher in the world?) States, counties, and cities also produce information, and, of course, the United States is only one country among many around the world. Add it all up, and we're talking about a goldmine—many goldmines—of information about business, law, education, geography, health, energy, and more.

This chapter will provide you with an overview of government sources, as well as six strategies you can use to evaluate and find these sources:

1   Beware of bias.
2   Search your library's catalog, but limit your search to government documents.
3   Search or browse the FDsys database.
4   Run searches in the U.S. government's online portal.
5   Search for bills and laws.
6   Check microforms.

Once you are familiar with these strategies, you will be able to tap government sources for statistics, facts, insights, maps, charts, tables, photographs, and more.

Examples: Types of Information Available from Government Sources

The terms *government sources* and *government documents* are accurate, but can be misleading. While most government documents are produced *by* committees, agencies, and other entities associated with a national, state, county, or municipal government, most of the information they contain is not *about* government, laws, or politics. Lawmakers and other people involved in government need information to make decisions about the economy, energy, education, the environment, and many other things (including many that don't start with the letter *e*), so it makes sense that government entities should make this information available to them. Besides, one way that governments serve their citizens is providing them with information that can help them improve their country, as well as their own lives.

Here are just a few examples of the types of information that are available through federal documents:

1   How should a local government proceed following a disaster? The answer can be found in *Planning for Post-Disaster Recovery and Reconstruction*, published by FEMA.
2   Get the latest news on the SARS virus in the journal *Environmental Health Perspectives*, published by the National Institute of Environmental Health Sciences.
3   Find out about water quality around the country in various circulars published by the U.S. Department of the Interior.
4   Learn how to create a safety network and reduce illegal firearms trafficking through various reports published by the Bureau of Justice Assistance, part of the U.S. Department of Justice.

5 How are public lands being used? Check out *Public Land Statistics*, published by the Bureau of Land Management, part of the U.S. Department of the Interior.

6 How has the federal minimum wage changed over the years? The Wage and Hour Division of the U.S. Department of Labor has produced a table showing minimum wages over the years. (It was $0.25 an hour in 1938, by the way.)

7 How safely can you travel through space? The National Aeronautics and Space Administration has published an informational kit with an answer to this question.

8 Is climate change affecting our marshlands? See the *Proceedings of the Smithsonian Marine Science Symposium.*

9 How much money can your senator have in his or her savings account before it must be declared? The *Senate Ethics Manual* from the Select Committee on Ethics, part of the United States Senate, has an answer.

10 How are poverty-stricken people throughout Latin America affected by assistance grants from the United States? See the pictorial *Making Their Way*, published by the Inter-American Foundation.

You get the idea. For a variety of research projects, it's a good idea to see what government sources have to say.

Types of Government Sources

Government sources resemble some of the sources you have already seen in this book. Some, like the reference sources you studied in Chapter 8, provide an overview and background of an issue and define terms. Others, like the articles you saw in Chapter 10, are very specific and may present research conducted by experts, such as university faculty, working for the government. As you saw in Chapter 11, many government sources contain statistics. Still others consist of minutes from meetings of various ad hoc and standing government committees and thus constitute primary sources, which we discussed in Chapter 4.

Historically, government documents have long been available, to some degree or another, in print format—as small pamphlets, bulky reports, periodicals, and book-length or even multi-volume resources. Most government sources are now available online, although many federal documents are still made available to libraries in print format, microform, or CD-ROM. Libraries holding these tangible materials are called **federal depository libraries** and number more than 1,200. Each contains anywhere from 10 to 100 percent of all print and CD-ROM documents published by the federal government (those available through the U.S. Government Publishing Office or GPO). A regional depository typically collects close to 100 percent of all documents (which includes several thousand documents each year). In some cases, if you have borrowing privileges, you can check out government documents, but many libraries still limit access to in-library use only, especially in the case of older and hard-to-find items. All depository libraries involved in the Federal Depository Library Program (FDLP) must provide access, both in print and electronic (non-filtered Web access) formats, to a basic collection of documents. The basic collection typically includes, among other items, American FactFinder, Budget of the United States Government, Catalog of Federal Domestic Assistance, Catalog of U.S. Government Publications, various Census of Population and Housing documents, the Code of Federal Regulations, the Daily Compilation of Presidential Documents, the Congressional Directory, Economic Indicators, the Economic Report of the President, the Federal Register, the Occupational Outlook Handbook, the Public Papers of the Presidents of the United States, the United States Statutes at Large, the United States Code, and the United States Government Manual. Depository libraries then select additional documents that meet their needs, the needs of their students, and the needs of their local citizenry.

State documents are also very prevalent in libraries of all kinds. Like the federal government, each state has departments, offices, and agencies, and these entities also produce lots of resources that are available in print, CD-ROM, and online formats. If your research is particular to your local area, state, or region, then state documents are often useful sources for specific information that may have a large impact on you personally: information about crime, housing, poverty, domestic violence, geologic features, and more.

Just as we do in the United States, most foreign countries produce voluminous information in print and electronic formats. Furthermore, several international organizations provide informational resources. The African Union, European Union, International Monetary Fund, United Nations, and World Bank, just to name a few, all disseminate massive amounts of information—documents, meeting minutes, reports, and more. Whether you're studying business, political science, sociology, or another subject, there are numerous international information resources that you will find useful—and even if your research is about the heart of Kansas, national and international data can help you to place your research in a wider context.

Government documents, especially federal documents, are typically indexed in a library's catalog or other online catalogs and indexes, such as the Federal Digital System (FDsys). Each library may use its own local call number system, but academic libraries tend to use the **Superintendent of Documents (SuDoc) Classification system**. Like a Library of Congress call number, each SuDoc identifier starts with a letter. The letter *A* indicates that the document comes from the Department of Agriculture, *C* designates the Commerce Department, and so forth. Typically, a SuDoc identifier also includes a series designation, a report number (which indicates a specific title), and a publication year, volume number, issue number, or some combination of these items. (See Figure 12.1.)

Depository libraries typically have an area set aside just for government documents—anything from a few shelves to several ranges to entire floors (especially

Figure 12.1   Sample SuDoc call number. Source: Created by Michael C. Alewine.

in larger regional depository libraries). The end of each range generally will feature a finding aid, where the range of agencies and sub-agencies will be labeled. Larger academic libraries often have personnel dedicated specifically to government information. Even if a library does not have a specific section set aside for government documents, there should be reference personnel available to assist you with finding relevant government information.

Think Fast: Classification Systems

Compare the SuDoc and Library of Congress systems. Do you see any similarities? How are they different?

Like federal documents, state documents take many different forms. Most state governments have departments or entities that in some way mirror the federal government, such as a department of health and human services, so the variety of subject matter is about as broad as that of federal documents. States typically produce far less paper than the federal government, but they are prolific producers of online information, as well as CD-ROMs and microforms. Some libraries index these documents in their online catalogs. A library that has personnel dedicated to federal documents typically has staff for state documents, as well.

The Web provides access to a great deal of information from international government agencies, as well as organizations, such as the United Nations. United Nations documents are particularly useful for topics dealing with human conditions. For example, the World Health Organization (WHO), an agency of the United Nations, produces important data and research related to global health concerns. The United Nations also produces information related to economic development, human rights, and social conditions. For example, every five years the U.N. Department of Economic and Social Affairs produces the *World's Women: Trends and Statistics*, which might be a useful source for a researcher working on equality of the sexes. Typically, only large regional depository libraries and specialized research centers will actively collect international documents in paper format, and if they do, these are typically limited to materials from the United Nations.

Think Fast: Kinds of Government Sources

Name a few kinds of government sources. How are they similar to other kinds of sources you have seen in this book?

Beware of Bias

As you learned in Chapter 5, researchers have to be wary of bias when considering the information in sources, including government documents. Most government reports, such as information about beach erosion, are produced by government professionals and other experts, such as university professors, and generally can be considered accurate and objective. It's a different story when it comes to political debate, such as the kind that goes on in Congress, and political publicity on the Web. Let's say that you are researching a contested issue such as campaign finance reform or gun control. You might read transcripts of congressional sessions featuring remarks by people on various sides of the debates. What do you think you will find? Since each representative or senator has an agenda, you can count on seeing some differences, not necessarily contradictory "facts," but differences perhaps in the kinds of facts reported or in interpretations of those facts. It's not a bad idea to use this kind of information—a form of primary source—but use the critical eye you developed as you were reading Chapter 5 and try to find some more objective commentary in scholarly sources, such as articles in reputable journals.

Limit a Catalog Search to Government Sources

You can employ a variety of strategies to track down government sources. Let's start with something familiar. You already have learned how to set limits when searching for books or articles in periodicals. You can use limits when you are looking for government information, too. When you are using the library's online catalog, look for ways to limit the material type or even the location to government documents. (If the library has a special section for government documents, the catalog may allow for this kind of limiting.) Keep in mind that government information comes in a variety of formats, including CD-ROMs and small print documents, such as brochures and pamphlets. Once you take down call numbers and other useful information from catalog entries, you may need to seek help because actually locating the correct document in the stacks, file drawers, or microform may be difficult, even for experienced researchers. Take brochures, for example. You probably have never seen these little flimsy items lined up on library shelves, right? That's because libraries typically store them in a different way—in folders in a file cabinet, for example. Similarly, microfiche, like the ERIC documents you encountered in an earlier chapter, are typically stored in special file cabinets and are organized by some sort of number. Just ask a library staff member for assistance when you come across one of these kinds of government sources in the online catalog.

Search FDsys

Unless you know exactly what you are looking for, the best way to search for relevant government publications is to forgo the library's catalog and instead use the Government Publishing Office's **Federal Digital System (FDsys)**, which catalogs digital documents. The default search is the basic search, where you simply enter your keywords as you would do in any other database. There is an advanced search, which is useful for searching specific agencies or small groups of agencies, as well as limiting by publication date or date range. Within FDsys, you can search with Boolean operators, such as *and*, and complete phrase searches with quotation marks. (See Figure 12.2.)

The results list will display the PDF documents by relevance. Once you get this far, you again can impose a limit, this time by clicking on one of the links at the left, thus telling the system that you want to see only results from a particular collection, by a certain author, and so on.

You also can browse specific collections, such as the Code of Federal Regulations, Compilation of Presidential Documents, Congressional Hearings, Congressional Record, Economic Indicators, United States Code, and the United States Courts Opinions.

Quicktivity: Search FDsys

Pull a keyword combination or concept phrase from your research log and run a search in FDsys. Record the SuDoc identifiers (or other identifiers) from promising items in the results list. Practice using the links at the left to limit the results.

Figure 12.2 FDsys basic search. Source: Created by Michael C. Alewine.

Search the Government

| children and vaccines | Q Search |

Figure 12.3   United States Government Portal (USA.gov). Source: Created by Michael C. Alewine.

Run Searches in the U.S. Government Portal or on the Internet at Large

Another way to find government information is to use the U.S. government portal. (See Figure 12.3.) You can search by topic to retrieve results from relevant agencies or choose an agency and search its collection directly. The latter approach is useful when you know that the government may have published hundreds or thousands of documents on a broad topic and you want to zero in on the most relevant ones. For example, various government agencies may have had reason to publish material on children and vaccines. If your research focuses on the use of vaccines to prevent diseases (instead of policies, education of populations, political debates about vaccines, etc.), you may want to go directly to the page for a specific agency, such as the Centers for Disease Control and Prevention, and use its own search feature.

You also can find government documents by using a Google search, but be sure to include "… and site:gov" when you run your keyword search. (See Figure 12.4.) This phrase will limit the results to only those from federal and state government agencies, including those of other countries. You can google specific committees, such as the House Armed Services Committee, and find their individual sites and records of meetings and special reports or legislation. Keep in mind that the Senate and the House of Representatives have similar committees, some with similar names, such as Armed Services. Make sure that you look at both to get a clear picture of how legislation is developing.

education and reading assessment and site:gov

Figure 12.4   Internet search limiting to government sites. Source: Created by Michael C. Alewine.

Quicktivity: Run Online Searches

Choose a keyword combination or concept phrase from your research log and search for it in the U.S. government portal. Next, run the same search within a specific government agency. Finally, run this search in Google with "and site:gov." Compare the results lists. What did you learn about these different search strategies?

Search for Bills and Laws

One specialized form of government information worthy of special mention is legal information. This kind of material is of interest to those studying political science and history, of course, but it also has relevance for people in business, social work, education, and other fields. Unless your school has a law library or there is one nearby, it is unlikely that you will have access to a significant collection of printed legal resources, but you can find a wealth of information online. For example, past and current legislation, as well as the Congressional Record, is available through Congress.gov. You can search by specific bill number or use keywords, such as *immigration reform*. Links can help you navigate among related laws and even to the histories of various bills.

There are other ways to get to legal information online. Google Scholar has published a significant number of state and federal case laws in full text. The U.S. Supreme Court (supremecourt.gov) posts all judgments, as well as audio clips and transcripts of actual arguments. Landmark cases, such as *Roe v. Wade*, are generally freely available online as well. Finally, if you have access to it through your library, one of the best suites of databases for the average student is LexisNexis Academic Universe, which includes several specific search capabilities for state and federal cases, as well as law reviews.

Check Microforms

Remember microforms from Chapter 4? If you are not finding what you want in your online searching, you might want to see what is available in microform, particularly if you are looking for government documents from many years ago. After all, millions of pages of information have been printed on microfiche and microfilm, and no one has gone back and digitized all of this information. (It may be that no one ever will.) For this reason, you should be aware of these sources, which have vast amounts of valuable information you cannot find anywhere else. If you were researching oil spills and prevention, for example, you would have trouble finding "Gulf of Mexico Oil Spill Prevention and Response Act: Hearing before the Committee on Energy and Natural Resources, United States Senate, One Hundred First Congress, first session, on Amendment no. 229 to S. 406, July 24, 1989"; however, this document is available in microfiche in many libraries. Similarly, some older ERIC documents (government reports about education and related fields) are available only in microform. Although many ERIC materials are available online, thousands were taken down from the Internet until each document had been cleared of personal information (such as Social Security numbers) to protect privacy. Many academic libraries have retained the microfiche versions of these documents, which often are available through document delivery.

Think Fast: Uses of Microforms

When might you want to take the trouble of checking microforms for government information?

Conclusion

You may have never realized how much information was available from the U.S. government, as well as other political entities here and abroad. Now you do. You also know the basics of the SuDoc system for classifying information from the U.S. federal government, and you have several strategies you can use to find government sources. Specifically, you know how to search libraries' online catalogs for government sources, run searches in FDsys and the U.S. government portal, and search for bills and laws. Finally, you know that a vast amount of information is available only on microform. The next chapter surveys a familiar kind of source: webpages.

Steps to Success

1   Using what you have learned in this chapter, search for information on your topic in government sources. Try to find a federal document, a state document, something from the government in another country or an international organization, and a state or federal law, all somehow related to your topic. How did checking different kinds of government documents broaden your information or even your perspective?

2   Visit your library's government documents section and browse any sources on display or in open stacks. Note some distinctive features of these sources. What kinds of information might you find there for current or future research projects?

3   Focus on one of the government sources you have found. Evaluate it carefully and determine whether it shows any signs of bias. How does your evaluation shape the way you might use this source, or would you discard it because of excessive bias?

13

Webpages

Types of Sources

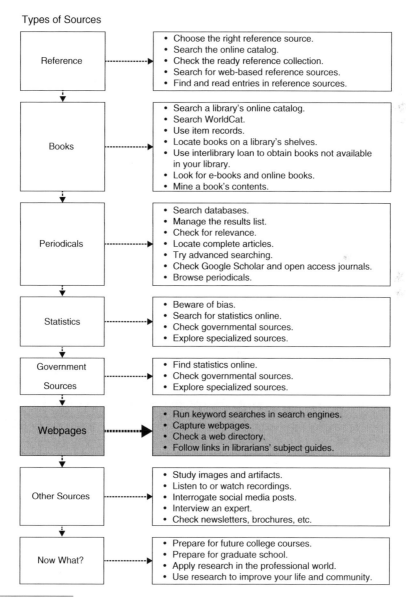

Reference	• Choose the right reference source. • Search the online catalog. • Check the ready reference collection. • Search for web-based reference sources. • Find and read entries in reference sources.
Books	• Search a library's online catalog. • Search WorldCat. • Use item records. • Locate books on a library's shelves. • Use interlibrary loan to obtain books not available in your library. • Look for e-books and online books. • Mine a book's contents.
Periodicals	• Search databases. • Manage the results list. • Check for relevance. • Locate complete articles. • Try advanced searching. • Check Google Scholar and open access journals. • Browse periodicals.
Statistics	• Beware of bias. • Search for statistics online. • Check governmental sources. • Explore specialized sources.
Government Sources	• Find statistics online. • Check governmental sources. • Explore specialized sources.
Webpages	• Run keyword searches in search engines. • Capture webpages. • Check a web directory. • Follow links in librarians' subject guides.
Other Sources	• Study images and artifacts. • Listen to or watch recordings. • Interrogate social media posts. • Interview an expert. • Check newsletters, brochures, etc.
Now What?	• Prepare for future college courses. • Prepare for graduate school. • Apply research in the professional world. • Use research to improve your life and community.

Introduction to Information Literacy for Students, First Edition. Michael C. Alewine and Mark Canada.
© 2017 John Wiley & Sons, Ltd. Published 2017 by John Wiley & Sons, Ltd.

Chapter Summary

Travel the world—the World Wide Web, that is—in search of information, using tools and strategies that can help you get the most out of your expedition.

Key Terms: cloud, cyberspace, domain, Internet, natural language search, server, sponsored link, results list, subject guide, URL, Web directory, website, wiki, World Wide Web

Chapter Objectives

- Distinguish among various top-level domains.
- Decipher a URL.
- Effectively capture and preserve information stored on a webpage.
- Use search engines, Web directories, and subject guides to locate information on the Web.
- Distinguish between wikis and other kinds of sources.

An Old Friend in a New Light

A chapter on using webpages for research might seem about as useful as a chapter on breathing. Who needs to know how to use the Web? After all, people of all ages—from children to octogenarians and beyond—practically *live* on the Web.

That's the just the thing, though. *Living* on the Web—that is, gaming and shopping and tweeting and YouTubing—is not the same as *researching* on the Web. The latter is a special skill involving a lot of tools and knowledge that the vast majority of people, even people who spend virtually every waking hour online, simply don't know. This chapter begins with an overview of the structure of the Web and then walks you through several strategies you can use to mine it for credible information:

1   Run keyword searches in search engines.
2   Capture webpages.
3   Check a Web directory.
4   Follow links in librarians' subject guides.

Now, Web-ster, here's a bet. You know the Web, right? You've spent countless hours on it, and you've even used it for research for your classes, right? Do you think that maybe, by the time you have finished this chapter, you will know at least five new things about this very familiar place? Start counting.

Cyberspace: It's Real—and Manageable

We'll start with a couple of terms you may have thought you already knew: *Internet* and *World Wide Web*. They're synonyms, right? Get ready to learn your first lesson about the online world. Although you will often hear the two terms used interchangeably, they actually mean different things. The **Internet** is a massive collection of computer networks, connected in a wired or a wireless way. It includes email and information retrievable through FTP protocols. The **World Wide Web** is the protocol that provides access to some of the information on the Internet—specifically documents known as **webpages**. Usually a number of webpages appear together as part of a **website**, often sponsored by a single organization, such as a business, university, government agency, or nonprofit organization.

When referring to the billions of documents, images, and other materials available on the Internet, people often use a misleading term: **cyberspace**. Perhaps because "cyberspace" sounds like "outer space" or because we see the stuff on the Internet through our computer screens and not on tangible pieces of paper (unless we print it, of course), some people may consciously or unconsciously think of online materials as intangible, mysterious, ethereal, or elusive, as if they were existing in a cloud. We even use this term—"the **cloud**"—to refer to space where we can store our own documents, photos, and contacts. It's worth remembering, though, that all the words, images, and software on the Internet are stored in physical locations—namely, computers called **servers**. When you connect to a website, you are simply accessing a server through another computer. Everything in cyberspace is actually stored on a computer somewhere.

Every webpage has a Uniform Resource Locator (**URL**), its "address" in cyberspace. Typically, as the box below shows, a URL consists of *www* (although you usually can omit this prefix), a name or acronym referring to the sponsor, and the domain, sometimes followed by a slash and other letters, numbers, or symbols.

Example: Anatomy of a URL

Do you remember reading about call numbers in the chapter on books? (The correct answer is "Yes, of course, I do. How could I forget something as important as call numbers?") Call numbers, as you may recall, are systematic labels in which each letter or number captures something about the book. URLs are also systematic. Let's break one down.

http://www.cdc.gov/healthyyouth/physicalactivity/facts.htm

- *http://* stands for "Hypertext Transfer (or Transport) Protocol." (There's another thing we bet you didn't know!) This prefix once was a necessary part of the URL, but now you usually can omit it.

- *www* stands for World Wide Web, of course. It, too, is usually optional. By the way, not all webpages will have *www* in their addresses.
- *cdc* refers to the Centers for Disease Control and Prevention. (The last two words were added to the name years after the institution was established, but no additional letters were added to the abbreviation.) This part of the URL represents the sponsor, which might be a government agency (as in this case), a business, a college or university, a nonprofit organization, or some other entity. Sometimes this part of the URL is an abbreviation (cdc, nih, uva), and other times it is a full name (chevrolet, whitehouse, marines).
- *gov* is the domain. This first part of the URL (www.cdc.gov) refers to the website. The remaining parts refer to more specific parts of the site.
- *healthyyouth* is a section of the site. Think of it as a folder containing documents or even other folders.
- *physicalactivity* is another, more specific section (a folder within a folder).
- *facts.htm* is a single webpage stored inside the "physical activity" folder, itself stored inside the "healthy youth" folder.

Standard rules of capitalization and spacing don't apply in URLs; thus, you often will see lower-case letters where you would expect capital letters, and you will not see spaces between words (since spaces are not allowed in URLs). Also, let's get something straight. A mark that travels from the lower left to the upper right is a *forward slash*, or simply a *slash*. One that travels from the upper left to the lower right is a *backslash*. (If you are one of the 7.2 billion people who call every kind of slash a "backslash," you can check off another lesson in this chapter.)

Examples: Web Domains

Depending on its affiliation, each website has a top-level **domain**, or category of site, indicated by the suffix. Here are the original domains, most of them still very common:

- *com*: Although many businesses use this domain, some non-profit organizations use it, as well. Even some educational sites, such as The SocioWeb (an online guide to sociology-related resources), use this domain. Examples: www.wiley.com, www.target.com, www.socioweb.com.
- *edu*: With some exceptions, U.S.-registered and accredited post-secondary educational institutions and educational consortiums, districts, or systems

use this domain. Since students at some of these institutions can store information on the schools' servers, the actual creators may be students, not employees. Some research institutes, or "think tanks," such as the Brookings Institute, have this domain, as well. Examples: www.stanford.edu, www.indiana.edu, www.brookings.edu.

- *gov*: All federal government sites, except for military entities, have this domain. State governments use .gov in combination with a state designation. For example, a site sponsored by the state of New York should end with ny.gov. A number of foreign countries use .gov, too. Latvian government sites, for example, end with .gov.lv. Examples: www.senate.gov, www.nps.gov, www.dnr.wi.gov, www.csb.gov.lv.
- *mil*: Most sites related to the U.S. military use this domain, although a few use .com or .edu. The military makes available (both freely on the Web and in various article databases) a wide range of factual information and various scholarly studies in fields ranging from engineering to medicine to military science to politics to psychology. Examples: www.marines.mil, www.uscg.mil, www.navy.mil.
- *net*: Networking agencies, companies, and organizations use this domain. You can find almost any topic covered on a .net site. At one time, it was used interchangeably with .com, but you probably will see fewer and fewer .net sites as time passes. Examples: www.java.net, www.fanfiction.net, www.wordle.net.
- *org*: Any initiative or organization can use this domain. Many sites here are sponsored by nonprofit groups, such as Mothers Against Drunk Driving (MADD). Examples: www.madd.org, www.aclu.org, www.one.org.

As you can see in the examples above, a domain generally tells you something about the sponsoring organization. As you learned in Chapter 5, you can use this information as part of the process for evaluating a source's credibility. Many sites using the .edu domain, for example, are run by universities, whose missions generally involve education, not profit. In theory, the creators of the site should be objective when it comes to discussions of academic topics (but keep in mind that students sometimes post material on .edu sites, and some of them may not have mastered objectivity). Many sites using the .com domain, on the other hand, are businesses seeking to make a profit, so the creators may include information that makes their products look good and exclude information that makes them look bad. As you can tell just from the sketches above, however, there are many nuances that make these simple characterizations less than perfect. Always use what you learned in Chapter 5 to go beyond the domains in trying to determine what is credible and what is not.

Think Fast: The Nature and Structure of the Internet

What exactly is the Internet? How does understanding its structure help you to use it as a researcher?

Run Keyword Searches in Search Engines

If you want to find something on the Web, you just google it, right? Brace yourself for another surprise. Actually, no single search engine indexes the entire Web. (Google does not, but it has access to a vast number of webpages, far more than any other search engine). Much of the Web—variously called "The Deep Web," "The Hidden Web," and "The Invisible Web"—is not indexed by standard search engines, although some search engines claim to search this region of cyberspace. Many of the documents and other material on the Deep Web are on private networks or intranets. For example, in theory, all of our medical records are secure on "The Deep Web."

Then there is the Neglected Web (not an official term, but a useful one): material that no one is updating or managing. (Maybe you yourself have neglected pages you created.) As long as this material remains on a server and the server is still connected to the rest of the Internet, it is available, but no one is minding the store. You might be surprised by how many of these "unmanned" webpages are drifting through cyberspace. In fact, because the federal government has lost track of so many of its own webpages, President Obama actually prohibited the creation of new .gov sites by the federal government. Because this orphaned material is often still indexed by search engines, you may come across it when you run searches. When you come across these neglected webpages, use what you learned in Chapter 5 to evaluate them critically. They may not pass the "Recent" test.

Although they don't index a lot of material on the Deep Web (and may take you to some questionable material on the Neglected Web), search engines are very useful. In fact, they often are the best tools to locate relevant webpages. They will accept the kind of keyword searches you studied in Chapter 3, but they also are capable of "understanding" everyday language and completing what is termed a **natural language search,** which employs sophisticated programming to figure out what you are trying to say and then match the words you have typed with what seem to be the best and most relevant results. In this respect, searching the Web is different from searching online library catalogs and other databases. For example, you can type "what happens if you have an extra y chromosome" in a Google search box (or dictate it to a smart phone) and get some useful hits, but this same search would not work nearly as well in a library catalog or periodical database. (Try it.)

What you see after you run a search is a results list—that is, a list of links to sites that the search engine found (similar to the results lists we saw in the chapters on books and periodicals). Be careful because many search engines will also present

african -american and hunger and relief and site:gov

Figure 13.1 Internet search combining limiting techniques. Source: Created by Michael C. Alewine.

you with **sponsored links**—which they place in prominent places in exchange for a fee they charge the sponsors. The webpages these links take you to might be very good, but just keep in mind that they appear prominently not because the algorithm the search engine used indicated they were good, but simply because someone paid for the prominence.

Although you *can* use natural language searches on the Web, you don't have to limit yourself to them. You often also can use Boolean operators, which you probably remember from Chapter 3. For example, some search engines allow *or*, which is useful when a keyword has a common synonym (teen OR adolescent). You can also use quotation marks when you want to locate webpages with exact phrases ("No Child Left Behind"). To limit your search to a certain top-level domain, use *site:* (e.g., unemployment and site:gov). You can even limit your search to a particular website by including the site's sponsor and domain (drunken driving and laws and site:madd.org). All search engines come complete with search help and even some limiting capabilities. If you are not finding what you need using a basic search, try using one or more limits. In the example below, you can see that *–american* eliminates "American" (in the same way the Boolean operator NOT would in other databases) and "site:gov" limits to government sites. (See Figure 13.1.) This search should turn up government webpages that have the words *hunger*, *relief*, and *African*, but not pages that have *African-American* (unless they also have the word *African* by itself). Some search engines allow you to run highly specialized searches—for just images, for example, or just videos, blogs, social media sites, or online discussion forums. Some government search engines allow you to search for grants or jobs.

Think Fast: Limitations of Web Searching

What are some limitations of using a search engine to find information on the Web?

Capture Webpages

The Web can be a magical place. Consider the disappearing act that involved the "Information Literacy Competency Standards for Higher Education," posted on the website for the Association for College and Research Libraries (ACRL).

For years, the URL was http://www.ala.org/ala/mgrps/divs/acrl/standards/standards guidelines.cfm. One day, it disappeared. What happened? Apparently, someone working for the ACRL reorganized folders on the server, so the URL changed. That could be a problem for someone who found the original page and wanted to return to it. Some organizations post announcements when a webpage is going away or moving to a new URL, perhaps even providing a forwarding service (automatically sending you to the new address). Still, many sources just seem to vanish with no warning.

You can see why librarians (who are familiar with the permanency of books and periodicals) have a line for webpages: "Here today, gone today." Of course, books and other print materials can be moved, too, but they retain their basic identifying information (author, title, publisher, and so on), whereas webpages lose their URLs when they disappear or move. If you have the citation for a book, you could order it from a different library through interlibrary loan even if your library's copy is lost, but a URL is of little use if a webpage moves.

To protect yourself, capture valuable information on the Web while it's still "here today." First, highlight key text, copy it, paste it into a Word document, and record the URL. Now you have the main parts you need. Even if the URL changes, you should be able to google some of the language you recorded and locate the information at its new URL. So that you can see the original context, even if the page disappears, it's also a good idea to capture the original page in one of three ways:

1   Download and save the webpage.
2   Use the "Print Screen" key on your computer keyboard, copy the screen capture to a Word document, and save the Word document.
3   Take a picture of the webpage with your phone.

If you do lose track of a webpage, check the Internet Archive (www.archive.org), which stores more than 400 billion webpages, including many no longer available at the URLs where they used to be.

Think Fast: Capturing Material on the Web

Why is it important to capture what you find on webpages? What are some ways to capture this material?

Check Web Directories

A different approach to locating webpages is using a **Web directory**, an organized list of links to relevant sites. Many search engines—including Yahoo!, DMOZ (Open Directory Project), the Internet Public Library, and the WWW Virtual Library—maintain Web directories. While these lists might be useful, you may be better off searching for lists of resources more related to the *specific* topics that you are

campaign finance reform libguides

Figure 13.2 Internet search for LibGuides about campaign finance reform. Source: Created by Michael C. Alewine.

researching. For example, if your topic is campaign finance reform, you can google *political science links* or *voting and elections links* or more specifically *campaign finance reform links* or *campaign finance reform resources*. This kind of search often will take you to a Web directory, where someone has compiled lists of numerous links and perhaps even provided annotations with information about the various sources. If the compiler has been careful (and used the kind of strategies you learned in Chapter 5), the sources listed on a Web directory should be credible ones worthy of your attention.

Follow Links in Librarians' Subject Guides

Many librarians create **subject guides** featuring links to free online resources, not just proprietary databases. The creators of these guides typically evaluate sites and provide brief annotations concerning the subject matter for each site. To find these subject guides, search for your keywords, along with *libguides*. (See Figure 13.2.)

For example, the search "campaign finance reform libguides" produces more than a dozen relevant libguides, just in the first two pages of results, that list only sites that have been critically evaluated and annotated by librarians. These guides and others like them are goldmines for researchers, since they list relevant pages that librarians have vetted and annotated for you. Like bibliographies and Web directories, subject guides can save you a lot of time, since you don't have to run keyword searches to learn about the sources they list.

Be Wary of Wikipedia

Wikipedia pages often appear near the top of the list of links when you google people, places, events, just about anything. It seems like one-stop shopping. Why would anyone need anything else? Having read this far in the book, you know the answer, of course. You realize that reference sources, books, periodical articles, government sources, and statistical sources are invaluable sources containing information you will never find in Wikipedia. Still, it's worth asking what, if any, value can be found in Wikipedia.

Wikipedia indeed has some attractive assets. For one thing, as a **wiki** site—that is, a website that anyone can alter by adding, deleting, or changing material—it allows lots of participation. For that reason, it has thousands of entries of all kinds of topics, including ones that generally don't make their way into standard reference books and sites. Little-known television shows, short-lived clubs and organizations, and very small towns and elementary schools generally don't draw a lot of attention from professional researchers, but someone with some interest in or connection to one of these subjects just may have contributed an entry on it to Wikipedia, and others can add to this entry.

Alas, the advantage here is also a disadvantage. The key word here is *anyone*. Research, as you have learned in this book, is not an easy thing to do well. Good researchers not only know how to locate information and evaluate its credibility, but also can understand, synthesize, quote, paraphrase, summarize, and cite the facts and interpretations they find in sources. Professional scholars, who are the authors of many entries in standard reference sources, have learned these skills, and the editors of these sources screen and edit the entries that these authors write. While not all of these entries wind up being perfect, the authors' skills and the editors' oversight help ensure that the information is credible. When you are reading a Wikipedia entry, you can be far less certain that an expert researcher or an editor had anything to do with it. Factual errors, questionable interpretations, and outright fabrications could lead you astray. For this reason, you should be very wary of Wikipedia. Some instructors, in fact, will outright forbid students from citing any Wikipedia entries.

Think Fast: Wikipedia vs. Traditional Reference Sources

Compare Wikipedia and traditional reference sources. What key differences do you need to keep in mind when you are conducting academic research?

Conclusion

Well, did you learn anything about the Web? Perhaps you supplemented what you already knew about webpages and basic searches with some useful information about cyberspace and servers, the Deep Web and the Neglected Web, the Internet Archive, the anatomy of a URL, and the powers and limitations of search engines, as well as some strategies for preserving records of Web material and some tools you can use to limit searches. Maybe you also learned about some lesser-known tools: Web directories and subject guides. Finally, this chapter gave you a chance to review much of what you learned about evaluating sources. The Web has billions of pages, but you need to think critically about each one. If you have doubts, don't spend a lot of time on it. After all, in a typical results list, there is another link right below this one (and another below that one and another below that one …), so whenever possible, use webpages created by librarians and scholars (such as many Web directories and subject guides). Librarians and scholars have already critically evaluated thousands of credible, useful sites, so put their work to use for you. The next chapter will focus on some additional online sources, such as social media sites, as well as other kinds of sources that can inform your research.

Steps to Success

1 Use two search engines, a Web directory, and a librarian's subject guide to find information on a single topic. Note the different kinds of sources you found. What are the advantages of the different tools?

2 Study the links that appeared when you used search engines for the above activity. Which are sponsored links? Now focus on the other links. Why do you think some appear higher than others?

3 Now do another search on the same topic, but this time use some of the limiting techniques discussed in this chapter. For example, use "site:" or the − (minus) sign. How are the results different from the ones you found with a basic search?

4 Try to think of an obscure topic, such as a very minor historical event or a little-known television show. Google this topic and note what appears. Do you see a Wikipedia entry on it? Are there links to any webpages that have the same amount of information but are more credible? Where else might you find information on this topic? Use what you have learned about reference sources, books, periodical articles, government sources, and other sources and tools to try to locate credible information on this topic. Now compare the facts and interpretations in each source. Consider the credibility of the information in each source.

14

Other Sources

Types of Sources

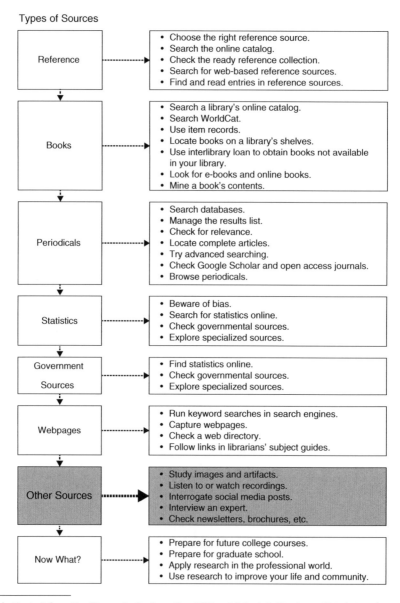

Introduction to Information Literacy for Students, First Edition. Michael C. Alewine and Mark Canada.
© 2017 John Wiley & Sons, Ltd. Published 2017 by John Wiley & Sons, Ltd.

Chapter Summary

Expand your research to include a wide range of sources, from social media and interviews to images and recordings. In this chapter, you will learn how to transform various primary sources into information that will broaden and deepen your research.

Key Terms: artifact, podcast, vodcast, social media, interview, newsletter, brochure, pamphlet, factsheet, monograph, white paper, report

Chapter Objectives

- Locate and mine images, recordings, and social media.
- Identify interview sources, write appropriate questions, and conduct interviews.
- Find and use newsletters, brochures, pamphlets, factsheets, and reports.

But Wait, There's More!

Many of the sources you have studied in the preceding chapters probably look familiar. Almost certainly, you have used the Internet in your previous research, and you probably also have some exposure to reference sources, books, and periodicals. You may have even dabbled in government sources. Maybe you thought that research ended with these sources.

Hardly.

The spectrum of sources is infinitely broad. After all, since every object in the universe constitutes a kind of reality—a fact, if you will—everything can be a kind of source. Now, unless you are an astronomer or a physicist, you may not be spending a lot of your research time studying dark matter or quarks, but you get the point. Everything—that is, every thing—is a kind of information, and information is what researchers study to understand the world.

This chapter surveys several of these less familiar sources—not just "things" (often known as "artifacts," especially in history and anthropology), but also social media, television shows and other kinds of video, various types of audio sources, and more. After reviewing the basics of evaluating and mining sources, you will learn some strategies for expanding your research into the realm of lesser-known sources:

1 Study images and artifacts.
2 Listen to or watch recordings.
3 Interrogate social media posts.
4 Interview an expert.
5 Check newsletters, brochures, etc.

As you will see, working with these sources can be especially stimulating and rewarding because you often will be doing your own analysis and interpretation. In short, you probably will be acting and feeling more like a professional researcher—such as a detective, historian, scientist, or journalist—than you ever have.

Take the Broad View

Reference sources, books, periodicals, statistical and government sources, and many webpages have a certain amount of built-in credibility because they have become known as the conventional sources researchers use. You still have to be careful with them and use the strategies discussed earlier in this book to evaluate them, but at least they *look* like sources. Tweets, YouTube videos, and homemade vlogs, on the other hand, are, well, different. Do they count as credible sources?

Actually, many things that you may not have thought of as credible—or did not even think of as *sources*—actually can be both. Their credibility has come partly from their use by established sources, such as major newspapers and news magazines. For example, the 2010 Arab Spring uprising and related violence were captured by cell phone cameras, employed by protestors and bystanders alike, in different countries. As the video footage that these amateurs generated made its way to the Internet piecemeal, major news organizations incorporated it into their own coverage of the events, in turn building the credibility of the amateur coverage.

Whether conventional sources have used a tweet or a blog, you can use what you have learned about evaluating and mining sources to do your own evaluation and interrogation so that you can judge whether a source merits consideration. If you are listening to a lecture in iTunes, for example, look for its thesis and evidence. Many of the sources discussed in this chapter—social media posts and vlogs, for example—are primary sources, which you can analyze just as you would a poem or a letter. What emotions might underlie a tweet? What might have motivated someone to post a particular picture on Instagram? Why did a YouTuber include some footage, but not other footage? What do the facial expressions of people in an image reveal? What do you hear in the tone of voice of a person speaking in an oral history? What is your interview subject *not* saying? Asking the right questions about social media posts, recordings, images, and other sources will help you tease out the kind of information that can deepen your understanding of your topic.

Quicktivity: Explore Nontraditional Sources

Run another keyword search for your topic on the Web. This time, as you scan the results list, zero in on an image, a video, a blog—anything that does not look like a traditional source. If you don't see anything, check Facebook, Instagram, Snapchat, Tumblr, Twitter, or another form of social media. What do the images, recordings, or posts you found say about your topic?

Study Images and Artifacts

We all have heard the expression "A picture is worth a thousand words." While it probably isn't a good idea to respond to a 4000-word paper assignment with four pictures, you should consider images as part of your research. In some cases, you may want to integrate images into a paper, blog, or presentation to complement your explanations or argument. Remember, though, that images can be tremendously useful to you even if you don't include them in your project. Simply examining an image—a photograph of an event or a person or an artifact, a painting, a drawing, a map—can tell you a great deal about a topic. To take just one example, a photograph of the 1968 My Lai massacre in Vietnam captures the emotional side of this historical event.

Many such photographs have earned the Pulitzer Prize or other accolades for photojournalists, but other images have been captured by ordinary people. Because of the explosive growth of digital cameras, especially those built into cell phones, many of us are documenting our lives practically every day or even every hour: how we live, how we love, how we work and play and organize and interact. Historic and contentious moments—such as the Arab Spring mentioned at the beginning of this chapter—have been caught on camera, and the images of these moments in turn become invaluable sources. No matter what your topic, an image search on the Web may produce relevant and useful results that can be used to bolster your points. Images can also help to clarify something for your audience. For example, let's say you are researching the use of interactive whiteboards in an education class and you want to show a particular teaching strategy for mathematics using one of these boards with kindergarten students. An image of a teacher using this strategy could help to illustrate it. Keep in mind that most images come with copyright implications. Under the "fair use" allowance in copyright law, you are permitted to use images for your research projects, but use them sparingly. In other words, try not to use multiple images from a specific author or book. Again, always cite your sources. You can copy and paste the images into your research paper or project, but try to use large images and then resize them smaller instead of the other way around. (Making a small image larger can compromise quality.) Search engines allow you to select different image sizes. You can also set a date range if you are looking for something relatively recent.

Quicktivity: Study Rules for Using Images

Do a search on the Web and locate the "fair use" guidelines for using images. Use what you have learned about evaluating sources to make sure the site presenting the guidelines is credible.

Just as you can study and interpret images to learn about the people, places, and events they represent, you can learn a lot from objects, such as the ones found in museums. When such objects tell stories about the eras that produced them, we call them **artifacts**. Artifacts include not only vases and jewelry from ancient civilizations, but also clothing, toys, decorations, and more from the recent past. If you have been to the National Museum of American History (one of many museums that constitute the Smithsonian Institution), you may have seen many such artifacts, including famous ones such as Dorothy's shoes from the movie *The Wizard of Oz*, the original Star-Spangled Banner, and dresses belonging to America's First Ladies. Whether you examine artifacts in person or study pictures of them online, you can draw conclusions that you can then use in your research projects.

Think Fast: Artifacts

What is an artifact? How might studying a relevant artifact inform your research?

Listen to or Watch Recordings

Podcasts and **vodcasts,** audio and video recordings available from the Internet, are also wonderful sources of information. They are typically audio files (such as mp3 files), although some (sometimes known as *vodcasts*) are video files. They may be freely available for download and transfer across various mobile devices, or they could have digital rights management (DRM) features that limit access and transfer. The Web has tens of thousands of free podcasts that provide credible information. Many are attached to online collections or news services. One valuable source of audio reports is National Public Radio (NPR), which covers a wide variety of topics in politics, law, science, education, entertainment, culture, and more. (One of its best-known programs is called *All Things Considered*.) The programs, prepared by journalists and other professionals, air on the radio, but they also are available—in parts or in their entireties—online. You can listen to the recordings online or download them to your desktop or mobile device; you also can read text accompanying the recordings.

Quicktivity: Search for NPR Recordings and Transcripts

Go to npr.org and search for some keywords related to your topic. Locate a relevant audio clip and listen to it. Try to find a transcript of the report on NPR's site.

Oral histories are also useful for various research topics. For example, the University of North Carolina's *Documenting the American South* features audio interviews—as well as textual interviews and personal narratives—on a wide range of topics: business, civil rights, education, family, farming, history, politics, race, religion, slavery, women's studies, and more. Since the interview subjects are people who lived through a time period or experienced an important historical event, these interviews can be rich sources of firsthand information. Many other sites—sponsored by universities, as well as the Library of Congress—provide free partial or complete access to a wide range of oral histories from ordinary people who lived during extraordinary times, as well as famous scientists, historians, politicians, and so forth.

You can find still more podcasts through iTunes, where you can gain access to, among other things, free lectures by university professors (in a special subset called iTunes U) on business, history, science, and more. ITunes requires a download, but this download makes it easy to organize and manage podcasts that interest you.

You also can find tens of thousands of videos taken by ordinary people, security cameras, and professional news cameramen that capture world events as they are happening. For example, consider the problems across the United States with law enforcement and its relationship with communities. In response, we are now seeing the use of more cameras in law enforcement and specifically body cameras. If you were doing a research project on police and community relations, you will of course find news videos, but you also could watch raw footage of actual events and their aftermath (from multiple angles), as well as interviews with people talking about how they feel about the police and interviews with police officers discussing what it is like to work in a specific community. When searching for video recordings, you often can limit your results by date, duration, and source (e.g., CBS News). If you are putting together a presentation, blog, wiki, etc., you can even embed full or partial video clips into your project.

Quicktivity: Find a Recording

Use a search engine to find a recent recording related to your research topic. Are there particular sections of the video that you find useful for your project? Who created the video? When was it created? What other information do you need to properly cite a video?

Interrogate Social Media

Most organizations, including libraries, have a presence on **social media** sites, such as Facebook and Twitter, where they can deliver news about events, programs, and such. (See Figure 14.1.) Some organizations use these sites to reach out to people, particularly the younger set. (Studies have found that even some homeless teens have Internet access and make use of social media to stay connected with other people.)

For updated information (catch us here):

Facebook   Instagram   Twitter   YouTube

Figure 14.1   Social media links at the bottom of a webpage. Source: Created by Michael C. Alewine.

For example, the National Institutes of Health (NIH) uses Facebook and other social media to highlight new studies related to the treatment of paralysis. In some cases, these sites have links that will take viewers to other webpages or even to scholarly publications, but quite often the social media pages will present unique content. As business, education, and government are already on social media, we can expect more and more credible, useful content to appear there.

Of course, much of the material posted on social media sites is personal, not professional, but this material can be invaluable, particularly when you are doing research in the social sciences. Do you remember what you learned about primary sources, such as diaries and letters, in Chapter 4? While some people in our own time keep diaries and write old-fashioned letters, many prefer to share their personal news about their adventures, family activities, and such through social media. All of this material constitutes a new form of primary source—one that could prove invaluable to you if you are studying, say, social life in college, family dynamics, or any number of other topics with social dimensions. Imagine you are preparing a presentation on the sociology of college spring break. How much could you learn from various college students' YouTube videos, Instagram posts, and tweets? Carefully interrogated, these primary sources could provide you with a wealth of information about peer pressure, self-image, and much more. Furthermore, since you would be providing your own analysis, you would be developing the crucial skills of interpretation and sense-making.

When citing social media, check the appropriate publication manual and citation guide you are using for your project, but note that not all publication manuals have caught up with social media. If you don't find what you need in the manual or guide, search the Web for the citation style and the words "social media" to see if you can find any guidance.

Quicktivity: Interrogate Some Social Media

Visit a social media site and search for posts relevant to your topic. What do these posts reveal about your topic?

Interview an Expert

Schools, colleges, and universities are cool places—and not just because of their lively social scenes. They are packed with people who have immense amounts of expertise about a wide range of subjects, from art to zoology. In short, when you walked onto your campus, you entered a world of highly knowledgeable experts, men and women who conduct their own research, share it in books and journal articles, and teach it to other people (you, for example). Sometimes journalists and documentary filmmakers **interview** these experts for their own research. Why shouldn't you? These people have the equivalents of whole books—or bookcases—of information in their heads, and you don't need a keyword or a catalog to get to this information. You just need to find the right people and ask the right questions.

Let's start with finding the right people. You may already know one—your professor. After all, this person already knows enough to teach the course; he or she probably knows something, perhaps a lot, about your topic. Since the two of you probably already know each other, you don't have to worry about any awkward introductions. Besides, who knows more about the kind of information you need to put into your project than the person who made the assignment? Your professor also probably knows other sources, including not only books and articles, but also colleagues. For example, a typical biology professor knows the basics of genetics, but a specialist in ecology generally doesn't know as much about the subject as a geneticist. If your professor is an ecologist, he or she could point you to one or more geneticists in the department and maybe even introduce you. (Many professors spend a lot of time outside their offices teaching their classes, doing research in labs or libraries, or working in the community. If you have trouble getting in touch with a professor, check with the department's administrative assistant, who probably can help connect the two of you.) You also can carry out interviews with practitioners who are experts because of their professional expertise. For example, let's say you are in a social work class and you want to research "client confidentiality policies" that are actually used by professional social workers. Odds are, there is a local health and human services office nearby. Locate the website and see if you can find the email address or phone number for the supervisor. Of course, you don't have to limit yourself to experts who work at your own university or nearby. Look back at the books, articles, and other sources you have found over the course of your research. The authors of these sources are usually clearly identified, and their institutional affiliations sometimes appear along with their names. (See Figure 14.2.) If you don't see an affiliation, just google the author's name, along with the title of the source, and try to find an email address. You then can arrange an interview or send an email questionnaire. Make sure to read the article or at least some of the book first.

Listen to What They Have to Say!
Assessing Distance Learners' Satisfaction with Library
Services using a Transactional Survey

By Michael C. Alewine
Mary Livermore Library
University of North Carolina at Pembroke
Pembroke, North Carolina

Figure 14.2 Author and affiliation listed on scholarly journal article. Source: Created by Michael C. Alewine.

Insider's Tip: Experts Are Real People—and Great Sources

When I was an undergraduate at Indiana University, I noticed what I thought was a funny habit of my grammar professor. When talking about our textbook, he used the author's first name, "Martha," or just "she" instead of "the book" or "it"—as if he knew the person behind the book. Now that I am a professor, researcher, and author myself, I understand why he talked that way. To many students, books are just that: books—inanimate objects with information in them. To professors, on the other hand, books are creations, things made by real people. In many cases, we professors *are* those real people, or we know the real people because we work with them or met them at a conference. I don't know if my professor, Bill, actually knew Martha. I wouldn't be surprised if he had met her at some point in his long career, but, even if he didn't, he knew that behind every book is a real person or a group of real people.

There's value in this knowledge. As a researcher, you don't have to settle for what is there in the books or articles you are reading. You can consult the people who wrote that information. Email is a great way to reach out to these experts. Because I have posted a lot of information on the Web, I have heard from many students and other people who want to ask me questions, interview me, or seek my consultation on Edgar Allan Poe, Benjamin Franklin, Harriet Beecher Stowe, the Lewis and Clark expedition, and English grammar. I always respond, and I am happy to provide any assistance I can. Because I also have been on the other end of this process—reaching out to other experts, that is—I know that other scholars are equally happy to offer their knowledge. Just look at the other "Insider's Tips" features in this book.

Don't be shy. Email the authors who have written the books and articles you find. Ask questions. Conduct interviews. Build relationships. You may find this approach the most valuable and enjoyable part of your research.

–Mark

Once you have identified an expert, you need to know what to ask in the interview. Before you meet, write down several specific questions. ("Soooooo, tell me about chromosomes" is not the best way to start an interview with a geneticist. You may get a funny look or a three-hour impromptu lecture, neither of which is your goal.) After you have done a little reading on your topic in a subject encyclopedia, book, article, government document, or website, make some notes along these lines:

What do you need to clarify? An interview with an expert is a great opportunity to fill any gaps in your knowledge or clear up confusion. ("What exactly is the difference between a stem cell and other kinds of cells?" "What do federal laws say about the use of stem cells?")

What are the issues or controversies? Chances are, experts disagree on certain aspects of a topic—perhaps not the facts (although some debate is possible even here), but probably interpretations of those facts. You may want to ask your subject about his or her own position. If you do, follow up with questions about his or her reasons and evidence for this position. Consider playing devil's advocate and asking your subject to respond to the other side of the argument. ("In my reading in *CQ Researcher*, I saw that some people are concerned about the ethics of using stem cells. How would you respond to these people?")

What else do you need to know? One of the challenges that beginners or outsiders have when doing research on a topic is knowing what they don't know. It's like walking into an unfamiliar building with only a flashlight: you can see a few things in the light and have some sense of things in the dim areas, but you have no idea what lies out there in the absolute darkness. Ask your subject what other facts, statistics, concepts, and issues you need to explore. ("We've talked a lot about the connection between stem cell research and abortion. Are there other aspects of stem cell research that make it controversial?")

What are some other useful sources to investigate? As noted above, experts know where to go for more information on their subjects. Take advantage of the interview to ask about other sources you should check: books, articles, government documents, websites, and other people you could interview. ("You mentioned Francis Collins. Where might I learn more about him and the Human Genome Project?")

Next, you need to set up the interview. Consider the format: in-person interview, telephone conversation, or email questionnaire. The first is usually the best if the person you want to interview is nearby and you are pursuing an in-depth understanding of the subject. When you are meeting a subject in person in his or her workplace, the subject can show you relevant images or objects, take you on a tour, and introduce you to other people. A telephone conversation is appropriate when the subject is farther away. Finally, an email questionnaire may help you to gather basic facts or brief explanations, but it doesn't allow for spontaneous, rapid give-and-take and is impractical for lengthy explanations. Whether you are visiting, calling, or emailing the person you want to interview, provide a little context. ("I am a student in Professor Lorraine Baker's social work class at Big State University, and I am preparing a presentation on confidentiality policies in rehabilitation clinics. One of my classmates, Yuto Satou, works at your clinic and suggested that I get in touch with you about this topic. Would you be available for a 30-minute interview on any afternoon of this week?") Be patient. Like you, professors and practitioners are busy people. It may take a while for them to answer phone messages and email. For this reason, you don't want to be trying to set up an interview two days before an assignment is due. Also, keep in mind that many professors have limited availability during the summer months, when they may be out conducting their own research.

Finally, when you actually conduct the interview, take accurate, comprehensive notes, even over things you think are not directly related to your topic. Don't be afraid to ask your subjects to repeat or clarify something they have said. Be respectful of your subject's time, but be willing to stick around as long as your subject is willing to talk. Sometimes, it takes a person a while to warm up to a topic, and the best material may come only after you and your subject have been talking for an hour. Remember, many of these experts are teachers at heart and enjoy sharing their knowledge with others. If you have a digital recorder, ask permission to record the conversation, but still take good notes; later you can use the recording just to flesh out quotations and review things you missed instead of taking the time necessary to listen to the entire conversation again. If completing the interview via email, be succinct and state your questions as clearly as you can. (After all, the subject won't have the luxury of asking for a clarification on the spot.) In an email questionnaire, you may want to include one or two open-ended questions, thus giving your subject room to expand upon his or her thoughts, but keep in mind that many people probably will not be inclined to spend a lot of time typing responses. (Again, email questionnaires are not ideal for in-depth explanations.)

Think Fast: Preparing for an Interview

What are some things you should do before carrying out an interview with an expert?

Check Newsletters, Brochures, Etc.

You may have noticed that the survey of printed publications in Chapter 4 did not include newsletters and other common kinds of printed matter; then again, maybe you didn't notice. After all, even though you see these publications all the time, you may not have thought of them as *sources* you could use in your research.

Take, for example, **newsletters,** small publications aimed at employees of a company or members or an organization. Since they come out on a regular basis, they are a form of periodical, but they may not be indexed in databases, and you may not even think about them when you think of periodicals. In fact, they generally provide little depth of explanation and thus pale in comparison with journal articles, but they still can be useful. Whether they are published by universities, organizations, companies, or government agencies, they may alert you to projects, people, or events related to your topic. For example, a newsletter written by a faculty member in a university's biology department about a recent research project might provide you with the name of someone you could interview or some keywords you could use for a Web search. Newsletters may appear in print or on the Web.

Brochures, **pamphlets**, and **factsheets** are, like newsletters, small publications published by organizations, government agencies, and other entities, but they do not appear regularly the way newsletters do. Almost certainly, you have seen them in the waiting rooms of doctors' offices or credit unions. While they do not necessarily go through a peer-review process, they are often written or sanctioned by experts. For example, a pamphlet on recognizing the signs of depression in college students was probably created by an expert in that field or made available through an association, such as the Anxiety and Depression Association of America. Like a reference source, such a publication might provide you with some useful facts and background, lead you to other sources, and provide you with contact information you can use to set up an interview with an expert.

As you already know, educational institutions and think tanks are overflowing with experts who spend a lot of their time studying things and publishing their findings. Often they publish these findings in books and journal articles, but they also may share them in stand-alone forms that are shorter than books, but may be significantly longer than periodical articles. Such materials go by a variety of names— **monographs**, **white papers**, **reports**—and may appear in print or on the Web. They may or may not be indexed in databases. For example, a consulting agency might produce a white paper on the effects of drought on economic development in a community. If the source is an expert or group of experts, this kind of source can be as credible as a journal article. It may contain statistics and other facts gathered through research, as well as analysis, explanations, footnotes or endnotes, and a list of references or works cited.

Think Fast: Articles vs. Reports

Compare journal articles and reports, or white papers. What do they have in common?

Conclusion

As you saw in this chapter, literally everything can be a source. A few particularly useful ones are images and artifacts, various kinds of recordings, social media sites, interview subjects, newsletters, brochures, pamphlets, factsheets, and reports. What's next? During this information revolution, even more forms of communication are just around the corner. For that reason, you should not limit yourself to any of these sources. Keep your eyes and mind open and be ready to learn from anything.

Steps to Success

1   Find some images, including at least one image of an artifact, online and study them. Take notes on facial expressions, colors, shapes, wear and tear, anything that might reveal something about your topic. Use what you have learned to interpret these details.

2   Find some podcasts online and listen to them or watch them. Take notes on theses, evidence, and examples.

3   Run keyword searches on various social media sites to locate posts related to your topic. Take notes on these posts, paying close attention to content, word choice, and other details that may reveal emotions, motivations, consequences, and more.

4   Identify a professor at your own institution and another individual, such as a practitioner or a professor at another institution, who could be appropriate interview subjects for your topic. Get in touch with them and schedule interviews. Prepare a list of questions.

5   As you visit offices, libraries, and other locations, pay attention to the newsletters, pamphlets, and other printed materials lying on tables or stored in bins on walls. Skim them for information, such as keywords or names of experts. Take notes on anything you might be able to use in your research.

6   Google some keywords for your topic, along with "white paper" or "report." Skim the results list and identify one or more items that look relevant. Interrogate anything you find and take notes.

15

Now What?

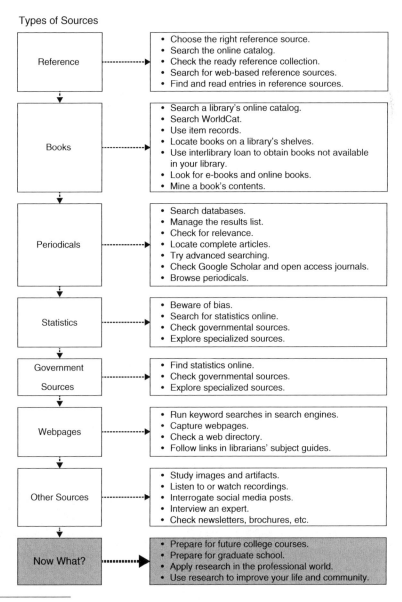

Types of Sources

Reference
- Choose the right reference source.
- Search the online catalog.
- Check the ready reference collection.
- Search for web-based reference sources.
- Find and read entries in reference sources.

Books
- Search a library's online catalog.
- Search WorldCat.
- Use item records.
- Locate books on a library's shelves.
- Use interlibrary loan to obtain books not available in your library.
- Look for e-books and online books.
- Mine a book's contents.

Periodicals
- Search databases.
- Manage the results list.
- Check for relevance.
- Locate complete articles.
- Try advanced searching.
- Check Google Scholar and open access journals.
- Browse periodicals.

Statistics
- Beware of bias.
- Search for statistics online.
- Check governmental sources.
- Explore specialized sources.

Government Sources
- Find statistics online.
- Check governmental sources.
- Explore specialized sources.

Webpages
- Run keyword searches in search engines.
- Capture webpages.
- Check a web directory.
- Follow links in librarians' subject guides.

Other Sources
- Study images and artifacts.
- Listen to or watch recordings.
- Interrogate social media posts.
- Interview an expert.
- Check newsletters, brochures, etc.

Now What?
- Prepare for future college courses.
- Prepare for graduate school.
- Apply research in the professional world.
- Use research to improve your life and community.

Introduction to Information Literacy for Students, First Edition. Michael C. Alewine and Mark Canada.
© 2017 John Wiley & Sons, Ltd. Published 2017 by John Wiley & Sons, Ltd.

Chapter Summary

This book has to end, but your research does not. Plan to apply what you have learned in this book to succeed in the research you may do for future classes (including online classes), your career, and your personal and civic lives.

Key Terms: original research, literature review, specialist librarian

Chapter Objectives

- Identify uses of research in undergraduate and graduate education, the professional world, and personal and civic lives.
- Prepare for literature reviews and original research.
- Prepare for a job interview.

The Value of Information in *Your* Life

If you have studied all of the chapters in this book carefully, completed the Quicktivities and other exercises, and applied what you've learned to one or more research projects, you probably have a very sound foundation in research. In fact, you probably know more about finding, evaluating, and using sources than most students and even a lot of professionals.

Now what?

It's a fair question. You have had to work hard to absorb all of this information about Boolean operators, primary and secondary sources, subject encyclopedias, item records, bibliographies, government documents, and dozens of other tools and sources. How is all this work going to pay off for you?

The short answer is "splendidly." One word doesn't make much of a chapter, though, and besides there is a bit more to say about the value of research knowledge and skills. This chapter will highlight some specific ways you can use research in various aspects of your life:

1 Prepare for future college courses.
2 Prepare for graduate school.
3 Apply research in the professional world.
4 Use research to improve your life and community.

If information is the most powerful tool on earth, it ought to empower you. It will. Let's see how.

Prepare for Future College Courses

By now, it should not take much to convince you of the value of research knowledge and skills in high school and college. After all, you probably are using this book in a class that requires research, or you are taking other classes in which you have to complete research projects. Just think how much more tedious and difficult all of your projects would be if you didn't know how to ask a good research question, narrow a topic, keep a research log, truncate and combine keywords, distinguish a credible website from a questionable one, take notes strategically, follow the leads in a source to find other sources, or collect and mine information from books, periodical articles, social media sites, interviews, and many other kinds of sources.

The key point here, though, is not that you got your money's worth out of this book. (But you did, right?) More important is what you do going forward. Too many times, students leave a class and then "clear their cache," forgetting most of what they learned. When they do, they cheat themselves out of a lot of really valuable knowledge and skills that could have served them in future courses and beyond. That's especially true of information literacy and research because many courses, especially upper-level ones, require you to know how to find, evaluate, and use information. In fact, as the first chapter explains, one of the main purposes of academia is to expand humans' understanding of the natural, social, and cultural worlds. Academia and research go hand in hand.

That point leads to the first piece of advice for going forward with your research abilities. Hold on to what you have learned here. OK, you probably will not remember everything this book has been teaching (or preaching) about the nuances of item records and call numbers, but you don't want to lose the valuable tools you picked up here. The big-picture concepts, such as credibility and synthesis, are essential to success in many advanced courses—and the little hints and shortcuts, the specialized sources, and the general step-by-step method outlined in the chapters here are sure to make all of your future research much more manageable and successful. In particular, remember to work with both your instructors and your librarians as you choose and narrow your topic, search for sources, and evaluate and use these sources.

One more thing: keep this book. You may be surprised how many times you return to it when you need to refine a search, find a government document, prepare some interview questions, or take notes on a source.

Quicktivity: Think Ahead about More College Courses

Think ahead to some courses you will take next semester, as well as one or two upper-level courses you will need to take for your major. Reflect on a few terms and concepts you learned from this book and jot down some ways that you could use your knowledge of them in these future classes.

Insider's Tip: If You Lose It, You Can't Use It

Chances are, I've never met you, but I'll bet I can tell you something you've said at one point in your high school or college career:

"When am I ever going to use this?"

I can virtually guarantee that you asked this question about something you were covering in one or more of your classes. (Math seems especially prone to this question.) How did I know? Everyone says it. I've heard my son say it. *I've* said it!

Maybe, once you completed a class, you also have said something along these lines: "Whew, I'm glad that's over." Again, the sentiment is natural. Learning is hard, and sometimes the subject is, well, not something you want to hold close to your heart—or even remember.

I won't try to talk you into cherishing every class you have ever taken and every fact you have ever learned, but I can tell you that I have used more of what I've learned in school than I ever thought I would—and not just to help my kids with their algebra homework. To take just a few examples, I have used what I learned about ellipses in a math class to design a coffee table, what I have learned about history and meteorology and criminal justice to understand the world around me, and what I have learned about literature and psychology to understand myself.

Every class eventually will end, but the value of the material you learned in each class doesn't have to end. (After all, if you're going to forget everything you learned in a class, why learn it in the first place?) That's especially true of information literacy in the Information Age.

When are you ever going to use information literacy? Hold on to it, and you'll see.

−Mark

You may be reading this textbook for a course that you are taking online or off campus. No matter how or where you take a course, you can use what you have learned here. From developing topics to consulting a librarian for assistance to locating and using various kinds of sources, you can conduct research successfully even if you never set foot on the main campus of your school.

Most academic libraries have an authentication process that allows you to log into proprietary databases from off campus. These libraries also usually have an interlibrary loan process you can use to obtain electronic versions of periodical articles and even have books mailed to your home address. Many academic libraries even have at least one librarian who is responsible for distance education services, and some larger academic libraries have whole teams of personnel devoted to working with students who take courses off campus. Some of these librarians have "Distance Education" in their titles.

Figure 15.1 Student working with a reference librarian. Source: Photo taken by Christopher W. Bowyer; permission given by Christopher W. Bowyer.

If you are taking courses remotely, try to find contact information for library personnel dedicated to distance education, read any related policies and procedures, and begin your research as soon as you can, since you may need to allow time for books to be sent to your home. Even if you need items or chapters from reference books, most academic librarians responsible for distance education services will scan these items and email them to you as PDF attachments (within appropriate copyright limitations of course). Librarians can also suggest alternate sources, depending on your topic, or steer you toward mostly online resources.

You sometimes may want to consider visiting libraries other than your own academic library, especially if you are a distance education student. All public libraries are, by definition, open to the public, and most academic libraries in the United States allow at least some access to their resources and services. Most, for example, provide access to reference librarians (see Figure 15.1), reference books, and open stacks, and many allow access to electronic resources when you visit in person.

Prepare for Graduate School

If you are not in graduate school, you may assume you can skip this section. Don't! At some point in your life, immediately after graduation or in the years ahead, you may join the millions of Americans who have enrolled in graduate school. If you want to become a pediatrician, psychiatrist, lawyer, public school principal, dentist, pharmacist, family nurse practitioner, or physical therapist (just to name a few), you will have to have a graduate degree. In many other fields, such as social work and business, a graduate degree is necessary for career advancement. Indeed, just as a bachelor's degree eventually became the norm for good jobs in the United States in the twentieth century, a graduate degree is becoming much more common for satisfying, well-paying careers in the twenty-first century.

If you are already in graduate school, you probably know that research is even more a part of your daily life than it was when you were an undergraduate. Most graduate courses require research projects, and the culminating project in many master's and doctoral programs—a master's thesis or a doctoral dissertation, for example—generally requires extensive research. For this reason, the skills you have learned in this book can enrich and facilitate your experience in graduate school by making you an effective, efficient researcher. Let's take a look at a few specific considerations for research in graduate school.

One key difference between the kind of research done by undergraduates and the kind done by graduate students is the demand for originality—that is, the requirement that the student researcher expand the understanding in the discipline. Some undergraduates may do **original research** for an honors thesis or capstone project, and the increasing emphasis on faculty-mentored undergraduate research outside the classroom means that more undergraduates are blazing new trails—studying the habits of amphibians in a particular river, for example, or offering fresh interpretations of art, drama, music, or literature. Still, the stakes are higher in graduate school, where covering new territory or offering original interpretations is often the norm. In many cases, particularly in the sciences, graduate students begin working with faculty early in their careers, long before they begin working on their theses or dissertations.

What does this expectation mean for you as a researcher? For one thing, it means that you need to be comfortable with a **literature review**, or "lit review" for short. Very often, writers of original research, especially dissertations, examine many—ideally all—of the sources focusing on their topic and summarize all of this scholarship, or "literature," in their own words. The value of this practice is twofold. First, as the researcher, you familiarize yourself with the discoveries and interpretations already made by others. All of this information can then inform your thinking *and* ensure that what you are doing is truly original. Remember what we said about reinventing the wheel in the first chapter? The process of conducting a lit review helps you avoid wasting a lot of your time, say, discovering the moon (been there) or inventing solar panels (done that)—or, for that matter, describing a sociological phenomenon already well known to others in the field, interpreting a historical event just as a previous historian has done, or proposing an economic or educational theory that already has been proposed. Second, the lit review shows the *reader* what already has been done on this topic and helps to set up what is original about your research.

The research skills you have learned in this book perfectly equip you to conduct a slam-dunk lit review. Using what you have learned about keywords, Boolean operators, databases, and bibliographies, you can look broadly and deeply for sources on your topic, greatly minimizing the possibility that you will waste your time on research that already has been done. (Your professors, particularly your thesis or dissertation advisor, will help you avoid this pitfall, too, since they ideally are well-versed in the subject; however, in many cases, your particular topic will be so precise or extraordinary that your professors will not be experts in it. By the time you are done, you will know more than they do about this particular topic.) To take just one example, making extensive use of bibliographies can help you identify all of the major and many of the minor studies done on your topic, since the sources you are studying while conducting your lit review will cite these studies. If you read all of the books and articles listed in the bibliography for one source, then all of the articles listed in the bibliographies for all of these books and articles, and so on, you eventually would have read everything—or, at least, everything generally regarded as important—on your topic. (Remember to use a research log to keep track of all of these sources.)

Original research, by definition, requires the use of primary sources. If all you are using are secondary sources, you are merely reviewing what already has been done—and that's not original research. To offer a new discovery or interpretation, you need to be considering raw data (such as statistics you have located or generated) or other kinds of material (diaries, newspaper articles, social media sites, images, recordings, poems, chemical reactions, fossils, experimental subjects, and so on) that you yourself can interpret. Here again, the concepts and sources covered in this book (especially the types of sources covered in Chapter 14) will prove very useful.

You already know two other resources who will be very useful. Faculty are even more important to graduate students than they are to many undergraduate students, since they serve as mentors on original research. Librarians may prove even more important, too. At many large universities, the library systems have **specialist librarians**, people who have expertise in research on particular subjects. Indeed, many universities have whole libraries for law, health sciences, and other fields. Take advantage of the expertise of the librarians in these libraries.

As you can see, research and graduate school go hand in hand—another reason to exult in the foundation in information literacy you have built while reading this book.

Quicktivity: Imagine an Original Angle

If you have done any research that was not original, as most students have, imagine that you are trying to do *original* research on the same topic. That is, you are not merely surveying what others have said and adding your own two cents, but seeking to expand the knowledge in the discipline. Try jotting down a few angles you could take. What would you do to find out whether these angles would provide fresh insights into the topic?

Apply Research in the Professional World

Even if you decide not to head off to graduate school—not right away, at any rate—there's a good chance that you will have a chance to use your research skills in your career right out of college. Consider, for example, these scenarios:

- Your company is considering rolling out a new product line, but executives want to be sure that all the investment in product development, manufacturing, and marketing will pay off with substantial sales. You may be involved in doing "market research" to gauge demand for this product.
- The elementary school where you teach has the opportunity to pursue a grant to fund a project that would pay social workers to spend time in the school each week. Your principal may ask you to conduct research on your students to see if they would benefit from interactions with social workers. (By the way, agencies that distribute grants—"free money" to help promote potentially valuable projects—often require schools and organizations requesting the grants to demonstrate a need or make a case that the funds will pay dividends.)
- The city park where you work as a recreation planner has the opportunity to build a new baseball diamond. You may be tasked with a proposal, for which you would need to do research on the number of spectators to expect, the current requirements for safety features, and so on.

Professional people in every field use research to make progress—and money. It goes back to a point made at the beginning of this book. In this Information Age, knowing how to find, evaluate, and use information can help you thrive in the professional world.

Actually, research will be important to you even before you take a job. After all, before you can work in a job, you first need to *get* the job, and research can play a key role here, as well. Many employers will tell you that one key to succeeding in a job interview and ultimately landing the job is demonstrating knowledge of the employer and the job itself. You might even hear some people in charge of hiring say things like "Do your homework" or, more to the point of this book, "Do your research." You can use what you learned in this book to search an organization's website for its strategic plan (or for profiles of the people who will be interviewing you), find and study financial statistics for a publicly held company, and much more. Don't stop with researching the company. Use what you know about research to study current issues and trends in the industry. Identify the appropriate trade journals and read some articles. Follow up on what you see by using a keyword search in an appropriate database and read even more. Some employers—in public relations, for example—may expect you to propose a possible project or campaign in the interview process. You could study social media sites to learn more about the audience for a publicity campaign or examine websites where you might propose purchasing advertising space. You could also schedule interviews with other people in the field—at different organizations or in different companies—to broaden your knowledge base. Research, in short, could make you the kind of informed candidate that employers want to hire.

Finally, remember that information literacy encompasses more than just research for big projects and job interviews. Being able to process information will be key to success in your everyday working life. You may frequently find yourself studying statistics, reading formal or informal studies of your field, and, yes, interviewing other job candidates. Being information-literate—that is, being able to make sense of numbers and facts, evaluate the credibility of sources and candidates, and more—is a very important asset that will serve you even when you are not working on a proposal or presentation.

Insider's Tip: Stand Out in Your Job Search

A bit of extra research can make the difference between a successful search and a long, frustrating one.

For starters, research the culture of an organization to assess the potential fit between its culture and your strengths, interests, and values. You can learn a lot from its website, information in the public domain, and present or past employees. Don't think you know anyone who works there? Use your LinkedIn network to find second- and third-degree connections who have experience with the organization, ask your mutual connection to make an introduction, and ask for an informational interview. Almost all professionals are willing to help, particularly if you have a common link such as an alma mater or a mutual acquaintance.

Research can help you prepare for the interview, as well. Search the web to find out if the organization has recently won an award, released a new product, or been in the limelight for other reasons. If so, prepare to talk about this development. Sites such as glassdoor.com and vault.com also contain "insider information" on many organizations. Insights gleaned from such sites can help you decide how to dress for your interview, how to prepare answers to possible questions, and what questions to ask at the end of the interview.

My office recently worked with a student who went into an interview having researched not only the position for which he was applying, but also the next position in the organization's career path. When asked where he saw himself in five years, he answered with details about the more senior role. The employer was so impressed that the student got an interview for the more senior role and got the job. Doing your research pays off!

–Emily McCarthy, Career Development Director, Northern Arizona University, and former human resources manager and hiring manager in multiple large, global organizations

---

Think Fast: Research on the Job

What are some occasions for research in the professional world?

Use Research to Improve Your Life and Community

On some level, you probably knew that research skills and information literacy could serve you well in school and on the job, but did you ever think about how it could serve you at home?

All over the world, people consult experts to help them make decisions about their marriages, health, finances, and more. When they are expecting a baby, for example, many couples take classes in delivery or parenting. An increasing number of adults have consulted personal trainers and dietitians to help them exercise and eat properly. Financial consultants are popular resources for people planning for retirement or otherwise trying to maximize their savings and earnings. Consulting all of these experts is a kind of research. You will be better off if you know how to evaluate their credibility before you hire them—and if you know how to ask the right questions, since a productive conversation with a consultant should, in some respects, be like an interview.

While talking with consultants can be a very valuable form of research, remember, too, that you can learn a great deal through the other forms of research we have discussed in this book—by reading credible websites and journal articles, for example. If you know where to look—and public libraries are a great place to start—you can find enough books, articles, diagrams, statistics, websites, images, and podcasts to improve your parenting, exercising, eating, saving, and more by leaps and bounds.

Information literacy can help you outside your home, too. Democracy depends on a knowledgeable electorate—that is, voters who can make informed decisions about local, state, and federal programs and policies. Should a city increase hotel taxes to support a new stadium? Will a proposed change in educational policy help or hurt students in your state? (Even if it could help the students, is it worth the price tag?) Should the federal government increase tax credits for people who adopt solar energy for their homes? Countless questions come before the legislators and others we rely on to make decisions. The more we ourselves know about community development, education, energy, and other topics, the better we will be at talking to these legislators, electing the best ones, and, for some of us, *being* those decision-makers. The same goes for political activists and volunteers of all stripes: information is essential to good decisions, and research is essential to getting that information.

Even when you are not deliberately looking for information—in a library or on the Internet—your newly developed information literacy will serve you well.

Information, after all, is everywhere, whether it takes the form of tweets, books, articles, documentaries, advertisements, speeches, graphs, maps, logos, vlogs, podcasts, songs, photographs, signs, posters, or something else. When you know how to interrogate all of these sources of information, you are in a much better position to make sense of the world and act in constructive ways. You are less likely to fall victim to ploys, less likely to waste your money and time, more likely to build productive relationships, and more likely to make decisions that lead to success and fulfillment. It's no exaggeration to say that information literacy is a key to a better life.

Insider's Tip: Use Research to Improve Your Health—and Your Game

As a professional basketball player, I need not only strength, stamina, and agility, but also highly refined skills in shooting, passing, rebounding, and defending. In short, I have to be able to do things that will make me stand out from other players, who also work hard at being fit and developing their skills.

I turn to research to help me become the most competitive player I can be, as well as an effective coach. I often read books and articles about basketball and watch training videos on YouTube. Since doing the same drills over and over can become monotonous, I am especially interested in learning about new routines. For example, I like to check out the drills developed by basketball experts, such as Dirk Nowitzki, who is known for his unusual training techniques. When I see something I like, I add it to my own training regimen.

Of course, professional basketball players are not the only people who want to be in good shape and play competitively. Whatever your game or level, you can use research to build your own training regimen, improve your health, and realize your potential on the court, the field, the diamond, or the track.

–Mike Oppland, professional basketball player (Black Star Mersch, Luxembourg) and youth basketball coach

---

Think Fast: The Uses of a Public Library

Identify three things you might research at a public library after college. Where in the library would you look for this information?

Conclusion

As you can see, the ability to find, evaluate, and use information is one of the most important skills any college student, graduate student, professional, or citizen—indeed, any human being—can possess. For the rest of your college career and the rest of your life, you will have plenty of opportunities to use your information literacy and practice your research skills. The method presented here will serve you in just about any research situation where you find yourself. For one thing, it is scalable—that is, no matter the breadth or the depth of the research need, it can work for you. Furthermore, it makes research both manageable and productive. Finally, it is variable, allowing for multiple source types–even ones not yet invented—and it emphasizes critical thinking, a skill at work across all disciplines and research situations.

Do you agree? Did you learn skills that you used to do effective research in your classes? Can you imagine how you might use these skills on the job, in your family, in your community? Well, guess what? You now have another Quicktivity—a whole lifetime of Quicktivities, in fact. Get out there and apply your research skills to make better grades, better families, better organizations, better communities, and a better world.

Steps to Success

1 Write down three skills or tools that really struck a chord with you after you read about them in this book. Make some notes about how you could continue using them in a future course, on the job, and in your home or civic life.

2 Consider some research tools or skills that are still a little fuzzy for you—government sources, for example, or partial quotations. Revisit the relevant section of this book and refresh your memory. Make some notes on ways that this information can help you in future projects.

3 Use what you have learned in this chapter, as well as the entire book, to learn more about a career that interests you, as well as a specific opening in this career. What are some trends or issues that people in this career face? Does the hiring organization appear to be credible and financially healthy? What kind of knowledge (of both the industry and this particular organization) would you bring to an interview? If you are nearing graduation without a job lined up, consider applying for this job.

4 Take a minute to reflect on something that could help you improve your health, your family, your community, or some other aspect of your non-scholastic life. Use what you have learned in this book to locate some credible information on this subject. The Web, of course, is a logical place to start, but consider visiting your public library, as well. You may be surprised how much a brief conversation with librarian—an information expert if there ever was one—could reveal about sources that never occurred to you.

Glossary

abstract: a summary of an article or book. You will frequently see abstracts in item records that you find when you run searches in article databases indexing scholarly journals.

academic: a professor or researcher associated with a college or a university.

academic library: a library, usually on a university campus, that specializes in research materials. Unlike many public libraries, academic libraries typically provide access to a wide selection of scholarly books and journals.

academic press: a publisher specializing in scholarly books. Many academic presses are affiliated with universities. Examples include Oxford University Press, Harvard University Press, and University of Chicago Press.

academic research: research on academic topics, often performed for the sake of advancing knowledge in a field. Academic research involves locating credible sources, such as journal articles and government documents.

access: the ability to see the information in proprietary resources, such as periodicals. Libraries must require authentication for access to proprietary resources. See **authentication**.

access services: the division of a library that typically involves circulation (where you check out books and other library items), course reserves (a system that college instructors use to make sources easily available to their students), and document delivery, or interlibrary loan. Access services also commonly maintains the library stacks—making sure, for example, that library items are correctly shelved and accessible to all patrons.

advanced search: a search function that allows users to set various parameters, such as format or date range, and combine keywords, title, and other language with established search boxes. Many advanced search interfaces automatically

Introduction to Information Literacy for Students, First Edition. Michael C. Alewine and Mark Canada.
© 2017 John Wiley & Sons, Ltd. Published 2017 by John Wiley & Sons, Ltd.

show three search fields and allow users to add fields. Others allow users to build searches one field at a time. Many advanced searches allow for additional search fields.

agenda: a particular political, commercial, or other purpose, often one that shapes the inclusion or presentation of facts in a source.

almanac: an annual compilation of various kinds of information, such as statistics and brief accounts of events.

analogy: a comparison, often one used to make a point.

annotated bibliography: a kind of bibliography that includes annotations.

annotation: a note, such as one appearing in a bibliography and containing a summary and/or an evaluation of a source.

appendix: a collection of additional information, such as a list of survey questions used in a study, appearing after the text of a scientific report or other text.

archives: collections of special library items (within academic and public libraries), such as manuscripts, typescripts, rare books, and artifacts. Academic libraries typically archive materials related to the history of a college or university, as well as the local history. Because such materials typically are rare, valuable, or delicate, archives have special requirements for handling them, and items in the collection are not available for checkout.

article: a piece of writing on a particular topic. Articles typically are much shorter than books, ranging from a sentence or two to many pages, and can appear in scholarly journals, popular magazines, and other periodicals, as well as other sources, such as reference sources, edited books, and webpages.

artifact: a physical or digital object, such as metalwork or a digital image, that researchers can use to understand a subject.

Ask a Librarian: a service, commonly accessible via a link on a library's website (but possibly going under a different name), that enables researchers to request assistance from reference librarians via a face-to-face visit, telephone, email, instant messaging, or other forms of communication.

atlas: a collection of maps, typically bound in the form of a book.

attributive phrase: a reference to a source in a sentence.

authentication: the process of "logging in" with a username and password to a database or other electronic resource, typically from off campus. This process shows that the user is affiliated with the school (as a student or an employee) and thus eligible to use proprietary resources.

author search: a search for an author's name as a way to locate a book, article, or other kind of source via a database. An author search should turn up anything written by this author and indexed in the database where you are searching.

back files: periodical or other older data available in electronic format or in hard copies stored separately from other materials. Libraries typically purchase access to electronic back files depending on academic need or space considerations within a library. Access to hard copies of back files, whether they are stored in a special section of the library or in a facility outside the library, usually requires submitting a special request. Staff then retrieve the requested material and provide it to the person making the request, either in its physical form or in the form of a pdf made from scanning the relevant pages.

bias: a tendency to favor something or someone over something or someone else.

bibliography: a list of source citations. Bibliographies appear at the ends of sources (where they are sometimes called "Works Cited" or "References"), but also can stand alone as research aids. Bibliographies on large topics, such as the Civil Rights Movement, may take up entire books and often are shelved with other books in libraries.

biographical dictionary: a reference source featuring information about the lives of notable people.

biography: a narrative of a person's life, often in the form of a book.

blog: an online source featuring posts written by experts or laypeople about one or more topics.

book: a bound written document, usually longer than 100 pages. Although some books are published on a regular basis—almanacs are published annually, for example—most books are intended to be published only once. Some books are updated and come out in later editions. Libraries typically keep books on shelves—or, in the case of rare books, in archives—and organize them by some kind of identifier, such as a Library of Congress call number.

book review: an article, typically found in periodicals, that offers critical evaluation of a book. Book reviews can help researchers identify relevant books.

Boolean operators: words used to combine search terms to narrow or broaden a search. The word *and*, for example, narrows a search by requiring that more than one search term appear in the item record or text. Other Boolean operators include *or* and *not*.

brainstorming: an idea-generating process in which a person or group freely lists all ideas that come to mind.

brochure: a small publication designed to describe a program, resource, product, etc.

call number: a unique number (or combination of one or more letters and numbers) that identifies a particular book or other item in a library's collection. Two popular systems of call numbers are the Library of Congress system and the Dewey Decimal system. Items in both general and reference collections are arranged by call number in numerical/alphabetical order.

catalog: a database housing identifying information about the books, media, and other materials that are physically available in the library. Unlike the older catalogs, which consisted of alphabetized index cards stored in narrow drawers, modern catalogs (sometimes known as online catalogs or online public access catalogs, or OPACs) are available online and thus are searchable. Item records in catalogs typically provide citation information, subject headings, tables of contents, locations and call numbers, and notes on whether items are available in the library or checked out. Catalogs also often provide access to virtual materials, such as databases and online journals. Many are branded with a name associated with the library or university. For example, one university library calls its online catalog "BraveCat."

cataloging: the process by which librarians assign call numbers and item records to books and other library items.

CD-ROM: a disc containing data. Some CD-ROMs contain digital databases that index sources. They require a computer with a CD-ROM drive. These databases often contain not only citations, but also the full texts of articles.

circulation: the process by which a library lends books to borrowers or the branch of the library in charge of managing this process.

citation: basic identifying information for a book, article, or other kind of source. A full citation typically includes the name of the author or authors, the title of the source, date of publication, and the name of the publisher or the periodical in which the source appears. Full citations appear in bibliographies and item records in databases. Parenthetical citations are shortened citations that appear inside parentheses in the text of a source, usually at the ends of sentences.

citation style: prescribed format for citations indicating order of information, capitalization, and punctuation. Common citation styles are APA (American Psychological Association), Chicago, and MLA (Modern Language Association).

collection: a body of materials in a library. Most libraries contain two or more collections, such as general collection, government documents collection, juvenile collection, reference collection, and one or more special collections or archives.

concept-mapping: an idea-generating process in which a person or group records a concept, writes a cluster of words or phrases around this concept, and then repeats the process with the new set of words and phrases.

conclusion: a summary appearing at the end of the text in a scientific report.

controlled vocabulary: a specific set of words (placed in a specific order) that is used to describe an idea, person, place, or thing as prescribed by an organization, publisher, indexer, or cataloger. For example, Dewey and Library of Congress cataloging systems have controlled vocabularies. Most electronic resources allow for the efficient use of controlled vocabularies and more forgiving keywords (which are less controlled). Some even allow for the kind of natural-language searches that Google allows.

correlation: a phenomenon in which two things happen together even though they may not be causally related.

credential: something, such as education or experience, that lends authority to an author.

credibility: the believability of a source. Various factors, including the credentials of the author, go into making a source credible.

critical evaluation: the process by which someone determines the value of a source. When evaluating a source critically, researchers should take into consideration factors such as credibility (including accuracy of facts and soundness of reasoning), timeliness, and the author's credentials.

critical thinking: the process by which a person analyzes, evaluates, and interprets information.

curriculum materials center: a space featuring educational materials and teaching aids for education majors completing coursework or student teaching assignments.

cyberspace: the realm where information is stored on computer servers.

database: a collection of data, or information. Today, the term typically refers to information that is stored in digital format and therefore searchable. Two common databases used in research are online library catalogs and article databases such as Academic Search Complete, ERIC (Education Resources Information Center), and PsycINFO.

database publisher/vendor: a company that has the publishing rights to certain databases. Common database publishers/vendors include ABC-CLIO, EBSCO*host*, Elsevier, Gale Cengage Learning, JSTOR, ProQuest, and ScienceDirect. Some databases, such as ERIC, are made available by more than one vendor.

demographics: data dealing with age, income, and other aspects of people.

depository library: a library housing printed copies of federal documents. The U.S. government designates only some libraries as depository libraries.

descriptors: linked subject headings found in various article databases, such as ERIC.

Dewey Decimal Classification system: a classification system, created by Melvil Dewey in 1876, that uses numbers to organize materials by subject. Most public and school libraries in the United States, as well as other libraries throughout the world, use this system. Some academic libraries use Dewey, especially for items in juvenile collections.

dictionary: a source that provides definitions, pronunciations, and other information about words.

digital collection: a collection of sources available in electronic format. For example, many libraries have digital collections of books—that is, e-books. In many cases, images, old yearbooks, and other such archival materials are available in digital collections available via a library's website.

Digital Object Identifier (DOI): a unique set of numbers and letters used to identify specific electronic objects, such as online journal articles and other electronic documents. Some citations in bibliographies and reference lists include DOIs.

directory: a reference source featuring contact information for associations, corporations, and the like.

discussion: a section of a scientific report in which the researcher or researchers remark on the significance of the results found in the research.

dissertation: a lengthy document typically based on original research and completed by a doctoral student as a requirement for completing a degree. Dissertations are made available publicly for researchers, but they are not widely available in hard copy in libraries. Many dissertations are accessible through databases such as ProQuest's Dissertations & Theses database (PQDT).

document delivery (interlibrary loan): a system by which library patrons can request and receive books, articles, and other sources from other libraries, often in digital form (such as a pdf of a periodical article).

documentation: the use of citations to show the sources of information.

domain: the category of a website, indicated by a suffix such as .edu and .com.

e-book: a digital version of a book. Many libraries have large collections of e-books made available by vendors such as EBSCO*host* and ebrary (ProQuest).

edited book: a book that has been read and evaluated by an editor. Editors typically work to ensure that the facts, interpretation, and language of a book are sound. For this reason, edited books are generally considered more credible than books that have not been edited. In the case of collections (of essays, for example), editors may select the book's contents. In the case of transcriptions of manuscripts, editors read handwriting and transcribe it to type.

electronic book: See **e-book**.

electronic resources: a common generic term for databases and other digital materials, such as e-books or online collections of reference sources, such as Oxford Reference Online or Sage eReference. Libraries typically provide access to online article databases, as well as databases that provide other forms of information, such as statistical data.

encyclopedia: a book or set of books containing information about a wide variety of subjects, including people, places, and events.

endnote: a note appearing at the end of an article, chapter, or book. It may contain a citation or explanatory material.

entry: a small or large section of a reference source with information on a specific subject.

evaluation: the process of determining the value of something, such as a source.

factsheet: a one-page publication summarizing facts about a product, program, etc.

false hit: website or other source that turns up in a search but is not related to the topic for which the researcher is searching.

federal depository library: a library that provides access to certain government sources, such as the Budget of the United States Government and various U.S. Census publications, in both print and electronic formats.

Federal Digital System (FDsys): a tool that people can use to find digital government sources.

federated search: a tool that allows researchers to search for information in a variety of different sources, including books and periodicals, simultaneously.

folio: a large book. Technically a printing term for a book published with sheets of foolscap folded only once and gathered in signatures, the term *folio* today refers to any large book stored in a library's folio collection. In a catalog, an item record will include *Folio* or *Oversize* to indicate that a book is in this part of the library. (Folios are shelved separately to conserve shelf space.) Some books are too big even for folio shelves; these books may be stored in another section of the library.

footnote: a note appearing at the bottom of a page in a source. It may contain a citation or explanatory material.

full quotation: See **quotation**.

full text: the entire text of an article or other source. The term **full text** is often used in databases to indicate that readers will find all of the original source, not just a portion of it.

general collection: the main collection (also sometimes referred to as "stacks") of "normal" books in a library. These books are smaller than folios and, unlike books in the reference collection, are available for checkout.

Google Scholar: a tool that allows researchers to locate scholarly materials that are freely available on the Web.

government documents: reports and other documents published by a government, such as the federal government of the United States. The term also refers to the part of a library where these documents are made available to library patrons.

guide: a specialized, practical reference source created for use by practitioners, researchers, and students.

handbook: See **guide**.

hypernym: a word that is more general than another word.

hyponym: a word that is more specific than another word.

hypothesis: an idea that a researcher tests, often by conducting an experiment.

idea generator: a list of topics, often found on the Web.

index: a tool designed to help someone find information. A common form is the index at the end of a book, where researchers can look through an alphabetized list of names and subjects to find the page numbers where these names or subjects appear in the book. The term *index* is also used to mean other kinds of tools, including databases that researchers can use to find articles in periodicals.

information: facts and interpretations, presented in the form of words, images, artifacts, etc.

information literacy: the "set of abilities requiring individuals to recognize when information is needed and have the ability to locate, evaluate, and use effectively the needed information" (as defined by the Association of College and Research Libraries).

information overload: a paralyzing sensation associated with an abundance of information. A researcher suffering from information overload has become so bogged down in the gathering of sources that he or she loses sight of the primary objective—that is, to complete an academic research project. To prevent information overload, try to find sources in small bunches, evaluate them, read and make notes, cite them, and then add textual information and notes into your outline.

information timeline: a way of describing the relationship between various source packages and the points in time when they cover topics.

interlibrary loan: See **document delivery**.

Internet: a collection of computer networks, connected in a wired or wireless way.

interrogate: to ask one or more questions of a person or a source.

interpretation: the process by which a person draws conclusions from facts

interview: a process by which a person collects information by communicating directly with someone else, usually via oral conversation or email. The term also refers to a written record, audio recording, or video recording of an interview.

in-text citation: a citation appearing in the text of a source (rather than the end of the text). Examples include attributive phrases, parenthetical citations, and footnotes.

introduction: the opening section of a scientific report, often containing a review of previous research on the same topic.

issue number: the number assigned to an issue of a periodical. Typically—but not always—each issue of a periodical in a given year has a separate number, beginning with *1* for the first issue, *2* for the second issue, and so on. In some citation styles, citations for periodical articles should include issue numbers. See also **volume number**.

item record: a brief collection of information about a book, article, or other source. Item records appear in databases and provide citation information and, in some cases, a summary, table of contents (for a book), and other details.

jargon: specialized vocabulary used by professionals.

journal: See **scholarly journal**.

juvenile: designed for children. Libraries typically shelve juvenile books in a separate section.

keyword search: a search using keywords as a way to locate sources via a database. A keyword search is typically very broad in nature and searches the maximum number of indexed fields (author, title, subject, abstract, etc.) in an item record or the full text of a document.

keywords: words that describe a particular topic and that are used to search for information on that topic. Researchers often combine keywords with **Boolean operators**.

lab report: See **scientific report**.

lay audience: audience of non-experts.

librarian: someone with expertise in organizing, storing, and using the materials stored in a library. Typically, librarians have master's degrees in library science (MLS); however, people with many different types of degrees work in libraries. In the United States, most academic libraries require a master of library science degree from a program accredited by the American Library Association (ALA). Academic librarians often are faculty members at the colleges and universities where they work. All libraries have people who want to help you find what you are looking for and succeed.

library: a physical collection of sources, such as books, periodicals, and DVDs. Modern libraries collect both physical and virtual resources. What makes something a "library" and not just a repository of books or other printed matter is that librarians have organized a library's contents and provide continuous appropriate guidance, finding aids, and search tools, such as online catalogs.

Library of Congress Classification system: a classification system used to organize materials in the library by subject. It uses an alphanumeric system consisting of an initial set of letters, followed by numbers and more letters. Most academic libraries use this system.

limit: a restriction placed on a search.

link resolver: a specialized database/item-finding tool that connects researchers with library periodical holdings. When a database does not provide direct access to the full text of an article, researchers can click a link in a link resolver to try to acquire indirect access to the full text in a different location, such as another database.

literature review: an essay that summarizes—and sometimes evaluates—sources on a particular topic. Researchers sometimes write literature reviews, or "lit reviews," to broaden and deepen their understanding of a topic they are exploring in their own research and to show readers what is already known about the topic.

magazine: a kind of popular periodical that generally contains a variety of articles written by journalists. Some magazines, such as *Time* and *The Atlantic*, cover a wide range of subjects while others, such as *Yarn* and *Canadian Dog Fancier*, focus on particular hobbies or interests.

manuscript: an unpublished document, often one with handwritten text on it.

manual: See **guide**.

media literacy: the set of skills involved in working with images, film clips, web-pages, and other forms of information found in the media.

medium: the form of an information source.

methods: a section of a scientific report in which the author or authors describe the way an experiment was conducted.

microfiche: See **microform**.

microfilm: See **microform**.

microform: a format for various kinds of sources, especially newspapers, magazines, and other periodicals. Microforms, including both microfilm and microfiche, feature very small photographs of printed documents on sheets (microfiche) or film on reels (microfilm). Because the images are much too small to read with the naked eye, microforms require special reader-printers to view and print them.

monograph: a publication that offers analysis of a subject.

natural language search: a tool that allows researchers to type search questions or phrases in conversational terms ("When was Denver founded?") instead of using the controlled vocabulary ("Denver and found*") required by some search tools.

newsletter: a small periodical featuring news aimed at members of a company or other organization.

newspaper: a type of periodical that carries a variety of articles about current events and, typically, features about celebrities, entertainment, hobbies, and other topics of interest. Most newspapers are published daily or weekly.

objective: free from influence by emotions or opinions.

off-campus login: a process by which users can obtain access to a library's proprietary materials, such as digital versions of periodical articles or subject encyclopedias, when they are not on campus. To acquire access, the user logs in to an electronic resource on the library's site with either a generic login or one that is unique to a user. College students often have unique usernames and passwords they can use to access campus resources, including library resources. See also **authentication**.

offsite storage: storage of library materials in a location other than the library itself. To conserve space, libraries sometimes store a portion of their holdings, such as books and periodicals that are not frequently used, off site. Library patrons still have access to these holdings, but they may need to wait a day or more to use them.

online book: a book available on the Web.

online reference sources: electronic sources, such as Merriam-Webster's online dictionary, that can be used for reference.

open access journal: a journal that is freely available on the Web.

original research: See **research**.

pamphlet: a small publication designed to describe a program, resource, product, etc.

paraphrase: the use of different words to capture the meaning of words in a source.

parenthetical citation: See **citation**.

partial quotation: See **quotation**.

peer review: a process by which experts evaluate research conducted by other experts. Reputable scholarly journals and academic presses use peer review to try to ensure that what they publish is credible.

periodical: a publication that comes out on a regular basis. Many popular magazines, for example, appear monthly, and most newspapers come out daily or weekly.

photograph: an image of a person or thing as recorded by a camera.

plagiarism: use of another person's ideas or exact words without proper credit given to this person. Some definitions of plagiarism include the word "intentional" or "deliberate"; however, because it is difficult to prove intent, some teachers may consider any use of another's words or ideas as plagiarism if the author has not identified this person with an attributive phrase or citation or enclosed exact words in quotation marks.

podcast: an audio recording of a lecture, interview, personal narrative, etc., often found on the Web.

popular book: book intended for a general audience.

***post hoc* fallacy:** the assumption that one thing caused another simply because it came first. The Latin phrase *post hoc* means "after the fact."

primary source: a source that a researcher is analyzing or interpreting. Common primary sources include artifacts, poems, letters, and diaries. If a researcher conducts a survey or observation, the raw data collected is a form of primary source.

public library: a library tied to a specific location and generally supported by city, county, or state tax dollars. Public libraries are generally open to anyone who wants to walk in and make reasonable use of them, but borrowing materials generally requires proof of residency.

publication information: details—specifically, place of publication, name of publisher, and year of publication—for a book.

quotation: the use of exact words from a source. A **full quotation** is a complete sentence. A **partial quotation** is an excerpt from a sentence in a source.

ready reference collection: a section of a library containing atlases, almanacs, manuals, and other reference sources handy for answering common questions.

reference collection: the section of a library containing encyclopedias, subject encyclopedias, dictionaries, manuals, and other sources used primarily for general information and basic facts. Unlike items stored in the general collection, items in the reference collection are generally not available for checkout.

references: a list of sources appearing at the end of an article, chapter, or book.

reference source: a source, such as an encyclopedia or manual, providing general information, such as overviews, or basic facts, either on a range of subjects or a specific subject. Examples include *Encyclopedia Britannica, Goode's World Atlas,* and *The New Grove Dictionary of Music and Musicians.*

reflection: the process of thinking about an event, phenomenon, etc. Reflection commonly involves consideration of relationships, causes, effects, and meaning.

relevant: related to a subject. **Relevant** sources are those that contain information directly related to a research question.

report: a source, often relatively brief, generally providing some combination of facts, analysis, and interpretation regarding a specific subject.

research: the process that scientists, scholars, and others use to find answers to questions by consulting various kinds of sources, such as books, websites, and artifacts. While some research—particularly in traditional college classes—may turn up existing knowledge, **original research** produces new interpretations, findings, and proposals.

research log: a set of notes on keyword searches conducted, databases consulted, citations of sources, and other information related to the process of conducting research for a project.

research question: a question posed about a specific person, thing, phenomenon, etc. Scientists, scholars, and others begin with a research question and then conduct research to answer this question.

results: the section of a scientific report reporting what the researcher or researchers learned. The results section typically contains tables or graphs showing data collected from an experiment.

results list: a list of sources found in a search on a database or the Web.

review article: a scholarly article that summarizes other articles or studies, presents conclusions based on their contents, and offers generalizations based on the findings.

scholar: a college professor or other person who studies something and produces research about it.

scholarly book: See **scholarly source.**

scholarly journal: See **scholarly source.**

scholarly source: a book, journal article, or other source written by experts, such as university professors, for other experts.

school library: a library found in an elementary, middle, or high school. A school library may not have a librarian on staff; some schools have teachers share the duties of the librarian. Some school libraries are called "media centers" and have librarians called "media center coordinators."

scientific report: a summary of a scientific research. Sometimes called a **lab report**, a scientific report typically consists of an abstract, an introduction, a discussion of methods, a summary of results, discussion, a conclusion, and a list of references.

search engine (or Web search engine): a tool in which a researcher can insert words, phrases, and some Boolean operators to search for sources on the World Wide Web. Examples include Google and Bing.

search limits: restrictions used to limit results in searches conducted on the Web and in other databases. Researchers often can limit results by subject, publication date, document type, author, and so forth. Some databases offer very advanced and detailed search limit options.

secondary source: a source providing some kind of secondhand account. A secondary source may interpret primary sources or draw from other secondary sources. For example, a novel is a primary source whereas critical studies of the novel and biographies of the novelist are both secondary sources.

serials: See **periodicals**.

server: a computer that stores information accessible to other computers, often via the World Wide Web.

service desks: resources providing a variety of public services within a library. Service desks include circulation desks, course reserve desks, government document desks, periodicals/serials desks, reference desks, and so forth. Many libraries have combined circulation and reference desks into something sometimes called "customer service." Service desks are staffed by librarians, support staff, and trained student workers and volunteers.

social media: interactive websites and tools, such as Facebook and Twitter, used by people, governments, and organizations to communicate in both formal and informal ways.

source: anything that provides information. Most sources, such as books and websites, contain at least some text, but photographs, paintings, musical recordings, silent video recordings, sculptures, and artifacts also can be sources.

special collections: See **archives**.

special library: a library serving a special purpose or type of patron. For example, a law library is a special library that serves lawyers, judges, and law students. Other special libraries include those dedicated to art, health sciences, history, and music.

specialist librarian: a librarian with expertise in research in a particular discipline, such as law or health sciences.

sponsored link: a link that appears near the top of a results list because a sponsor, such as a company, has paid to have it appear there.

statistics: numbers of people or products, sizes of cities, rates of changes, and the like.

streaming video: video recordings provided through streaming servers (thus preventing proprietary content from being downloaded or copied). Streaming video databases often provide access to documentaries and other educational videos. Like any other proprietary electronic resources, video databases will require students to log in when they are off campus.

subject encyclopedia: a specialized form of encyclopedia containing information about various aspects of a particular subject, such as medicine or religion.

subject guide: an online resource featuring links to webpages related to a particular subject.

subject heading: a word or phrase assigned to a source in an item record to indicate a major subject covered in the source. The Library of Congress has a system of thousands of subject headings, which library cataloguers use when completing item records for books.

subject search: a search for a subject as a way to locate a book, article, or other kind of source via a database. Unlike keywords searches, subject searches do not cover all the words in an item record or in the text of a source; rather, they cover assigned subject headings in an item record.

subjective: shaped by emotions or opinions.

summary: a condensed version of information in a source.

superscript: appearing above a line of text. Superscript numbers in a text refer readers to footnotes or endnotes.

supplement: a published collection of articles coming out separately from a periodical, serial, or multivolume reference set. Because a supplement is not part of the regular run of a periodical, serial, or set, researchers need to pay close attention to citations when trying to locate one.

SuDoc (Superintendent of Documents) number: a code in the classification system used specifically for U.S. federal documents. It is based not on subject, but rather on the department that created the document. For example, E stands for the Department of Energy.

synonyms: words that mean roughly the same thing.

syntax: the way words are put together to create meaning in a sentence.

synthesize: to use various pieces of information to construct something meaningful.

table of contents: a list of chapters or sections in a book, along with the numbers of the pages on which these chapters or sections begin. The table of contents appears near the beginning of a book.

tertiary source: a source that provides indexing, synthesis, or both of other sources. Common tertiary sources include annotated bibliographies, directories, and print indexes.

text: words and sentences found in books and other documents.

thesaurus terms: sets of terms (broader terms, controlled vocabulary, descriptors, keywords, narrower terms, subject headings, etc.) that are specific to a database or subject. Most electronic resources allow you to browse or limit to specific thesaurus terms, especially useful when you are unaware of all of the terms that are related to your topic.

thesis: a statement of a position in a book, article, or other argumentative piece of writing.

three R method: a method for evaluating sources. It requires three questions: "Is it relevant?" "Is it recent?" "Is it reliable?"

title search: a search for the title of a book, article, or other kind of source as a way to locate it via a database.

topic: a specific aspect of a subject, an area that a researcher explores in a paper, presentation, or other kind of research project.

top-level domain: category of a website, indicated by a suffix such as .com, .edu, .org, or .gov.

trade magazine: a periodical aimed at professionals in a particular field. Trade magazines include *Latin Finance* and *Construction Weekly*.

truncation: a process by which a researcher can substitute a **wildcard** for unknown letters at the end of word and thus broaden a search.

typescript: an unpublished document with typed text on it.

Uniform Resource Locator (URL): the "address" of a website. URLs typically contain the letters *www* (for "World Wide Web"), a name for the overall site, an extension identifying the kind of sponsoring organization (.edu for a university, .com for a commercial entity, .org for an organization, .gov for a governmental agency, and so on), and, for subpages, additional words, letters, numbers, or symbols. For example, the URL for the U.S. Postal Service is www.usps.gov. Browsers typically do not require *www* at the beginning, so usps.gov generally will work, as well.

vanity press: a press that charges authors to publish their work.

video recording: a visual recording of an event as captured by a video camera.

virtual library: a library providing access to digital content. In a sense, all libraries are virtual libraries to some degree, since even those that house books and other printed materials also provide access to online sources, such as periodical articles accessible through electronic databases.

visual literacy: the set of skills involved in working with images.

vlog: a video version of a blog.

vodcast: a video recording of a lecture, interview, personal narrative, etc., often found on the Web.

volume number: number assigned to a run, or series, of issues of a periodical. Often, but not always, a year's worth of periodicals are considered a single volume, and each issue is assigned a different number; thus, in the first year a magazine is published, the first issue would be Volume 1, Issue 1, or 1:1. In the second year, the first issue would be Volume 2, Issue 1, or 2:1. Some citation styles require volume numbers in citations for articles in periodicals.

Web: See **World Wide Web**.

Web address: See **URL**.

Web browser: software, such as Firefox or Safari, that allows a person to visit material posted on the Web.

web directory: an organized list of links to websites.

webpage: a single part, or "page," of a website.

website: a source of information, often consisting of a collection of interconnected pages, available on the World Wide Web.

white paper: a report, often published by a government entity or other organization, providing information on a subject.

wiki: a website that anyone can alter by adding, deleting, or changing material.

Wikipedia: an online reference source featuring entries on a wide variety of subjects. Unlike the entries in printed encyclopedias, many Wikipedia entries have been written and revised by people without traditional credentials and have not undergone a thorough, systematic editing process before they appear.

wildcard: a symbol used to indicate an unknown letter or number in a search. Researchers can use a wildcard, such as * or ? or !, to broaden a search if they wish the database search engine to consider variations of a word. For example, in some databases, a search for *teen** would turn up any item records containing *teen*, *teens*, or *teenagers*.

works cited: a list of sources appearing at the end of an article, chapter, or book.

World Wide Web: a network of online pages connected via links and visible via an interface. The information that appears on these pages is stored on physical servers and made available to users whose computers are connected to the network.

WorldCat: a tool that allows researchers to search for books stored in thousands of libraries around the world.

Index

Introduction to Information Literacy for Students, First Edition. Michael C. Alewine and Mark Canada.
© 2017 John Wiley & Sons, Ltd. Published 2017 by John Wiley & Sons, Ltd.

Printed and bound by CPI Group (UK) Ltd, Croydon, CR0 4YY